DAILY LIFE IN COLONIAL MEXICO

Title page of Ilarione's manuscript.

Daily Life in Colonial Mexico

THE JOURNEY OF
FRIAR ILARIONE DA BERGAMO, 1761–1768

Translated from the Italian by William J. Orr

Edited by Robert Ryal Miller and William J. Orr

UNIVERSITY OF OKLAHOMA PRESS : NORMAN

Also by Robert Ryal Miller

For Science and National Glory: The Spanish Scientific Expedition to America, 1862–1866 (Norman, 1968)
Arms across the Border: United States Aid to Juárez during the French Intervention in Mexico (Philadelphia, 1973)
Mexico: A History (Norman, 1985)
Shamrock and Sword: The Saint Patrick's Battalion in the U.S.-Mexican War (Norman, 1989)
Captain Richardson: Mariner, Ranchero, and Founder of San Francisco (Berkeley, 1995)
Juan Alvarado, Governor of California, 1836–1842 (Norman, 1998)

Also by William J. Orr

(editor, with Robert Ryal Miller) *An Immigrant Soldier in the Mexican War* (College Station, 1995)

Daily Life in Colonial Mexico: The Journey of Friar Ilarione da Bergamo, 1761–1768 is Volume 78 in The American Exploration and Travel Series.

Library of Congress Cataloging-in-Publication Data

Ilarione, da Bergamo, fra, d. 1778.
    [Viaggio al Messico. English]
    Daily life in colonial Mexico : the journey of Friar Ilarione da Bergamo, 1761–1768 / translated from the Italian by William J. Orr ; edited by Robert Ryal Miller and William J. Orr.
        p.   cm. — (The American exploration and travel series ; v. 78)
    Includes bibliographical references (p. -) and index.
    ISBN 0–8061–3234–5 (hc : alk. paper)
    1. Mexico—Description and travel—Early works to 1800.   2. Mexico—Social life and customs—18th century.   3. Ilarione, da Bergamo, fra, d. 1778.   I. Miller, Robert Ryal.   II. Orr, William J.   III. Title.   IV. Series.
F1211.I4213 2000
972'.02—dc21   00–025949

The paper in this book meets the guidelines for permanence and durability of the Committee on Production Guidelines for Book Longevity of the Council on Library Resources, Inc. ∞

1 2 3 4 5 6 7 8 9 10

To
Ana Eva Cárdenas de Orr

CONTENTS

ILLUSTRATIONS

FIGURES

Unless otherwise indicated, illustrations are from Ilarione's manuscript.

MAPS

ACKNOWLEDGMENTS

The editors wish to thank Dr. Giulio Orazio Bravi, director of the Biblioteca Civica Angelo Mai in Bergamo, for access to the original manuscript, for providing a microfilm copy of it, and for permission to publish this English translation. Dr. Bravi kindly assisted the translator, who visited Bergamo in November 1997, with a few particularly perplexing passages containing words and expressions not found in standard Italian dictionaries; and he provided additional information about sources bearing on Ilarione's work. We also acknowledge the contribution of Maria Laura Bruno, editor of the Italian edition. In addition, we are grateful to librarians at the Library of Congress in Washington, D.C., and the Bancroft Library of the University of California for locating and making available pertinent books and documents that we used in editing the account. Stafford Poole and John Frederick Schwaller, both authorities in Mexican colonial history, read the manuscript and provided many valuable suggestions. Thanks to Kathy Lewis, whose superb copy-editing prepared the manuscript for publication. Ana Eva Cárdenas de Orr also caught many errors, anomalies, or obscurities that would only be evident to a native of Mexico. To her this volume is gratefully dedicated.

DAILY LIFE IN COLONIAL MEXICO

EDITORS' INTRODUCTION

Although the colonial era spanned nearly three centuries of Mexico's history, few eyewitness accounts remain that describe everyday life—where people lived, what they ate, how they amused themselves, what foibles or vices they indulged in, what they experienced strolling through the cities, towns, and countryside. Extremely low literacy primarily explains the scarcity of these accounts, but shortage of paper and the destruction wrought by the wars for independence and later civil conflict hindered as well the creation and preservation of such primary source material. Narratives by foreign travelers are also rare because Spanish policy barred foreign visitors from the colony of New Spain, except for a few clerics and scientists who received special royal permission. Although many histories of the conquest, government reports, church records, and missionaries' accounts of Indian affairs are extant, there are only about a dozen substantial published diaries, journals, or memoirs that provide details about daily life; and few of these have been available in English.[1]

The recently discovered account of a voyage to Mexico by Ilarione da Bergamo (1727?–78), an Italian Capuchin friar, with details of his residence and travels in the colony from 1763 to 1768, marks a valuable addition to the firsthand literature of colonial

Mexico. Fra Ilarione spent several years in silver mining towns north of Mexico City. He also lived in the capital for some months and journeyed to Guadalajara before returning to Italy. His narrative provides unique information about many aspects of Mexican life in the second half of the eighteenth century.

Almost nothing is known about the author. Indeed, the only information about his life before the journey to Mexico is contained in the profession of just a few words made on September 24, 1747, when he entered the Capuchin order. At that time he was about twenty years of age—hence probably born in 1727—and had been baptized with the Christian name of Gaetano. Even his surname is unknown. His birthplace may have been the city where he spent much of his life, Bergamo, then at the westernmost extremity of the sprawling Republic of Venice. However, Ilarione made his vows not at the principal monastery in Bergamo, but at Sovere, a small town nearly 25 miles away. In 1769 this smaller establishment was dissolved and merged with larger monasteries, but Ilarione seems to have transferred to Bergamo before his journey to Mexico. In keeping with the practice of his order, he assumed the new name "Ilarione da Bergamo" (Hilary of Bergamo in English), after the city from which he came, where he was to spend the last years of his life.[2]

Located thirty miles northeast of Milan, Bergamo had a long, eventful history, dating back to pre-Roman times. During the Middle Ages, Bergamo, like many other medium-size Italian municipalities, pursued a turbulent autonomy, succumbed to factional strife, and eventually lost its independence to larger neighbors. In the fourteenth century it fell under the harsh, unwelcome hegemony of Milan, but in the fifteenth century it passed to the rule of the more distant, less domineering Venice.

A modern visitor strolling the narrow, winding streets of Bergamo amidst the ancient brown and gray buildings of the old city, perched on a hilltop overlooking the Lombard plain, can still sense much of what Ilarione experienced more than two centuries ago.

Besides its scenic location, the town is graced by several monumental buildings, notably the twelfth-century Romanesque church
of Santa María Maggiore, with its baroque interior and splendid
paintings; the Renaissance Chapel of Colleoni, noted for its
sculptured façade and marble tombs; and the main cathedral of
Saint Alexander, richly ornamented in the baroque style.[3] Ilarione
had reason to be proud of Bergamo, and the city served as a recur-
ring point of reference and comparison in his Mexican narrative.

Ilarione's order, the Capuchins or Order of Friars Minor Capuchin, was recognized as an independent branch of the Franciscan
order in 1628. Like two other major Franciscan branches, the Order
of Friars Minor (Observants) and Order of Friars Conventual,
Capuchins observe the vows of poverty, chastity, and obedience
and follow the rule of St. Francis. Their unique name was derived
from the pointed hood (*cappuccio* in Italian) attached to their dark
brown, coarse robe. They are discalced (go barefoot or wear sandals
instead of shoes) and do not shave their beards. Their rules call for
austerity, simplicity, and poverty; and their vocation involves
preaching, catechizing, and ministrations to the poor.[4]

There are two classes of Capuchins—members of both take vows
and wear habits—the "fathers," who are ordained for the priesthood; and the "lay brothers," who are not clerics and cannot admin-
ister sacraments, such as saying mass and hearing confession.
Ilarione was a lay brother. Both fathers and lay brothers are called
"friars," a term applied to members of mendicant religious orders.
In Spanish-speaking countries the contraction "Fray," in Italy
"Fra," was often used before the first name of a friar; thus: Fra
Ilarione.

In Italy the Capuchins were especially numerous and revered
by the general population—as exemplified in the saintly figure of
Father Christopher, that courageous and forbearing exemplar of
Christian charity, in the most celebrated of Italian novels, *The
Betrothed* (1825), by Alessandro Manzoni. Bergamo, a city long
reputed for its conservatism and piety, provided ideal soil for the

flourishing of the Capuchin order, which in the early eighteenth century was led by deeply pious and revered figures such as Fathers Gaetano Maria Migliorini da Bergamo and Francesco da Bergamo.[5] Whereas monastic life was in decline or disrepute in much of Europe during the Age of Enlightenment, in Bergamo the Capuchin order still preserved some of its traditional piety, discipline, and missionary fervor. Such was the ambiance that imbued the order in which Ilarione served, first as a lay brother then as a missionary.

This Capuchin lay brother displayed much of the simple piety that pervaded his order and, indeed, everyday religious life in one of the more devout regions of Italy. His devotion to the Virgin Mary is particularly evident—from his efforts after first setting out on his journey from Bergamo to Rome to visit leading shrines of Marian devotion, to his desperate prayers on a storm-lashed sea, to his keen interest in the Virgin of Guadalupe after his arrival in Mexico. To judge from occasional remarks in his narrative, Ilarione felt the greatest awe for the hierarchy, organization, and ritual element of his church but was less attentive to the charitable teachings that lie at the very heart of Christianity. Condescension toward the humblest classes, a note of reproof toward moral laxity, and impatience with the shortcomings of colleagues are often in evidence. Ilarione nevertheless does not strike one as humorless, austere, or ascetic. Many times during his travels he opted for more commodious lodging with private individuals rather than endure the rigors of a monastery. His appreciation for good food and wine is also evident. Clearly he enjoyed human fellowship and made friends easily, qualities that endeared him to Mexicans during his overseas mission.

From an early date the Capuchin friars undertook missions to Africa, America, and Asia.[6] Capuchin missionaries were active in Bengal, Bhutan, India, and Nepal in the eighteenth century, and from 1708 to 1745 a small group of Capuchin friars preached in Lhasa, the capital of Tibet. After that mission collapsed because of local persecutions and a lack of funds, the pope and a centralized missionary organization in Rome, the Congregation for the Propagation of the Faith (cited hereafter by its Latin name, Propaganda Fide), attempted to reintroduce Christian missionaries into Tibet. To aid this enterprise, Cardinal Girolamo Spinola advanced a considerable sum of money, with the debt being assumed by the king of Spain, who then ordered that the colony of New Spain should pay 10,000 pesos each year until the debt, totaling 134,073 pesos, was paid.[7] Mexico was targeted because it was at that time the most prosperous of all the Spanish colonies, and its mining industry was flourishing.

Between 1760 and 1768, Propaganda Fide sent seven Capuchins to New Spain to collect alms for the Tibet missions. One of these fund raisers was Ilarione da Bergamo. In 1761, having volunteered for missionary service, he left for Rome to expedite his assignment. Originally, Ilarione had planned on traveling to India, but at the last moment he was sent to Mexico instead as a replacement for another friar who had died unexpectedly. In the narrative of his overseas mission, Fra Ilarione mentions the six other Capuchin friars: Fermín de Olite, a Castilian; Filippo da Portogruaro, a Venetian; Francisco de Ajofrín, a Castilian; Jerónimo de Jerez, an Andalusian; Lorenzo da Brà, a Piedmontese; and Paolo Maria da Ferrara, a Bolognese. Ilarione da Bergamo and Fermín de Olite were lay brothers; the others were ordained priests.

Fra Ilarione's seven-year mission to New Spain was certainly the most memorable phase in an otherwise unremarkable career. He was thirty-four when he left Italy and forty-one when he returned to his homeland, evidently marking the end of his missionary work. In 1770 Ilarione began composing an account of his journey to the New World, entitled "Viaggio al Messico" (Journey to Mexico), which totals 293 manuscript leaves. Written in a very meticulous script, clearly the product of a disciplined monastic hand, the manuscript also includes two hand-drawn maps, two sketches of Indian huts, and thirty-eight illustrations of native plants—all in color—some of which are reproduced in this edition. Given the precise dating of many events, the numbers of crewmen and passengers aboard ships, and the highly detailed drawings of Mexican flora, Ilarione's account was undoubtedly based on notes, letters, or diaries and sketches since lost. The final years of the friar's life, like the beginning of his career, are shrouded in obscurity. All we know for certain is that he died on October 13, 1778.[8]

Sample page of Ilarione's manuscript.

After Ilarione's death his manuscript passed to his kin. To judge from a faint pencil notation on the inside cover of the manuscript, the first heir was Ilarione's nephew Felice Airoldi. For many decades the "Viaggio al Messico" probably remained a curious but unappreciated heirloom. Early in this century it had passed to the grandnephews, the Butturini brothers of Salò, whence it came to the attention of a scholar, Guido Bustico, who published a note on Ilarione's journey but apparently did no further research.[9] In 1929 Ilarione's manuscript was exhibited at the "First National Exposition of the History of Science" in Florence.[10] In 1953 the "Viaggio al Messico" was donated to the Biblioteca Civica Angelo Mai in Bergamo, where it remains today.

Normally, scholars would deplore a manuscript of this kind remaining so long in private hands, but in Ilarione's case this proved the most fortunate outcome. Troubled times befell the Capuchins of Bergamo soon after his death. The anticlericalism that increasingly dominated many governments of late eighteenth century Europe also influenced the Republic of Venice, which imposed ever more stringent restrictions on the order's activities and even dissolved some monasteries. When northern Italy fell under Napoleonic control, an even harsher fate was in store. In 1810 all monasteries and convents, with the sole exception of hospitals, were dissolved, their friars and nuns turned out onto the streets, and their fine libraries plundered and dispersed. For a time Ilarione's own monastery was converted to a tavern,[11] though eventually it was restored to its original ownership. Today the Capuchin monastery of Bergamo, first built in the sixteenth century, remains a functioning institution. Surrounded, however, by modern apartments, the building has been so renovated that it evokes little of the order's long, rich history. Given the vicissitudes of the monastery itself, it seems likely that had Ilarione bequeathed his manuscript to the monastic library, it would not have remained there and might never have ended up in safe hands today.

In 1976 an Italian geographer, Maria Laura Bruno, published an annotated edition of Ilarione's narrative.[12] She omitted interesting sections on religious orders and practices, however, as well as passages on indelicate matters, such as Mexican sanitation and sexual mores. Perhaps because this edition was issued locally by a publisher with very limited distribution, it never attained the wide circulation it deserved. In the entire Western Hemisphere the only known copy of the book is in the United States Library of Congress.

The first third of Ilarione's narrative recounts his journey from Italy to Spain and then to the New World. It vividly reminds us of just how perilous and arduous ocean voyages could be in that era. From the moment they left the coast near Rome in October of 1761, Ilarione and his fellow seafarers were on constant alert for Barbary pirates, the scourge of the Mediterranean, who as slave traders were never completely eliminated until the next century. After arriving in Cádiz, Fra Ilarione waited impatiently for four months before he could finally board a vessel bound for the New World. No sooner was he at sea than his ship was pursued, strafed, and captured by a British warship—Great Britain and Spain then being foes in the Seven Years' War—and the crew and passengers were taken to Gibraltar and released. From there, Ilarione returned to Cádiz to wait for the end of hostilities.

Five months later, on January 2, 1763, he set sail at last on an aged, perilously overloaded vessel, which traveled in a convoy to protect the fleet from pirates. Like countless other transatlantic voyagers, he suffered the terrors of a ferocious storm, which shredded sails, washed provisions overboard, and for a time left even the ship's captain despairing of survival. Gales gave way to long periods of becalming, oppressive tedium, and, eventually, depleted rations.

Before reaching Mexico, Ilarione's ship anchored for a week in the bay at San Juan, capital of the island of Puerto Rico. Among the first things the friar observed from his spyglass were the severed heads of criminals prominently displayed on a gallows. His offhand mention of that scene, as well as of the rotting corpses he earlier saw suspended from English gallows in Gibraltar, reflects the callousness of an era when severe exemplary punishment was taken for granted, as the price that must be paid to preserve order. Though this was the Age of Enlightenment and Ilarione's own countryman, Cesare Beccaria from nearby Milan, had just published an epochal treatise condemning torture and capital punishment and recommending the certitude rather than severity of punishment as the best deterrent to crime, Ilarione seems to have been oblivious to these intellectual currents.

Ilarione provides a brief glimpse of the Spanish island colonies of Puerto Rico and Cuba, the former visited on his way to Mexico and the latter on his way home five years later. He illustrates the major role slavery played in these societies and the abasement slaves were subjected to. Perhaps his account is most illuminating, though, in revealing the naive, condescending reaction of a reasonably well-educated European upon first viewing people of a different race. Ilarione's narrative also depicts the rudimentary living standards and amenities of these islanders, while at the same time acknowledging the cordiality and hospitality that made life there more bearable.

Ilarione arrived at Veracruz, the principal port of Mexico, on May 10, 1763. Wisely, he did not tarry long in this pestilential city, devoid of monumental architecture or other cultural attractions, but instead set out for the capital, following roughly the same route Hernán Cortés had taken two centuries before. Imprudently, he first attempted the journey on foot. Now he could marvel for the first time at the lushness of Mexican flora and profusion of fauna, including tiny insects that penetrated beneath his skin, causing him some discomfort and consternation. For the first of many times, he notes the humility and hospitality of the native Indian population, the most numerous ethnic group in New Spain. Eventually Ilarione borrowed a mule and in the end accepted a Mexican merchant's generous offer of a coach ride from Perote to the capital, where he arrived on June 1.

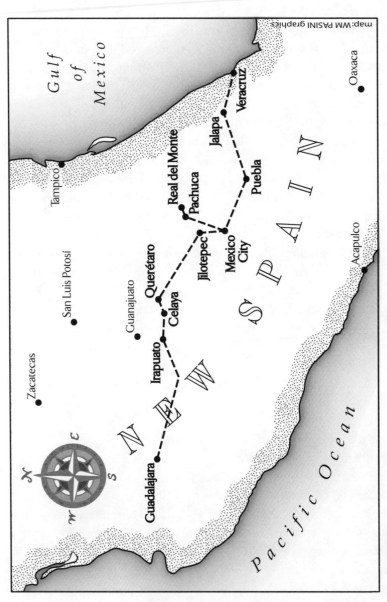

Ilarione's itinerary in New Spain. Map by William Pasini.

map: WM PASINI graphics

The viceroyalty of New Spain at the time of Ilarione's journey was enormous—it extended from northern California to Panama and was fourteen times the size of the mother country. Mexico City was then the largest urban settlement in North America; its population was 104,760 in 1790, whereas Philadelphia had 42,444 and New York City a mere 31,131 inhabitants.[13] Ilarione lived several months in the capital, and his account vividly recalls many bygone features of what was once one of the most enchanting cities in the world, girdled by lakes and snow-clad volcanos, with streets and canals faintly reminiscent of Venice. While recounting Mexico City's architectural splendors, its engineering works, and its commercial life, he also noted the squalor, crime, natural catastrophes, and other perils that dogged daily life in the capital.

Soon after Ilarione's arrival in Mexico City, his account changed from a day-by-day narrative of his journey to a topical discussion of Mexican life in the eighteenth century. Thus he describes native plants such as avocado, guava, maize, and vanilla, as well as typical meals consisting of broths, stews, or enchiladas, all prepared with chile peppers and accompanied by European vegetables like peas or onions. He notes popular native beverages such as chocolate and *pulque* and explains how they were prepared. Fond of birds, he records the varieties of parrots, parakeets, turtledoves, crows, and vultures. From his narrative we learn about the public baths (and their associated scandals), music, dances, games, and recreation; and there is a lengthy section on bullfights. Ilarione's account is unique for its detailed description of cockfighting, which he claims was widespread throughout the realm. In Mexico City he felt the tremors of an earthquake and inspected the elaborate drainage tunnels constructed to prevent flooding.

Ilarione provides much information about various occupations in the colony. The ubiquitous open-air markets featured vendors with stalls of foodstuffs, clothing, utensils, and cut flowers, for example. Many towns had small factories with ten or twelve employees who made cigarettes or rolled tobacco into cigars, smoking being a widespread practice. Tobacco was also used as a medicine applied to open wounds. Medical practices both paralleled and differed from those of Europe. Remedies used by physicians and *curanderos* (folk healers) included emetics, enemas, and hot baths; but bloodletting and cupping were rarer. Based on his long residence in a mining district, Ilarione describes in detail the work of silver miners, the mines themselves, and how the metal was separated from the ore. He also records a violent labor strike that occurred during his stay.

As a friar, it was natural that Ilarione would write extensively about the Roman Catholic church, which pervaded virtually every phase of life in New Spain. The church controlled education, hospitals, orphanages, and institutional care for the aged, destitute, and mentally disturbed. Clerics provided funds for the alleviation of suffering; were sources of information and solace for parishioners; and kept records of births, marriages, and deaths. In the 1760s Mexico City had 84 Catholic churches, 29 monasteries, and 20 convents, as well as a number of chapels, oratories, and other religious buildings.[14] Although there was a Capuchin convent for nuns in Mexico City, there were no Capuchin monasteries in any part of New Spain. Ilarione met and dined with the archbishop, made numerous visits to the cathedral of Mexico and the nearby shrine of Guadalupe, and witnessed many religious processions, as well as an Inquisition auto-da-fé. Some readers may be surprised to learn about the rivalry between religious groups and the contention within orders themselves, manifested, for example, in the competition between the Spanish and Italian Capuchin friars.

Ilarione's account tells us a great deal about Mexican colonial society. He was acutely aware of class and racial differences, the limits they imposed, and the interrelationships among various elements of the population. At times he provides a glimpse into the muted class and racial antagonisms that would erupt in full fury during the War of Independence fifty years later. The pervasive poverty and widespread criminality in colonial Mexico also come through clearly in the Capuchin's narrative—particularly in his treatment of the capital and his description of a journey to Guadalajara along brigand-infested roads. He notes disapprovingly lax sexual morality, widespread concubinage, and proliferation of illegitimate progeny.

Although Ilarione was a contemporary of the French Encyclopedists and other proponents of the Enlightenment, he never questioned the monarchical and ecclesiastical Spanish regime, with its concept of Divine Right and determination to impose European civilization on the native American cultures. He accepted the rigid class and racial hierarchy in Mexican society; and his class prejudice is much in evidence when he sometimes refers to members of the lower classes as "sluggards," "drunkards," "thieves," "swindlers," and "lechers."

For about four years, Fra Ilarione resided in the mining town of Real del Monte, near the village of Pachuca, about fifty miles north of Mexico City. Here he collected alms to support Christian missions in Asia. Dedicated and devout, he was nevertheless neither so aloof nor so austere as to antagonize or overawe those upon whose generosity his work depended. A certain worldliness and good humor undoubtedly endeared him to the local population. Because there were no monasteries or inns, he lived in a private house, where he was given free board and room and accepted as a member of the family.

Before beginning his solicitations, Ilarione called on the count of Regla, owner of most of the local mines, who gave him permission to solicit alms. Stationing himself daily at the entrance to various mine shafts, the friar appealed to the miners, many of whom gave him silver ore from their personal take, which he then sold to a broker. Other miners credited the friar's account for a specified amount. Ilarione never stated how much he collected, but a fellow Capuchin in New Spain, Francisco de Ajofrín, reckoned that the three active Italian friars collected 6,800 pesos. In 1765 and 1766 the total amount sent to the Rome headquarters of Propaganda Fide was 41,474 pesos.[15]

Fra Ilarione also visited nearby villages and made intermittent trips to the capital. Toward the end of his stay he traveled with a servant to Guadalajara, more than four hundred miles to the northwest, a journey that lasted eighteen days each way. This trip was in response to a directive of the archbishop that he collect a note for five thousand pesos, which had been deposited with a gentleman in that city. After six weeks in Guadalajara, he accomplished his purpose and returned to Mexico City. By now Ilarione had come to relish Mexico's climate, people, and cuisine, but his stay would come to a disheartening end.

In distant Spain the universalistic Catholicism that suffused the Habsburg monarchy in the sixteenth and seventeenth century no longer held sway. The Bourbons were now in control, and King Charles III hoped to apply to his realm some of the precepts of "Enlightened despotism," the guiding policy for many other European monarchies of the late eighteenth century. In particular, the king wanted tighter state control over church activity throughout his realm. The Jesuit order, that very embodiment of the old universalism, had no place in the new scheme of things. The Jesuits fell out of favor at the court, being accused, among other things, of favoring papal over national authority in ecclesiastical policy. In 1767 the king signed a decree, published throughout the realm, expelling all Jesuits from the entire Spanish empire.[16] Fra Ilarione provides details of how the decree was carried out in Mexico City—tears came to his eyes as he saw soldiers with fixed bayonets herding Jesuits into carriages for their long journey to Veracruz and then into exile.

Foreign missions and missionaries were next to follow. Indeed, there had always been some tension between the missionary efforts backed by European monarchs and Rome's efforts to maintain control of foreign missions through Propaganda Fide. Ilarione's own account devotes some attention to the rivalry in Mexico between the Italian Capuchins, who reported to Rome, and their Spanish counterparts, beholden to the Spanish monarchy. In March 1768 Archbishop Francisco Antonio de Lorenzana y Buitrón informed Ilarione and his countryman, Father Lorenzo da Brà, that they must leave the country as well, though their departure was handled with more delicacy than that of the Jesuits nine months before. The archbishop was adhering to a royal decree banning all foreign clergy from Spanish America. On May 10 Ilarione set sail for Cuba and eventually Europe. As he sadly noted:

> Truly, a malefactor condemned to the galleys or the guardhouse does not leave for his place of torment with such pain and regret as I was now experiencing on departing from Mexico, never to return. I had come to feel completely at home with the climate, the food, my work, the cordiality of the inhabitants, and, in the end, everything else.

Fra Ilarione's return voyage aboard a frigate from Mexico to Spain took a month less and proved far less arduous than the Atlantic crossing five years earlier, for there were no hostilities at sea and fewer perilous storms. The high point was an enjoyable stay of nearly a month in Havana. There Ilarione visited El Morro and the other impressive fortresses guarding the bay, witnessed elaborate military maneuvers, and observed religious processions commemorating the feast of Corpus Christi. After leaving Cuba, Ilarione's ship transited the Bahama Channel; then it passed by Bermuda and the Azores, eventually dropping anchor in Cádiz.

After three weeks Ilarione set sail for Genoa, the major Italian port closest to his home. From there, he walked to Bergamo, arriving on October 6, 1768—no doubt to the great astonishment of friends and family, who barely recognized their sun-bronzed countryman after an absence of more than seven years. In this staid but pleasant city, Ilarione spent the remaining decade of his life. He must often have recalled his sojourn in New Spain, a land so distant and different from his own homeland, and no doubt he regaled the other friars with tales about travel and customs in Mexico. It is fortunate that he did not leave matters at that but instead committed his memories to paper, unwittingly sharing his experiences with readers more than two centuries later, after the conditions he described had perished forever with few records to recall them.

Despite its immense value as a source of information on Mexican life and customs in the colonial period, Ilarione's account is not without flaws. Its hurried composition and uneven organization are evident throughout. Although the author provided a very detailed narrative of the various episodes of his voyage to the New World, once he reached Mexico City he turned to a description of various aspects of Mexican life, where he was often far too cursory. The many instances when he broached a particular subject then apologetically dropped it as being too trivial or tedious to be of further interest can only exasperate the modern reader. One wishes that he had risked "boring" his contemporaries by indulging in fuller detail.[17]

Nor is Ilarione's style always worthy of the subject matter. True, the author had some education: a less-educated friar would not have quoted the Renaissance poet Torquato Tasso or mentioned the journey of Pietro Della Valle to Persia a century before, as Ilarione does. He had read contemporary works on geography and the history of the New World, some of which he may have consulted in his monastic library after his return to Bergamo. Nevertheless, he was not a graceful stylist of the Italian literary language, a shortcoming probably resulting from patchy formal education. The text is replete with incomplete or run-on sentences, linked only by a series of "and"s. Some passages are vague. Occasionally, regionalisms, Mexican Indian words, or Hispanicized Italian creep into the text. The original text simply lacks polish.

To enhance the readability of Ilarione's account, the translator and editors have made some structural changes. Most importantly, we have divided an uninterrupted narrative into chapters based on unifying themes. On one occasion, we moved six paragraphs from one section to another; these paragraphs, describing Mexico City, were removed from a section dealing with Mexican occupations and inserted into an earlier section about the viceregal capital. We also broke down unwieldy sentences into more manageable units, and in a few cases we modified phraseology to improve the syntax. For example, we converted cumbersome passive constructions to the active voice.

Ilarione's original manuscript is illustrated with thirty-eight colored drawings of Mexican flora. Not all of these illustrations have scientific or historical value; thus the editors have made a selection of the better ones, reproducing them in black and white. A few phrases in Ilarione's text that refer to the omitted illustrations have been deleted. In a few instances bracketed material has been inserted to provide information lost by not reproducing certain of these illustrations.

The editors have made liberal use of brackets and endnotes to identify persons and places, add pertinent information or dates, and provide translations of foreign or unusual words. Although Ilarione did not know the Nahuatl language, spoken by the Aztecs and many Mexican Indians even today, he included two Christian prayers and the Apostles' Creed in that language. Scholars may find some fault with his transcription of the Nahuatl passages, especially the spelling and word divisions, but we have decided to keep them in the form he recorded. In addition, we have provided the English-language Roman Catholic version of these prayers.

Ilarione's manuscript contains numerous Italianized misspellings of Spanish words ("tortiglias" for "tortillas," "cinghirito" for "chinguirito," "ciamporrado" for "champurado," "Lameda" for "Alameda," "Cortese" for "Cortés," et cetera). We have silently corrected most of these, generally leaving the author's misspellings only for the few cases where there might be some slight ambiguity about his intended meaning. Similarly, we have converted archaic spellings into their modern equivalents (e.g., "Guadalaxara" to "Guadalajara"). As a result, this English rendition may actually read more smoothly than the Italian original. Nevertheless, we have attempted to remain true to the spirit of the text, avoiding, for example, contemporary words or expressions that might seem out of place for an eighteenth-century narrative.

We invite readers to share Ilarione's adventures as he journeyed from Europe to the New World more than two hundred and fifty years ago.

Santa Barbara, California   ROBERT RYAL MILLER
Rome, Italy   WILLIAM J. ORR

*The Journey of
Friar Ilarione da Bergamo,
1761–1768*

VIAGGIO
AL MESSICO
NELL' AMERICA SETTENTI ONALE,

FATTO, E DESCRITTO

DA F. ILARIONE DA BERGAMO

RELIGIOSO CAPUCCINO

CON FIGURE.

ANNO MDCCLXX.

Second title page of Ilarione's manuscript.

CHAPTER ONE

BY LAND AND SEA
THROUGH ITALY

It has long been customary for travelers to write accounts of their journeys for the edification of all concerned. Yet many of these individuals have injected into their writings fabrications of various kinds and stories about impossible events. That has been to no avail; for not only did they fail to enlighten posterity, but they cast doubt on what was true as well. I, too, have written an account of my recent journey, not for the benefit of others but solely for my own diversion. Nevertheless, I also alert whoever might happen to read this that it contains nothing concocted, just the unvarnished truth—regarding both the countries seen and what befell me.

I have not described the exceptional items seen in various cities of our Italian homeland, because there is plenty of information about them. I have limited myself to just naming the cities and principal towns I passed through. My travel account has been embellished with various illustrations of American plants, flowers, and fruits.

It was in the year 1761 that I wrote to the Very Reverend Father Amato da Lamballa,[1] our procurator and general commissary, to inscribe me in the registry of alms-gatherers for [foreign] missions. My request was promptly granted. To shorten the time needed to send me [on a mission], I wrote to Monsignor Marefoschi, secretary of [the Congregation for the] Propagation of the Faith [Propaganda Fide], now a cardinal, who worked with the new procurator, the Very Reverend Father Girolamo Maria da Caltanisetta, a Sicilian, requesting instructions to go to Rome to learn the Sacred Congregation's decision. I received the instruction, which included orders to transfer to Parma and from there be accompanied by Father Mariano da Borgo S. Donnino, as he had also been summoned to Rome to be sent to the missions of Georgia.[2] I thought it certain I would be sent to Tibet, but that did not happen, as will become evident. I bade farewell to my parents with mutual anguish, as everyone can well imagine.

I left Bergamo on July 8, 1761, and proceeded to the sanctuary of Caravaggio, where I commended myself to the Most Blessed Virgin for the good fortune of my journey.[3] Thereupon I headed to the city of Crema, then Piacenza, and passed in succession through the villages of Fiorenzuola and San Donnino. I arrived in Parma, where the aforementioned Father Mariano was awaiting me, and we decided to travel together through Tuscany to Rome. We spent a few days in Parma. Then we set out on our journey and headed to Reggio di Modena, Modena, Bologna, and Florence. There I received letters from Rome informing me that the cardinal prefect of Propaganda Fide had changed his mind about my destination: he was no longer planning to send me to Tibet but to Mexico. The reason for this change was that a certain Brother Lorenzo da Mentone, a Genoan Capuchin assigned to Mexico by Propaganda Fide, had just died. For this reason, I was substituted for him, and in my place someone from the Province of Tuscany was sent to Tibet. He later died en route in Bombay in [the district of] Malabar.

After Florence we passed through the cities of Prato, Pistoia, Lucca, Pisa, and Livorno, where we arrived around the middle of August. In all the aforementioned cities we stayed a few days to see everything of note—churches, palaces, galleries, gardens, antiquities, and other things. We spent ten days in Livorno. I had the good fortune to meet with Father Giuseppe da Rovato, who was returning from Rome and who had arrived in that port to embark for Alexandria or Aleppo. Embracing that father, I could not suppress my tears because, apart from the love I bore him, I would have been appointed his companion to Tibet were it not for the change in favor of Mexico.

It so happened that, at the moment my companion and I were boarding for Civitavecchia,[4] an order arrived from Rome for him to return to his province of Parma. He had to comply with the order, though reluctantly, and on the following day I embarked on a Livornese *felucca*.[5] Because it was heavily laden and the south-westerly wind rose, which always brings on seasickness, and because this was the first time I had sailed, I was quite apprehensive. After three days I arrived in Civitavecchia. I went to our monastery not far from the city, and on following day I left by myself for Rome by land. I passed by Tolfa and Bracciano and entered Rome on September 11.

I presented myself to the most reverend father procurator general, who affectionately received me. From him I learned that I had been assigned to Mexico in the capacity of alms-gatherer for Propaganda Fide—that is, to seek alms to maintain our missionaries in the Kingdom of Tibet and other nearby kingdoms, missionaries to whom Propaganda Fide remits a certain sum of money each year for their upkeep.

After a few days I presented myself to Monsignor Marefoschi, the secretary of Propaganda Fide. While my dispatches were being prepared by this prelate, I had a chance to see Rome. The Most Eminent Spinelli, prefect of Propaganda Fide, also wanted to see me.[6] For that reason he sent for me at the monastery. He kept me with him for some time and took leave of me with urgings to look after the interests of Propaganda Fide in Mexico. After a twenty-day stay, I received from monsignor the secretary credentials for the archbishop of Mexico, as well as letters of recommendation for the archbishop of Genoa and the bishop of Cádiz, with Propaganda

Fide's decree making me an associate of the Tibetan missionaries for ten years.

I left Rome and went to Albano[7] to visit the Most Reverend Father Francesco Maria da Bergamo, current pontifical preacher. After two days I returned to Rome, where at Ripa Grande[8] I embarked on a Neapolitan felucca heading for Civitavecchia via the minuscule stream, the so-called Tiber, which leads to the ancient port of Ostia. I arrived on October 4 at Civitavecchia, where I had to stay eighteen days for lack of a vessel to Livorno or Genoa. In this port I witnessed the launching of a war frigate of thirty-six cannons. There was an immense concourse of people, a considerable racket, and an artillery barrage from the castle.

Eventually I embarked on a Genoan *pinco*,[9] having made my own provisions for food and drink during the voyage because the ship's master, for charitable reasons, only granted me free passage. On October 23 we set sail, and after nine days at sea I arrived at Savona, where the ship docked. This town is small, as is its harbor, suitable only for small vessels. It is thirty miles away from Genoa along the western coastline. Within three miles of this town there is a celebrated sanctuary of a very miraculous Madonna of Mercy,[10] but I did not see it because I had to take another boat for Genoa, where I arrived in less than three hours.

Let it be noted that during this brief voyage from Civitavecchia to Savona I experienced the utmost dread in the sense that sometimes I deemed myself irremediably lost, expecting to be submerged by the waves at any moment. But that was the result of lack of experience in sailing. Seeing the sea wildly agitated, I suffered terrible anguish, and in that condition I stood off to the side uttering fervent prayers. This went on particularly while at sea around Tuscany, where not only I but other passengers and the crew were still quite distressed because, after many hours of rather stormy sea, we had to head inland into a kind of bay or inlet shielded somewhat from the wind. But having eluded one peril, that of the storm, we were confronted by another one, perhaps worse, because from another boat, which passed close to us, we learned that five Algerian xebecs [three-masted vessels] were not far away. So we spent the whole night keeping watch.

From there we left in the morning after the sea grew calmer. In the course of the voyage, however, another storm arose, which we had to pass through on the way to Livorno, where we arrived at night. As soon as we cast anchor, we realized that the ship had touched bottom, because the master and the sailors were greatly perturbed. There was at the same time a tremendous thunderstorm and pelting rain. The lights went out, and total confusion prevailed. Eventually, after tremendous effort, they steered the vessel away from that site.

To guide it to a better location, it was necessary to pass between two tall ships. Because the space for passing was narrow and the sea agitated, our ship was in great peril of being dashed to pieces by other larger ones. So the master and sailors cried aloud for mercy. But no one emerged. Instead, the crew of the two ships we had to pass between did not want us to pass through at all. With shouts, blasphemies, and threats, they wanted to force us to turn back, but such were our humble entreaties that eventually they let us pass. Meanwhile I took my crucifix along with the scriptures and a little money I had. Leaving my other things behind, I hurriedly clambered up, ready to exit on one of the nearby boats should a grim accident occur.

Upon arriving in Genoa, I headed to the archbishop, Monsignor Giuseppe Maria Saporiti, to whom I presented the letter from the most eminent prefect. On the order of the aforementioned cardinal, I received fifty Roman *scudi*[11] from the archbishop, allowing me to make some provisions for my journey.

I spent nearly three months in Genoa, waiting for a vessel headed to Spain. In the meantime, I managed to see the rare attractions of that dominion. Eventually I made an agreement about my transportation to Cádiz with Captain Orebick, from Ragusa,[12] on his 300-ton-frigate *San Nicolò*. I paid him one hundred Genoan lire to be a cabin passenger with a seat at his table. The expense was not excessive because I was treated well the entire voyage. On January 19, 1762, I took leave of some of my friends, and that afternoon they accompanied me on board.

CHAPTER TWO

ACROSS THE MEDITERRANEAN
TO SPAIN

On the 20th [of January 1762] we set sail and for two days navigated with a favorable wind; then we were becalmed. On the fifth day we reached the Gulf of Lions, which we crossed in two days, and despite the general apprehension (because it is always rough-going) we crossed without mishap. Then we were becalmed again, leaving us stranded for three days within sight of the Balearic Islands—Majorca, Minorca, and Ibiza. On the night of the 30th we had a wind almost directly behind us, and for two days we covered a considerable distance. The remaining leg of the voyage proceeded more or less favorably.

Every day, except when there was a high wind, Holy Mass was celebrated on board by the chaplain, Father Giuseppe Macali da Crema, a Carmelite.[1] The rosary was recited every evening, with all the passengers and sailors joining in; and other prayers were chanted for a prosperous voyage. In periods of calm some passengers sought a bit of diversion from the tedium endured through going nowhere by playing various musical instruments. In addition, the variety of passengers themselves, with their wealth of stories, left a marked impression on my spirit, which felt like it was soaring off to a new world. Nevertheless, starting out on my journey, I still lacked that experience acquired later on. There were more than a hundred and twenty passengers, but just four in the stern, including myself—as I have noted above. There were Venetians, Illyrians, Maltese, Neapolitans, Genoans, Piedmontese, and others, including a few women.

In the course of our voyage, a Moorish xebec was sighted off in the distance. When he caught sight of it, our captain had the cannons, twenty-four in all, loaded. He made ready rifles, sabers, and other arms; put out the pennants or streamers on the main-mast; and hoisted the top sails, as though this were a warship. This was to fool the enemy—and we succeeded. On the quarterdeck he displayed all those on board, and eventually everyone stood ready to defend himself in the event of an attack. But when the xebec was close enough so it could make out our forces, in part simulated, with a spyglass, it sailed away. I now thought we were heading straight to Cádiz, as the captain and I had agreed upon. But he duped me, bringing me to Málaga and dropping anchor in that port. He made up contrived excuses about needing water and other items, but in reality he wanted to dispose of his cargo.

The same day we dropped anchor—February 6, the sixteenth day after our departure from Genoa—I went ashore with the chaplain. We went to the Capuchin monastery, which is toward the north, a short distance outside the city. Here the friars welcomed me with embraces, as they are accustomed to receiving foreigners throughout Spain. They led the two of us to the refectory, where they served us dinner, but I ate little because this was the first time I had sampled food cooked Spanish style. Though the pot of soup they offered us is not bad when well prepared, we did not eat much once we saw that medley of meat, lard, greens, chick-peas, and rice.

That afternoon all those friars gathered round to converse with us. Because they did not understand us, nor we them, the conver-sation ended with a stroll through the orchard of the monastery, which was truly delightful, because here, among other things, there was a gorgeous lane of rather tall citrus trees laden with fruits. There were various date palms as well. There was something else that caught my eye. By happenstance I saw in a corner of that orchard five or six dead children laid out on the ground. I inquired, to the best of my abilities, what this meant, and I learned that here it was the custom to accept dead children from poor people and bury them in the orchard. Later I observed the same practice in Cádiz, and I believe they do the same thing all over Spain.

Situated along the Mediterranean [coast], Málaga is a city of medium size, celebrated for its wines. It is a minor port but can take large vessels. In the rest of the city there is nothing worthy of note. Our ship stayed more than twenty days in this port, waiting for a wind from the east, so it could head for the Strait of Gibraltar. Meanwhile, I stayed sometimes in the monastery, sometimes on board.

After fourteen days of delay, seeing that the departure was being postponed, I decided to go to Cádiz by land. I took two Genoan passengers with me on February 20. Bidding farewell to the captain and leaving my effects on board, I headed toward Cádiz, a journey that took six days. [Along the way] I saw nothing exceptional apart from some sugar plantations; I chewed cane from them for the first time in Málaga. The principal towns I passed through were Ronda, Arcos, and Jerez de la Frontera, all three large towns and classified as cities by the Spaniards. Jerez is renowned for the finest horses in all of Andalucía and for the most exquisite wines of Spain.[2] In this town there was a monastery of Carthusians[3] and another of Capuchins. On February 26 I arrived at Puerto de Santa María, a small city situated on the Bay of Cádiz. It belongs to the duke of Medina Coeli.[4] There is nothing worthy of note there except for a huge plaza in the center of the city, where the captain general of the Andalusian coasts normally resides. The next day I boarded a ship and at midday arrived in Cádiz. I went to our monastery, a magnificent structure, with its numerous friars, who welcomed me with embraces, in the same fashion as they did in Málaga.

Cádiz, or Gades,[5] city, port, and place of arms—which in ancient times was associated with Juno because of a temple here dedicated to that goddess—is situated at 36 degrees, 30 minutes [of northern] latitude.[6] It does not extend very far because it is surrounded almost entirely by water, and there is no vacant land left for building houses. Gemelli states that it is only a half-league in circumference, but I say it is greater.[7]

Cádiz is very densely populated, with people from every nation except Africans arriving there. When I landed at this port on my return from America—that was in 1768—I found the greater part of the houses, formerly of moderate height, raised two additional stories.[8] Because they could not be widened, they were raised. Many regard this as a peninsula, though some maintain that it is an island, the basis of their judgment being a canal that slices off a small isolated tongue of land, which is on the road to Chiclana.[9] That canal passes above [under] a very fine bridge and connects the waters of the bay with those of the ocean (which is then all the same water). It is as though this were nothing more than a narrow arm of land connected to the continent. From this section there is but a single gate—the earthen gate, to be more precise. It has very sturdy walls, ditches, ramparts, casemates, batteries, etc., like the rest of the city as well. Aside from having a naturally strong position, it is completely surrounded by water, as I have noted. It is well fortified by design too.

There are two fine castles, San Sebastián and Santa Catalina. This second one is at the inlet of the port, facing the other castle located on the other section of the canal. Ships are required to enter there if they want to drop anchor inside the bay. Enemy ships cannot enter without being harried by cannons from the two castles facing each other.[10] In the bay, however, there are two forts called Los Puntales, one positioned on the little island called Matagorda, the other near Puerto Real, both surrounded by water. Around the city, in the section that looks out onto the sea as well as in the sections looking out onto the bay, there are solid batteries

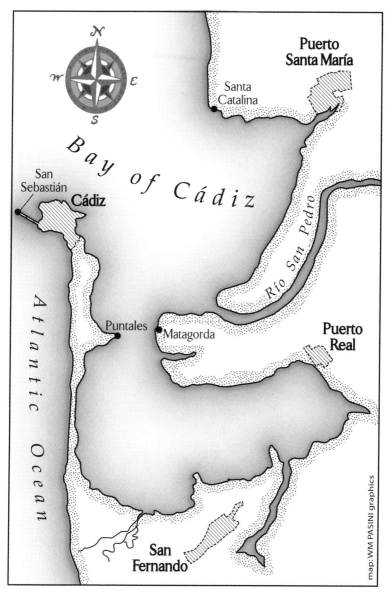

Bay of Cádiz, Spain. Map by William Pasini.

of cannons, always mounted, and mortars along every small stretch—all of them bronze. Some of these batteries were reconstructed in 1762, the year of the war with England.[11]

Besides the landward gate, there are three others toward the wharf. One near the great customhouse is called the Gate of Seville. Everything that is unloaded from the ships and brought into Cádiz passes through this gate, as do cargoes leaving the city. Of the other two gates, one is exclusively for those heading outside to stroll along the wharf or to embark. One can only enter through the other one. They do this to avoid the confusion generated by huge multitudes of people and to prevent fraud from being perpetrated on those handling customs duties.

The buildings are not inconsiderable, but the streets are nearly all winding, narrow, and very filthy because they throw refuse of every kind into the streets, as in Málaga (and, I believe, throughout Spain). For that reason there is a pervasive stench during the summer, particularly in certain areas. There is a small but lovely Alameda, or woods, for strolling, and it is located almost at the entrance to the port.

When I arrived in this city in 1762, they were engaged in constructing a sumptuous cathedral. On my return from Mexico in 1768, I found it well advanced, with its entire choir already roofed. It is a fine work of architecture adorned with massive marble from Carrara, and I believe the final result will be in keeping with Italian taste.[12] The other churches are all well maintained and generally opulent, the furnishings being of silver with all the *retablos* gilded.[13]

Among all the churches of Cádiz, I particularly liked the little church of the Divine Shepherdess, which looks like a paradise in miniature.[14] This name was devised by a Capuchin missionary father to honor the Blessed Virgin through this title. It then spread throughout not just Spain, but America and other regions as well. Of the various Capuchin styles, the church of the Capuchins is one of the finer ones I have seen. The main altar has fine paintings.

There are eleven other highly lustrous altars, and there is always a tremendous throng of people because of the frequent services. Confessions are heard, not just for nationals but in the Italian, French, and Irish languages as well.[15] Every Sunday a missionary father begins the rosary in our church and, accompanied by many people who form into a procession, goes around the districts of the city. In some spot heavily frequented by the people, he delivers a fine sermon, then returns to the church, bringing the rosary to a conclusion. Here he delivers another brief sermon, concluding the event by having everyone recite an act of contrition, giving the people a blessing with the crucifix. Often the Blessed Sacrament is then displayed for public adoration. Every Friday another Capuchin, with many people accompanying him, leaves with an elevated crucifix to undertake the Via Crucis [Way of the Cross], which begins at the three crosses, which are close to the victory monument near the monastery gate. All the crosses along the stations are of marble and quite large. The victory monument consists of a rather tall column with a very fine statue of the Immaculate Conception on top. At the base it is surrounded by balustrades with various statues of angels and saints of the order—and all of this in Carrara marble.

The Bay of Cádiz is eight leagues in circumference. Ships from practically every nation anchor here because it is one of the better and most frequented ports of call. Arriving here were Muscovite [i.e., Russian], Swedish, Danish, English, and Dutch ships, and those from all the ports of the Mediterranean, and even from Danzig, Prussia, and other seas farther north. It was like a perpetual fair with the immense throng of peoples from foreign lands. So it is a splendid sight on solemn days, and on other occasions, too, such as the birthday or related events for [members of] the royal family, when all the ships in the bay are adorned with flags and pennants of various colors. There is the boom of cannons too, customary on such occasions. There are many other things I could mention about this city and port, but to avoid delay I will move on.

On February 27, 1762, two or three days after my arrival in Cádiz, I paid a visit to Monsignor Don F. Tomás del Valle,[16] a Dominican, the bishop of Cádiz, to whom I presented a letter of recommendation from Propaganda Fide. He favored me with the most courteous expressions of esteem, and during the time of my stay in Cádiz I paid him several visits. I presented still more letters of recommendation to several gentlemen and merchants, and this effort was not in vain.

After a few days, a letter for me arrived from Madrid from his Excellency Monsignor Lazaro-Opizio Pallavicini, a Genoan, archbishop of Lepanto and apostolic nuncio at the Spanish court (he is now a cardinal).[17] He bade me to go to the royal ministry, the Casa de Contratación [Board of Trade] of the Indies there in Cádiz, to receive the royal dispatch for my passage to Mexico.[18] For that reason I headed to that ministry, but there I was told they had no such order from the court. I then informed monsignor nuncio by letter about what had happened.

Before getting to the response, let me return to our Ragusa ship, which, it will be recalled, I left in the port of Málaga. It lifted anchor from that port on February 24, heading for Cádiz, but was detained in Gibraltar for a period of fifteen days by the English. Eventually it was released and on March 14 arrived in Cádiz. I promptly boarded it to pick up my trunk and other items, which I brought to our monastery.

After fifteen days, monsignor nuncio replied to me that he had sent an order to the ministry or president of the Casa de Contratación to deliver the dispatch to me and that I should go back there. But that was to no avail because I received the same response as the first time. Therefore, I felt considerable affliction and sadness not only for the aforementioned reason, but even more because I considered it morally impossible for me to proceed to America because of the war declared in January of this year by the court of London on that of Madrid.[19] For that reason the king of Spain had issued a strict injunction that no ship should leave his ports because

English vessels in pursuit of Spanish vessels were always within sight of Cádiz. Because I would have to stay here a long time due to the uncertainty about when peace would be concluded, I indicated to the most reverend father procurator the difficulties noted above in proceeding to my destination. He replied that I should proceed to Madrid to obtain my dispatch. As for the war, he urged me to be patient until the return of peace; I should remain calm. Meanwhile, I would have the opportunity to familiarize myself with the city, visit many homes, and see churches and monasteries.

Often I went on board various ships and, among others, I once boarded a Spanish warship along with some students for the priesthood. After having provided us with refreshment, the captain had the soldiers on board perform exercises with two discharges of rifles. A few times I even saw the plying of oars by Dutch launches. Other times I attended the firing of cannons.

CHAPTER THREE

CAPTURED BY THE ENGLISH

I bided my time in Cádiz until the end of June 1762, when I learned that a wealthy local merchant named Ostaris, at his own expense and risk, had loaded two *saetías*[1] bound for America, which would serve as escort or courier ships. I wanted to take advantage of the opportunity even though many attempted to dissuade me, as there was a war going on and these craft were incommodious because of their small size. Weary, though, of my stay in Cádiz, I requested, through another round of letters to monsignor nuncio, that the dispatch be sent (because I decided not to go to Madrid in person to obtain it). Eventually this was sent to me. I delivered it to the president [of the Casa de Contratación], and he promptly gave the order to Señor Ostaris to take me aboard one of his two saetías. When I went to see this merchant to come to an agreement about the manner of my passage to America, he received me with a display of respect. He commended me to the captain with instructions to accommodate me in the stern and at his table, all this free of charge.

After having spent four and a half months in Cádiz, on July 9 I boarded the saetía, which was named *Nuestra Señora de la Merced*. Once I was aboard, a rather ludicrous incident occurred in the following way: A few hours after we set sail (and were already outside the bay) I was alone in the cabin below the stern and putting my effects in order, when I noticed that above deck various other passengers from the same room where I was accommodated were scurrying about. Also drawn by curiosity from ignorance about what was going on, I scampered above deck, like the others, and saw that the sea was quite agitated. One person was casting trunks into the water, another ropes; somebody else was tossing [overboard] whatever other item came into his hands; another person was lowering the sails; somebody else was summoning the chaplain; and someone else was making efforts to lower the lifeboat into the water. I did not understand the reason for this commotion. Suddenly I imagined that the trunks were being tossed to lighten the ship, and that the lifeboats were being launched to rescue people, and that the sail was being lowered because of the stormy sea. Considering myself irretrievably lost, I fell down on my knees to commend myself to God for a merciful death, the dread of which made me swoon. I was trembling all over from head to foot. Then, when I saw that all the activity was for the sole purpose of rescuing a sailor who had fallen from a yardarm into the water (whom they recovered alive, in fact), I laughed at my simplemindedness.

It was noon when we set sail. We traveled under a favorable wind until evening, when an English vessel was sighted. When it came within view, we headed toward the minor port of Sanlúcar de Barrameda, where we dropped anchor and spent the night. Early in the morning we set sail again with a reasonably favorable wind; but after navigating a while, we again sighted the English ship, which was heading our way at full sail. Our captain tried to escape by sailing away, but in less than an hour it was on top of us and suddenly began firing its cannons, loaded with grapeshot, to shred our sails. Indeed, with less than forty cannonades, it succeeded in shredding all the sails.

Meanwhile, I stayed in the room below deck with the other passengers. Because I thought they were firing cannons at us to send us to the bottom, I remained kneeling in front of an image of the Blessed Virgin and was weeping profusely, fearful of death, which I felt was imminent and inescapable. Great, otherwise, was my remorse for having embarked in time of war and finding myself in such peril of life; but I still have not finished my story, as you shall soon see.

Seeing the sails in shreds, our captain, unable to flee, cast into the sea the trunk filled with letters, including some from the court. Then he raised the flag of surrender—that is to say, lowered the Spanish flag to the foot of the mast as a sign of surrender. They quickly boarded and took possession of the vessel as a fine prize, hoisting the flag of England above that of Spain. Everyone, passengers as well as sailors, was led aboard their ship, each carrying items for personal use. As I was approaching the English ship, I heard some people remarking that the devil was nigh, and from this I could infer the kind of treatment I would receive.

The English vessel, a war frigate with forty-six cannons, was named *Pallas*. Its captain was a young man from the same nation, twenty-two years old, who was pacing the deck. The first meal I ate on the frigate was with those nasty sailors. We had some English pudding and salted meat. Fortunately for me, the captain's master fiddler was a Florentine Catholic, from whom I requested a bit more decent treatment. He spoke perfect English; so he talked to the captain, and I was assigned a more decent mess, i.e., with this Florentine and others from his circle.

For all that, I had a difficult time during the five or six days I was on board that frigate because they derided me, especially when they saw me, rosary in hand, reciting the Paternoster [Our Father]. And there was a cabin boy so insolent that, while I was standing at the table eating with my other mess companions, he took water into his mouth, stealthily headed toward a more prominent spot, and spat the water on my cape. But he paid dearly for this contemptuous deed because he was lashed to the cannon and received a good whipping on his buttocks.

My trunk and basket were examined, and only a few small, trifling items were removed from them. They took possession of the trunk of letters our captain had tossed into the sea. That chest stayed afloat because it had not been weighted down, and though all the letters were soaked, they were delivered to the English admiral whom we encountered in the Strait of Gibraltar. For this reason—i.e., for not having sent this trunk to the bottom—the Spanish captain was sent to prison upon his return to Cádiz.

Two days after our captivity, they discovered the other saetía, which had departed at the same time as our own on the same voyage—i.e., to America. They pursued it, and during the night there was cannon fire. Before the frigate *Pallas* (where I was) got close to it, however, two other English frigates, along with a Portuguese packet boat, were approaching, directing heavy cannonades its way. Because it was nighttime already, the three frigates armed two launches and dispatched them to board the saetía. Many people aboard it were injured by gunfire and sabers. Eventually they had to surrender and were all led aboard one of the two other frigates. The chief officers from the Spanish saetía were put in chains for having hurled overboard whatever they could of the merchandise on the ship. Once again I lamented my misfortune, seeing myself in constant peril of life, because on board the frigate I heard that if our captain had delayed just a little while longer before surrendering, the English captain was intent on sending us to the bottom, once and for all, with a full-scale broadside.

We spent a few days along the coasts of Spain, and they took us to within sight of Lisbon as well. Then they turned back and transported us in one of the two other frigates, called *Chinenson* [*Kensington*?], where I received better treatment by being admitted to the table of the higher officers and where I was respected. Once accommodated in the new frigate, we headed in the direction of Gibraltar and passed the strait with considerable effort because of the very heavy east wind, which was a headwind. With considerable tacking, which brought us near the coasts of Africa, then those of Europe, we eventually arrived in the Bay of Gibraltar. Before entering the strait, we encountered the English admiral on a ship with 128 cannons. It looked like a floating castle, escorted by a convoy of eighteen to twenty other very large and small vessels. Our captain halted and handed over to the admiral the letters from Spain, seized from the Spanish saetía, as I have noted above.

All told, I spent twelve days in English hands. When word arrived in Cádiz about our captivity, some Capuchin promptly wrote to the father procurator general in Rome about what had happened to me. He advised Propaganda Fide, whereupon they sought my ransom, believing me in distress. Before the letter arrived in Rome, though, I was already free.

On July 21 they dropped anchor in the port of Gibraltar, where we stayed the entire day and part of the following.[2] Through the spyglass I had the chance to view the plaza's fortifications, consisting primarily of a double wall, which ascends laterally to the summit of the mountain, at the foot of which is situated the plaza of Gibraltar. That mountain is entirely a natural rock formation and so steep that it resembles a high wall. It is packed with batteries, carved into the rock, positioned one on top of the other. On the summit there is a small but sturdy castle. I could not observe the fortifications facing the sea because we had dropped anchor in a location where they could not be discerned. I also saw four gallows, with [corpses of] men dangling from all of them; they are left there until they later fall apart. In the plaza there is a church where some Observant fathers officiate.[3] The English allowed this for the convenience of the Catholic merchants who live in this plaza or come there to do business.

On the final day our captain offered us a solemn repast aboard the frigate, but our table companions were just myself, our Spanish captain, three or four other respectable passengers, that same English captain, and a few officers. Then they put all of us aboard a launch, each of us with his own effects, and set us ashore. Meanwhile, to the beat of a drum, the English commandant left the plaza on horseback just as the Spanish commandant likewise arrived in the same manner from his guard post at the site called La Línea, near Gibraltar, not a quarter of a mile away. Here the English commandant handed over numbered lists [of released prisoners] to the Spaniard, and the ceremony thus came to an end.

I then wanted to enter Gibraltar, intending to stay there one or two days. For this purpose I had two letters of recommendation obtained aboard the *Pallas*. But due to the state of war, the guard did not let me. So I had my things carried by a porter and that same evening headed for a town called San Roque, where I found lodging with a benefactor. The following day, that is, July 22, I headed on to a small city called Algeciras, situated along the coast of the bay facing Gibraltar. There I stayed for four days in another benefactor's home, waiting while a ship headed for Cádiz was being loaded.

In the meantime I will briefly recount the daring exploit undertaken by the captain of the frigate *Pallas*, who took us prisoner. After having transferred us to the frigate *Chinenson*, the *Pallas* headed toward Cádiz. One fine afternoon it passed Los Puercos (which are some reefs visible at the mouth of the bay). There was cannon fire from the two castles facing each other, i.e., San Sebastián and Santa Catalina. But the balls did not reach the ship; instead, those from the ship hit the castles. It moved even farther in. Coming within range of the first Spanish ships—seven xebecs and one oceangoing one, which were scheduled to head out to sea in a few days—it began firing cannons at them. There was no response from even one of them because their captains and officers were disporting themselves on shore. Word had it that twelve Spanish sailors were killed. The captain-commandant, who was also ashore, was informed of all this and replied that he did not have an order from the court to defend himself (a truly preposterous response). Nevertheless, he gave orders for all the captains and officers who were on shore to go aboard [their ships] at once and promptly set sail to pursue the English frigate. But after having mocked the Spanish nation and destroyed its ships, it swiftly headed out [to sea] and escaped. Truly, this was a feat of memorable audacity and of no little glory for the English captain, and no less ignominy and consternation for the officers of the Spanish navy—all the more so since the news was disseminated all over Europe in public gazettes.

On July 26 I boarded a ship loaded with charcoal. Once more I passed through the strait [of Gibraltar] and again headed to Cádiz, where, upon my arrival, I gave notice, in a letter to monsignor nuncio in Madrid, about what happened to me. He promptly sent me a new dispatch to transfer me to America once peace was concluded. I also informed our most reverend father procurator in Rome about what happened to me; from him, too, I received a comforting response.

In September of the same year [1762] came word that the English had besieged Havana, a city and substantial Spanish port on the island of Cuba, indeed the gateway to all America. The siege lasted twenty-nine days and was undertaken by a very sizable fleet, whose admiral was Milord Pocock with the earl of Albemarle.[4] The governor of the celebrated citadel, called El Morro, was Captain Velasco, who died in glory, run through by a sword for refusing to surrender the flag to the aggressors.[5] Don Juan de Prado was governor of the city. The residents of Cádiz made light of that siege, believing El Morro was impregnable. In October, however, a flotilla of English and Dutch ships appeared with a white flag. That flotilla conveyed the garrison from the city of Havana and [personnel from] its fortresses and ships from there. Part of that garrison was disembarked in Cádiz and part in El Ferrol. [We learned that] El Morro had been taken by assault and the city had capitulated. This occurred in August 1762. Great was the consternation in Cádiz when this fleet appeared, and at once the terraces of the homes thronged with onlookers. This was beyond their comprehension, and many ascribed such a loss to treason.

About this time, in the vicinity of Cádiz, an English ship seized a Spanish frigate coming from Lima, Peru, with a cargo of four million [pesos], the greater part in coins. After having made such a long voyage and nearly reached port, this frigate fell into the hands of its enemies because no one aboard knew there was a war going on between the two powers. But in some ways they brought this loss upon themselves because they put up minimal resistance— with all the men, and the officers in particular, waiting to bag the money they had in their own trunks rather than fight as they were supposed to do. So they surrendered in cowardly fashion. The captain of this frigate, too, was sent to prison but soon released. If he had behaved this way on an English ship, he would have been summarily hanged.

CHAPTER FOUR

VOYAGE TO THE NEW WORLD

Having now grown weary of my stay in Cádiz, I felt ill-at-ease, not knowing what recourse remained. I was tempted to return to my homeland for the duration of the war because there was no way of knowing when it would end. On the other hand, going back struck me as unseemly. In November [1762], however, my courage rallied with news that the warring courts—that is, Spain, Portugal, and England—were discussing peace. Indeed, at the end of this month the preliminaries were announced—to universal jubilation. Havana was then restored to Spain, which ceded to England a tract of land from the Mississippi River to Pensacola, which is in the Florida peninsula.[1]

People promptly complied with the order for some transport vessels to send to America. So I headed for the president [of the Casa de Contratación] to obtain my vessel. At no cost, I got a frigate named *San José* from the Consulado [merchants' guild]. It was a small frigate, badly loaded, and poorly outfitted due to its age. But because of my tremendous longing to depart for my destination, I made do with this. Before long, though, I would regret my decision, as will be evident.

On January 2, 1763, I boarded with my effects, having spent, all told, ten months plus a few days in Cádiz. Due to the bad weather, we spent twenty-four days on board before we could set sail. One night we came perilously close to perishing because of a gale, which gave rise to a sizable tempest inside the bay where we lay at anchor—two hawsers being broken and [with us] holding out on hope alone. Finally, on the 26th we set sail, but that day we made little headway outside Los Puercos reefs because we were becalmed. At midnight a very powerful south wind arose, which was contrary to us, and it lasted several days.

It should be noted that when we left port we were a convoy of nine vessels—that is, with two line warships called *El Magnánimo* and *Eolo* that provided us escort against the Moors all the way to the Canaries, after which they would return to El Ferrol [Spain]. Another war frigate, called the *Venus*, had the same itinerary, purpose, and destination. Besides the ones mentioned above, [and a small vessel headed for Havana,] there were four large transport vessels to the Indies. With those remaining, we were to make the journey to America: one [ship] to Campeche, one to Cartagena of the Indies, one to Buenos Aires, one to Lima. Only the *San José* was destined for Veracruz.

The bad weather worsened, and the main- and foremasts toppled on one of our companions. Aboard ship, too, things took a turn for the worse because of our cramped condition. For that reason the discomforts of a stormy sea were felt in greater measure, and I spent most of the time standing on deck, very seasick, able neither to eat nor to rest. I was vomiting incessantly.

On the eleventh day after our departure from Cádiz, the sea grew calmer. We had a favorable wind, but we reaped no benefit from it because practically the whole convoy was dispersed. With us were just the flagship *El Magnánimo* and the *Venus*. We had to wait until the entire aforementioned convoy reunited because such were the orders and instructions for traveling in convoy, which is designed to ward off attacks by Moorish corsairs, should they appear. Word had it that various vessels of theirs were cruising the Atlantic. By this time we had covered not more than about one hundred leagues since leaving the port of Cádiz headed toward the Canaries.

On board we had a crew of sixty-four sailors and some officers, i.e., captain, pilot, second pilot, watchman, boatswain, chaplain, surgeon, etc. Cabin passengers included the deputy-viceroy of Yucatán, or Campeche, a brother of the bishop of Guatemala, two merchants from Seville, and myself. There was one woman, also a cabin passenger. Passengers in steerage included more than seventy riffraff, people who go to America clandestinely without the obligatory licenses required by the laws of Spain. Because we did not see the entire convoy emerge, we continued our voyage under minimal wind with the flagship, the *Venus*, and a small vessel with a single mast, which was making the voyage to Havana.

On February 11, the sixteenth day after our departure from Cádiz, a very powerful south-southwest wind arose, convulsing the ocean with such a storm that we all thought ourselves utterly and irretrievably lost. So high were the ocean's waves that the ship was tossed like a ball. The wind was roaring and waves raging, arousing terror. Enormous amounts of water surged into the ship so that we were continually on our feet day and night, working the pump (as they say)—that is, removing the water using suction. All of us, passengers and crew, were so exhausted from the toil and hunger that work was no longer possible. The rudder was out of control. There were no other sails except for the mid foremast, and the wind had ripped this to shreds, like the others. The midmast collapsed, and in the end we were totally at the mercy of the raging sea.

It was impossible to stand up straight. On deck it was always necessary to cling to something to avoid being tossed from one side of the ship to the other because of the tremendous undulations. All our provisions of fresh meat—veal, mutton, pork, chicken, and many other items—were washed overboard. From the beginning of the storm, I stayed in my *catre*, or small bed, and with one hand I always clutched a timber and in the other the crucifix, commending my soul because I deemed myself irretrievably lost. In this way I passed the last two days and nights without food, drink, and sleep, and unable to satisfy any other bodily need. For two days all the others, too, had a little biscuit and nothing else. All were weeping like children. One person was making vows, another person invoking a particular saint, and somebody else [asking] still another one to come to our aid. Various sailors, sotted on brandy to numb themselves against the sting of death, called upon all the demons in Hell. Others were blaspheming in such desperation that it was a horrifying spectacle.

There was a fine old man whose duty was that of boatswain. His son was a friar in the Order of Minims,[2] and he nurtured great devotion for the founding saint, an image of whom he carried on a card. In the storm's full fury, he attached it to the mainmast. Full of assurance—I do not know if I would call it filial, presumptuous, or desperate—he addressed it thus: *Padre San Francisco o libranos de esta tormenta, o yo riniego de vuestros milagros, y si puedo bolver a mi casa quiero sacar mi higo de vuestros Frayles, ni quiero mas hacer caridad ninguna a los mismos.*[3] Like everyone else, this poor man was weeping so profusely that it was truly a pathetic spectacle.

Finding themselves together, the captain, the helmsman, and all the other officers grew weary from struggling to withstand such a ferocious storm. Seeing that every effort was to no avail, the captain mounted the quarterdeck and, in a loud voice for all to hear, said that everyone should prepare himself for the life to come because there was no hope of salvation and we would definitely go under. With this pronouncement from the captain, who was a taciturn person and quite prudent, the weeping and screaming intensified. One person publicly confessed his sins. Another cried out to the Lord for mercy and to the Virgin for succor and to all the saints of Heaven. One person blasphemed more horribly than ever. When I heard this news, being in my cot as described, my whole body was bathed in sweat, which I thought must be the sweat of death. I was trembling from head to foot and performed nothing but acts of contrition and professions of faith. Now I bitterly repented the undertaking I had set out upon. I thought about my parents, and I cannot express the anguish and distress of heart I felt at that point. I continued this way until about midnight. All the lights had gone out. Tremendous quantities of water were constantly gushing into the ship, and, all told, there was confusion beyond compare.

The chaplain, a priest from Seville, also mounted the quarterdeck and in a loud voice gave absolution to everyone. Now let all who read this ponder the doleful state we found ourselves in. For a poor condemned wretch on the gallows, his dread and death agony last only a few moments, but to be expecting it for several days was onerous indeed. During this struggle all of us cabin passengers made our vow to the Divine Shepherdess that if we were delivered from death and brought to our port of call, we would present Her the sail from the foremast. Once we reached the port of Veracruz, we would proceed from the wharf to Her church, all of us barefoot, and there sing a solemn mass in Her honor.

Once this vow had been made and everyone was filled with hope in the Mother of Mercies, the captain undertook the final expedient, possibly not considered until now, of changing course and letting the ship move along with the winds because we were on the high seas and thus there was little peril from shoals. But could this be carried out if we were without sails, in the darkest night, with no lights, and with such a raging sea that it looked like it would lift the waves to the heavens? Nevertheless, the officers readied themselves for this final, very perilous measure. Once again, with loud cries, we appealed to Heaven to help us in whatever way possible. In particular, we turned to the Most Blessed Virgin, invoking one name or another. Slowly, the crew succeeded in changing course. But such was our peril during this quarter of an hour that one side of the ship was already well under water. God eventually had mercy, and by a sheer miracle the ship was turned and thus the primary danger averted for the time being.

Just when there was some slight hope of avoiding shipwreck, right after changing course, another ordeal transpired, no less

perilous than the first, but this passed quickly at least. Despite the
tremendous roaring of the winds and sea, voices could be heard of
people shouting, and that turned out to be from the frigate *Venus*
so close to us, also buffeted by the waves and winds that prevented
steering. It had come so close to us that it was nearly on top of our
ship. Such was its proximity that barely was there time to make it
out and shout *orsa! orsa!* [luff! luff!] to the helmsman. The poor
captain was stomping his feet and with other officers was again
beseeching God for mercy. Once more, when this frigate passed so
close to us while the sea was so stormy and the night so dark, it
was a miracle that, when it was time to luff, it did not collide with
us. If the disaster had come to pass with the two vessels colliding,
ours would surely have succumbed, being the smaller one and
poorly rigged. In that case death would have been inevitable. The
rest of that night and for the next two days we moved under the
power of the wind and waves without knowing where [we were
going]. Gradually, though, the wind began to abate and the sea
grew calmer; but not one of our companion ships could be seen,
and we did not know where they were headed.

    With a light but favorable wind, we picked up the course toward
the Canaries, from which we had strayed. So our spirits were
lifted—though not so much in my case, as I would have preferred
to return to Cádiz (there being rumors on board of such a likeli-
hood). In that case, I was bent on returning to my homeland
because by now I had suffered enough fear and peril of life from
the fickle elements. The favorable wind lasted a few days. Meanwhile they repaired the ship as best they could, and the people
recuperated after the poor food and even worse sleeplessness
during the stormy passage. But the supply of fresh meat had been
washed overboard, as I have noted; so at our table we had to settle
for salted meat.

    On the twenty-sixth day after our departure from Cádiz, on
February 20, land was sighted—the Canary or Blessed Isles.[4] That
was a very long period of time for such a voyage, as they are only

300 leagues away, a distance that can be covered in eight days. The sight of land filled all of us with gladness even though we had not reached the end of our journey and still had a long way to go. Yet it is only natural to take heart at the sight of land after so many days of privations and even more ordeals.

We passed between Grand Canary and Tenerife Island, which are only about ten miles apart. Here we were becalmed for two days until the wind picked up, allowing us to resume our voyage. Now I will say a few words about these islands.

In the division of the world into four quarters, the Canaries are adjacent to Africa and belong to the crown of Spain.[5] They are located between 26 degrees 30 minutes and 29 degrees 30 minutes northern latitude. The main ones are Grand Canary, the bishop's residence; and Tenerife, the site of that mountain so famous for its elevation. It is said to be the highest of those on the face of the earth; and it really can be seen from very far away—the Spaniards call it the Pico de Teide.[6] In addition, there are Hierro, the island from which most geographers and pilots take the first meridian; Madeira,[7] which belongs to the Portuguese; La Palma; Gomera; Lanzarote; and Fuerteventura. There are a few of minor importance as well. These islands enjoy a most felicitous climate, and they abound in exquisite wines, celebrated even in our Italian homeland. They also have abundant sugar, tobacco, coconuts, bananas, and other fruits from America. There is even an abundance of wheat and other products, which I will not enumerate in the interest of brevity. We did not go ashore. For this reason I could do nothing more than stand, gazing through a spyglass at the verdant shores of these islands.

After two days of calm, a favorable but light wind set in, lasting several days. We entered into a tremendous gulf a thousand miles long, called Las Damas by the Spaniards; they call it "the ladies" because normally there are no perilous storms there. During the passage of this gulf, lasting about a month, I enjoyed observing a variety of fish, and primarily some of enormous size, which are called *tiburoni*.[8] Following one after the other, they move ahead in the form of a procession, numbering forty, fifty, and even more. They are a splendid sight to behold as they move along because one emerges after the other, with the greater part of its body above the water, and then dives again. So they proceed on their journey, always in a northerly direction. We did not derive much enjoyment from the passage of these fish, however, because this was a certain omen of bad weather, as I actually observed to be the case. They are not good to eat, but if the sailors take some for sport, they extract only the blubber and the gall bladder. What purpose these two parts serve I did not bother to find out. In fact, they caught one—which they said was of medium size—with certain iron tools, which they carry on board for this purpose. They secure it with ropes passed through pulleys, and to do this several people were needed. It was situated on the quarterdeck and was tossing with such vigor that it was a sight to behold. Near the Windward Islands we saw a whale; various sea turtles; and a *bufeo*, as the Spanish call it, which expels water to a considerable height from its nostrils, like two fountains.[9]

Now the ship was nearly always accompanied by a goodly number of certain fish, called *dorados* [golden ones] from the color of their scales, which are the size of the largest pikes in Italy.[10] These fish like to follow the ships because they eat various items cast into the water. When we were not moving much, it was easy to catch some of them because they practically float on top of the water. They are very good to eat. But what I found even more delightful in this regard were the many schools of small fish, a little larger than our pilchard, leaving the water and soaring above it, to a height of more than six *braccia*,[11] for the distance of a pistol shot. Sensing that their fins were drying out, they submerged once more. They are called *voladores* [flying fish] by the Spaniards and are very good to eat. They leave the water in schools, and at times some of them collide with ships, as happened to us one day when three of them landed on deck. One of them was roasted and presented to me by the captain, and I actually found it quite delicate.

Another aquatic animal frequently seen resembled a bladder of spherical shape, always floating on the surface of the water, immobile and transparent like a crystal. They told me it had no body other than some very slender and very long appendages, but I did not see it outside the water to establish this with any certitude. This animal is called *aguamala* by the Spaniards because they say the water it contains in the bladder, which is seen floating on the water, is quite noxious. Others called it nautilus.[12]

I have noted the aforementioned minor details because during a long voyage every little trifle helps pass the time. I have not written about the points of the compass, the winds, and the manipulations of the sails because these are detailed matters and, furthermore, would be of interest only to specialists in nautical matters.

Likewise, on the ship there was nothing worthy of note except that we had to go without mass for more than a month because our chaplain, a priest from Seville, a stout and very fat man, had fallen out of his bed. Because he fractured his skull, the surgeon had to treat him, and he was bedridden. Once he got better, though, he wanted to celebrate mass out of a sense of obligation, even on the bad days when there was a raging sea, and against the advice of the captain and other officers. Thus twice he wanted to celebrate mass, even though there were tremendous undulations, making it hard for him to stay on his feet. So, at the captain's behest, since I was the only other cleric—I was put in position to hold the base of the chalice with one hand while two sailors sustained the celebrant.

CHAPTER FIVE

ISLANDS OF THE CARIBBEAN

On March 19, [1763,] the island of Saint Martin came into view. It is one of the Windward or Caribbean islands belonging to the English.[1] We moved ahead and in two days, to our immense relief, sighted the island of Puerto Rico, where we were headed for reprovisioning. As we continued our approach to the island, each person who had one took out his spyglass—with me, perhaps, being one of the first—to satisfy that natural curiosity about viewing a new land so far from one's own native soil. I saw, first of all, a vast multitude of people who were scurrying to the top of a small summit near the city to watch our vessel enter the port.[2] It struck them as a novelty that a Spanish ship should appear on their shores because they were unaware of the recent peace with England—our very ship being the bearer to that island of tidings about peace. In another place I saw a gallows on which there were four heads, which had not yet begun to decompose.

As we approached the port, the pilot arrived, as is the custom in every port. Guiding our ship, he conducted it into port; and we dropped anchor on March 21, 1763, after we had saluted the city with seven cannon shots and it had responded to us with five. Suddenly, various canoes arrived, which are, in fact, very long and narrow skiffs. They are used by those swarthy Indians who, thanks to their disfigurement, swarthiness, and many other factors, nearly took on a demonic appearance for me because I had not seen a race of people like this before.[3] They were carrying native fruits; thus I began enjoying the delights of America, forgetting the travails endured during the protracted voyage.

The following day I went ashore. There were no lodging houses or inns in this country, but every home takes in foreigners, who pay an agreed-on sum for lodging. So I, too, found a house and reached an agreement with the owner about how much I should pay every day for room and board. What little linen I brought for my own use was dirty, as were my habits, because keeping clean is hardly possible at sea. I had everything laundered and put all my things in order.

Before providing a brief description of this city and island, I will mention how I came to visit monsignor the bishop, who is a suffragan of the archbishop of Santo Domingo. He received me with a display of esteem, had me sit near him, and kept me for more than an hour to discuss various matters. I also paid a visit to the father guardian of the Observant fathers, who was kind enough to show me their monastic retreat. I did not want to accept lodging, though, having been told about the harsh poverty of this monastery.[4] Before long I took advantage of the comfort afforded by the house where I was lodged to put my things in order.

In olden times the Antilles Islands, of which Puerto Rico is one of the main ones, were called the Hesperides. Now they are called Antilles, or Caribbean, and the common people call them Barlovento [Windward] or Sopravento [Leeward]. This island was discovered by Christopher Columbus in 1493.[5] It lies between 17 and 18 degrees of northern latitude and was called Borichen [Borinquén] by the aborigines. From the eastern end of the Northern Sea [Atlantic Ocean], it is twenty-five or thirty leagues away from the island of Santo Domingo or Hispaniola. The island belongs to the king of Spain, who maintains a governor there with an adequate garrison. The island has one city, which is called San Juan de Puerto Rico.

The island is about fifty-five leagues long and eighteen to twenty wide.[6] It enjoys a very pleasant climate, on the warmer rather than the more temperate side, however. We arrived at this island on March 21, as I have noted. Nevertheless, I saw men as well as women very scantily clad because of the heat.

I witnessed a singular occurrence: every day a little rain falls and then, suddenly, a clear sky reemerges. Those islanders told me about this rare phenomenon, which would have struck me as incredible had I not seen it with my very own eyes during my seven-day stay on this island. They assured me that the same thing occurs every day of the year. Thus around noon some small clouds could be seen gathering; this is ordinarily followed by thunder, then a downpour, and, soon afterward, sun again. This is what keeps the surroundings more temperate and the soil quite fertile.

After two days of rest and putting my affairs in some semblance of order, I started going around the city to make observations and discover whatever might be worthy of note. I found little or nothing, though, because, to begin with, there are no palaces here. When I went to visit the governor's home, it turned out to be like a house for ordinary people in Italy. Nearly all of the other houses are of one story, made of wooden poles, and covered with a certain tree bark. I went to see the cathedral, which I found quite grimy, with the pavement consisting partly of tiles and partly of pure earth.[7] The church of the Observant fathers has mediocre maintenance; that of the Dominican fathers (of which I saw only a monastery, however) is in worse shape than the cathedral.[8] There is also a convent with a small but tidy church. The castle is a fine building, imposing, with good batteries, ramparts, ditches, etc. I was given a tour of that fortress by an official, who let me see everything down to the subterranean rooms at the end.

What a sight to behold, as I went about the districts of the city watching the people emerging in the doorways and windows of the houses, and particularly the women, who called out in Spanish, one after the other: *Ahí va el capuchino* [There goes the Capuchin]! How many women, in particular, called out to me wanting to confess, assuming from my blessings that I was a priest!

The island is impoverished for lack of substantial commerce. Ships arriving from Spain ordinarily land on these shores only to take on water and a few other minor provisions; then they continue their journey to America. Nevertheless, there is a cheerful atmosphere, a fine climate, and very friendly people. There is an abundance of tobacco, sugar, and numerous fruits—especially coconuts, bananas, pineapple, tamarinds, and others. (In the pages that follow I will provide illustrations of some of these fruits with their plants in their natural state.) Those Indians, who are mostly swarthy, made me a present of the fruits.[9]

Because little wheat is available, the bread they commonly eat on this island is cassava, called *mandioca* by the Portuguese. This cassava is made from a large, elongated root, which they call *yucca*.[10] When it is green, they grate it as we do cheese. Then they squeeze out the juice because it is toxic. After that, they immerse it in water and press it once more, and they do this various times until they have squeezed out everything noxious. Then they form the dough into the shape of a big omelette, as thick as one's finger. They bake it in an oven, and, when fresh, it does not have a bad flavor. After two days, though, it hardens and it is just like chewing wood because it no longer has any flavor. On my way back to Italy, I purchased two reals' worth on the island of Cuba. I brought it with me and still have some.

Inappropriately the Spanish and Americans call the fruit delineated *plátano*. It is more properly named *figo* by the Portuguese and the plant that produces it *figueira*. It is quite abundant all over America and the nearby islands, but these are warm countries. The plant from which it is collected is not woody like the true plátano [banana], but soft throughout and full of juice. For that reason, when ships leave America bound for Europe, they load up several stalks of this plant. Then, during the course of the voyage, they

Plantain.

chop them up and serve them as fodder to the animals they have on board—horses, oxen, calves, sheep, and pigs—thereby providing them food and drink simultaneously. They save considerable water this way. This plant or its fruit does not have seeds but reproduces with its roots, like our cane. When the fruits are removed from a stalk, they slice it at the base. Suddenly other stalks germinate and, without being cultivated, always produce abundant fruits, which are nearly as nutritious as bread. Indeed, in Puerto Rico they serve as a kind of bread, which, along with cassava, thus provides for the poor people as well. They are also roasted with honey and are quite good. In addition, they are dried like figs in Italy. All in all, it is a very useful fruit. There are two kinds, elongated and Guinean, which can be seen from their illustrations.[11]

This fruit is inappropriately called *piña* by the Americans because of its shape resembling an Italian pinecone, but its real name is *ananas* [pineapple]; and it is the fruit that the plant delineated on page 59 [of the MS] produces. It is a very singular fruit in America, too—though there it is found in abundance—because of its exquisite, sweet flavor with a tinge of sourness and because of its very delicate aroma. I liked them a lot and ate quite a few of them during the time of my stay in those lands. They thrive in warm climates, but the ripe fruits are taken everywhere to sell. The skin is cut the same way as a watermelon. Then it is divided into slices, with a little pulverized sugar on top. And when it is eaten, it fills the mouth and the chin with a very delicate juice. From this fruit American women make a preserve that is quite unique.

The coconut is a fruit with little or no flavor because when chewed it resembles, and is practically like, raw chestnuts. But the hollow area, in particular, holds about half of an ordinary glass of a special liquor, which these Indians hold in high esteem. This liquor is whitish in color. They say it is very refreshing, but I did not like either the fruit or its liquor. It is customary to eat them during Christmastime, especially, but they last a long time because

Pineapple fruit.

of their second, rather durable bark. For this reason they are used in some places for games similar to bowling in Italy. All over America it is the custom for close friends to wish each other a merry Christmas by sending coconuts and sweets. This gift is called an *aguinaldo*. They even make preserves from coconut, as they do with every other fruit. So I will not repeat this farther on for each fruit I describe.

The name for these fruits is little oil coconuts—exactly what one experiences by chewing them while sucking out a large amount of very savory oil. Now I will pick up the thread of my narrative.

In Puerto Rico I made another rather interesting observation: when the Indian women go to church to attend mass or whatever, they cover both their heads and faces so that nothing else can be seen except for their eyes and mouth. They wrap the forehead, cheeks, and chin with very white linen cloths. The remainder of their attire, too, is ordinarily of very white cloth, and the way they combine their clothes results in something pleasant to the eye (because of the novelty). At home and in the street, when they are not heading to church, they go almost from one extreme to another.[12] They are quite cordial and courteous, especially toward foreigners.

In this island the net, which they call *amaco* [i.e., *hamaca* or hammock], is used inside their homes, either because of the heat or for protection against the bites of various noxious insects in which the island abounds. The women, especially, spend practically the whole day inside this net (because they are lazy), seated and sprawled out as well, smoking tobacco, swinging the net around when they choose not to doze off. They have their slaves bring them something to eat inside it. Here they even nurse their children,[13] whom they allow to wander about the house stark naked, even though grown. Here I am providing a small sketch of the hammock, or net, attached to an islander's home, which more or less resembles all the dwellings of the Indian folk from the continent.

Woman in hammock.

Another house of poor Indians:

Cane hut in Puerto Rico.

This island produces guaiacum.[14] The woods are filled with lemons and oranges, the fruits of which they bring into the city in huge quantity, providing a plentiful amount for very little money—a half-real. Here there are no coins, just certain pieces of silver called "cut coins" by the Spaniards.[15] There is copper money as well. To sum up, I really liked the island a lot. I was quite content there, and I regretted having to go back on board to continue my journey to America.

In this island, as in all the other Antilles and Caribbean islands, the English carry on trade in men and women slaves whom they bring from Guinea.[16] They are black all over. Fortunate are those sold in Catholic countries because these poor Guinean Indians [African slaves] are not baptized and observe the religion imparted to them wherever they are enslaved. And because the Spaniards hold some of the aforementioned islands, the French others, the Dutch others, and the English themselves still others, it can be stated: fortunate are those who are sold in a country subject to Catholic Spain or France because, as they gradually learn the language, they are also taught the mysteries of Catholicism, along with Christian obligations. And once they have received adequate instruction, they are baptized.

In the house where I stayed a week—that is, in Puerto Rico—there was a young woman with lovely features, though Negroid in character, i.e., with very fat lips (this deformity comes from smoking so much tobacco). Not more than a year ago, she had been purchased for eighty Spanish pesos. However, she could speak little Spanish and for that reason was not baptized. These slaves, though converted to Catholicism, are quite prone to vice,[17] drink, and thievery.

To look pretty, the women cut their faces lengthwise, and these scars they deem to be the epitome of beauty, but once they [the women] are somewhat advanced in age they become frightening to Europeans. Around their necks they wear strings of pearls as well, and on their ears pendants of large pearls. Their attire consists

of shirts and other items, of very white cloth, all of which makes
their blackness stand out even more. In its darker tints it is regarded
as especially beautiful, in the same way as white is for other
nations. Both men and women are branded on their backs with a
hot iron, each slave-holding household using its own mark. Every
slave they buy must submit to the agony of branding so that, if
they flee and are captured again, their masters can immediately be
identified.[18]

As for these poor slave women, there is considerable dissolute-
ness, even among the Catholics. (Imagine what things would be
like in a non-Catholic country!) As I have already noted, they have
a very sensual disposition. . . .[19] Consequently, when they give
birth, the children all become slaves of their mother's master.
When a slave woman is of child-bearing age, she is held in all the
more esteem and becomes her master's favorite. He contributes
very little for the upkeep of these poor people because their attire
is quite scanty, especially for the men whom the master engages
as laborers in other people's workshops and in the performance of
other duties. Whatever they earn belongs to the master himself;
and it costs very little to feed them for, with a little cassava, fruits,
and water, they can get by the entire week. They send the women
to serve in other homes or to the plaza to sell pork and other items.
Everything they earn belongs to the master, who holds them to a
rigorous accounting. These slaves have little choice but to steal
when they can, even though they know they will pay with heavy
lashes. Everything is quickly forgotten, though, if they can get their
hands on some tobacco and brandy.

Before leaving this island, I should recount a minor incident that
befell me when I came close to drowning in that port. The master
of our launch had gone ashore to replenish our water supply. With
this launch or skiff fully laden with casks filled with water, there
were just four inches above the waterline. Nevertheless, I climbed
in to head back to our frigate. Some soldiers and other men jumped
on board after me, so that with just a slightly higher tide everyone

would have drowned. Because the sailors guiding this launch had been ashore and had drunk plenty of brandy (as is their wont), they were rollicking and had no desire to row, oblivious of the peril we were in. Despite all the master's shouting and commotion, they would not row on any account. So when we had to pass a little promontory, I was quivering with fear because water was already beginning to fill the launch. Nevertheless, we gradually approached our ship, from which the captain loudly excoriated the master of the skiff because he had overloaded it and taken so many people on board. Eventually, I was one of the first to grab a rope dangling from the ship, and with that I clambered on board, reaching safety.

On March 28, [1763,] having made the necessary provisions for the remainder of the journey, our ship, with a single cannon shot, gave the signal to weigh anchor. For that reason I quickly arranged to bring my trunk and other effects on board. I took leave of monsignor the bishop, the father guardian of the Observant fathers, and a nun whom I had befriended—but particularly my landlady, whom I deeply regretted leaving because she had treated me graciously and offered me her home at a decent rate during the time of my stay.

While standing on board waiting to set sail (which took place on the 29th), I happened to witness a rather odd scene. Not far from us, less than a rifle shot away, was a small French vessel. Its captain had ordered a sailor to be tied down stark naked on top of a cannon and was having him flogged with full vigor by another sailor. Because of the pangs from the lashes, the poor sufferer cried out so loudly as to arouse compassion. But because this captain thought the blows were not being dealt with the vigor his cruelty deemed desirable, he angrily seized the whip from the hands of the person administering the lashes, struck him in the face several times, and then ordered another sailor to perform the first person's duty. He obeyed and applied the lashes with all his might, with the victim crying out more loudly than ever. One of our passengers, moved to pity, began rebuking the captain, calling him inhuman, cruel, and beastly. After having responded to him in a very inappropriate manner, showering him with abuse in fluent Spanish, he grabbed a rifle and pointed it toward our compassionate passenger, who, seeing it, thought it advisable to duck out of sight.

On March 29 we set sail. Before recounting anything else, though, I will relate a brief episode. On the second day of our departure from Puerto Rico, I began to feel a certain itching in my fingers. I did not pay any attention to this for two more days. Eventually, I noticed that two of my fingers were considerably swollen. I had heard people in Puerto Rico talking about certain insects in which the country abounded, which these islanders call *niguas.*[20] From the information available regarding these creatures, I realized that I was contaminated by that pest.

These tiny creatures are nearly invisible to the naked eye. In particular, they attack those who do not wear tight shoes.[21] They slither between nails and flesh so imperceptibly that they pass unobserved. In the same impalpable way, they form a tiny hollow and a little blister for their abode, which they fill up in a few days with very minute eggs. If these succeed in hatching, they spread all over the toes. The malignity of these tiny creatures reaches such a point that, after working their way into both feet, these creatures cause swelling and eating away [of the flesh]. Some people, initially unaware of them, have had to have their feet amputated.

Apprised of these facts and realizing that this malady had infected me, I now asked the ship's surgeon if he could remove these creatures. But he excused himself, saying he did not have the keen eyesight needed for such an operation. A passenger offered his services and, with a needle and after considerable patience and suffering on my part, removed the two blisters under the toenails formed by these creatures. It should be noted that if, during the operation, the blister of eggs is ruptured, the greater part of them retain their foothold and cause tremendous damage as they swell up. But I was fortunate in that they were removed in their entirety, and with a little powdered tobacco the wound healed up again.

On March 30 the isle called Mona Island (i.e., Monkey Island) came into view. Perhaps it is so-named because these animals were encountered on this island. It is located at 17 [18] degrees of [northern] latitude, only fifteen leagues from Puerto Rico. It has a circumference of approximately five leagues. It is fertile and inhabited by Spaniards.

We continued our voyage with little wind, and in two days we sighted Santo Domingo or Hispaniola—in olden days called Haiti—an island that is presently occupied partly by Spain, partly by France. This was the first island of America that Christopher Columbus discovered, and he took possession of it in the king of Spain's name.[22] We approached this island sailing near Cape Tiburón, but here a calm set in, so tedious that for a period of ten days we not only made no headway but instead drifted backward a few leagues every night because of the countervailing current. Apart from that, the heat here was so intense that we almost felt like we were roasting under the sun's glare. For the period we were becalmed, I will make a brief note about this island.

The Spanish took possession of this island in 1492 under the leadership of Christopher Columbus, as I have noted above. It is located at 308 [70] degrees of longitude[23] and a latitude of twenty degrees with two or three minutes. From east to west it is 160 leagues long and 30 wide with a perimeter of 350 leagues. It is one of the greater Antilles, indeed the principal one. Cape Tiburón is at the southwest tip of the island, thirty leagues from the island of Jamaica. There are eighteen [leagues] between Cape dell'Espada [Cape Engaño], which is its eastern point, and Puerto Rico. There are only twelve [leagues] from Cape or Môle St. Nicolas, which looks northwest to the island of Cuba.

There are various other lesser islands there, all with the general name of Antilles or Windward Islands.[24] The most important ones are Saona Island, Beata Island, Santa Catalina, Attavela, Vache Island, Gonave Island, Tortue Island, Navassa, and Mona Island. Navassa is 10 leagues from Cape Tiburón toward Jamaica. There are also Guadeloupe and Marie-Galante, which belong to the French. Martinique, one of the principal Caribbean islands, is located at fifteen degrees and five minutes of north latitude and is also French. Jamaica is among the Antilles or Windward Islands and belongs to the English. Situated at seventeen degrees from the equator, it is south of the island of Cuba, and the channel separating it is only 15 leagues wide. It is 55 leagues long, 25 wide, and 150 around.

Then one encounters the island Saint Martin, which belongs partly to the French, partly to the Dutch—like Newfoundland as well.[25] Anegada is not far from Puerto Rico and is small and uninhabited. The Caymans, which include three islands, got this name from the Spaniards, I believe, because of the abundance of crocodiles (in Spanish cayman [*caimán*] means "alligator" or "crocodile"). They are located south of the island of Cuba and west of Jamaica. The first and smallest one [Little Cayman] is twenty-seven leagues from Cape Cruz; the second is called Cayman Brac; the third is the so-called Gran Cayman. I believe they are deserted.[26] Anyone who wants more information about the aforementioned islands should read the letters of Christopher Columbus and other conquistador captains, written for the king of Spain, as well as the history of the New World by Girolamo Benzoni,[27] and other voyagers, especially English and French, because we did not touch land in any of the aforementioned islands, except Puerto Rico.

In this period of calm, which lasted ten days without our advancing so much as a pace, scarcity of provisions began to be felt on board. We had a *repostero* or storekeeper, whose duty was dispensing needed provisions. Whether he had calculated [supplies] based on the days remaining to reach our port of destination or whether he was dominated by greed (which is most likely), he did not lay up the needed provisions of biscuits, salted meat, and other items in Puerto Rico, as he should have done. So even at the captain's table, where I also dined, we were given very limited food and water rations.

Meanwhile, our chaplain was performing novenas, processions, and prayers, imploring God and the saints for wind to speed us on our voyage because we still had a long way to go. After ten days of such a vexatious calm, a little wind arose. On April 15 we caught sight of the island of Cuba or Fernandina, [then] presently Havana (about which I will provide a brief notice later on).[28] With a little wind we proceeded along the coastline of this island, experiencing at this latitude another calm like the one that had just occurred. We were situated at twenty-two and a half degrees. The heat felt in this location was so intense that no exertion or effort could alleviate it. Not only by day but at night, too, it proved impossible to fall asleep, even though the air was calm. And eventually it nearly took one's breath away.

This second period of calm lasted twelve days, with provisions becoming scarcer than ever, so that the situation was much worse than the first time around. We were within sight of land. Because it was desert coast, however, there was no way of gaining relief, even if we had sent the skiff or launch there in search of water or other things. There was no point in catching fish other than as a minor diversion because there was no water to cook them, bread to eat them with, or oil to season them. (I do not know whether anyone would have enjoyed fishing anyway because everybody felt parched from thirst, enervated by hunger, languorous from sleeplessness, seared by the sun, and driven to boredom by the calm.) Meanwhile everyone was praying for wind. Water had been doled out to everyone in the smallest measure only at noon and in the evening. Furthermore, this paltry amount was turbid, malodorous, and warm. To avoid dying of thirst, I was forced to drink it; but with a kitchen cloth or napkin I covered the mouth of the jar into which it had been poured and in this way filtered it into my mouth. The food situation was perhaps worse because every twenty-four hours we were given nothing more than a very scanty portion of boiled rice seasoned with a little honey, without bread or anything else. Truly we stayed cool despite the great heat.

When it pleased God, on the 27th of that same month—that is, in April [1763]—we had a decent wind at last, which lifted everyone's spirits. That same day we passed the Isle of Pines, then Cape Corriente, then Cape San Antonio at the eastern edge of the island of Cuba. On the 30th we entered Campeche Sound or moved along the coast of the province of Yucatán, which is where the bay, or Gulf of Mexico, begins. Here we were also becalmed at times, though only for a brief period, but grievously afflicted because of the great scarcity of provisions. Slowly we proceeded with our voyage, and we passed the Alacranes, which are five or six small, uninhabited islands only twenty leagues from the coast of Campeche, or Yucatán, toward the north. Their location is about twenty [twenty-two] degrees of northern latitude.

On May 8, to our immense relief, we could hear the sailor who stood on the crow's nest shouting: "Land, land." We all congratulated each other because the hour of deliverance from a virtual purgatory seemed at hand. And truly, such were the travails everyone endured on that ship that the voyage proved a purgatory for practically all of us. Besides the terrible storm we had experienced before arriving at the Canaries (though this cannot be blamed on the vessel), the ship was badly loaded because it moved almost tilted to one side, even with a favorable wind. Then there were hunger, thirst, heat, sleeplessness, confinement, and so many other discomforts everyone shared. Apart from that, all of us were infested with lice, so that the captain, pilot, chaplain, and all the cabin passengers had no other occupation all day long than removing lice from their shirts and habits. All four habits I brought with me were also teeming, and I had nits everywhere up to my beard.

CHAPTER SIX

VERACRUZ TO MEXICO CITY

On the 9th [of May, 1763,] we approached the coast [near Veracruz, New Spain], and the captain, at the passengers' insistence, wanted to enter the harbor that same night. Accordingly, he fired off three or four cannon volleys so that the pilot would come and take us into port. Because it was already quite late, no one appeared; so we were forced to spend the night in that same spot. Since the anchors had not been cast, we risked shipwreck because the current had carried us into such shallow water so close to shore. It was a miracle that we did not run aground. The next morning we backed off somewhat. Having noticed a boat with fishermen, our captain summoned them with a cannon shot, and when they arrived, he climbed into the boat and headed for Veracruz. From here he promptly sent us a goodly quantity of bread and fruit. All of this was laid out on the deck for everyone to choose, and in a flash we consumed everything—we were so famished! Around noon the pilot arrived and gradually guided us into the harbor of Veracruz, where we arrived and dropped anchor on May 10. We all stayed on board until the following day, when royal officials came to inspect the ship, as they were wont to do. Once that was done, I went on land, which I kissed for joy, with that whole fiasco at last behind us.

I took up lodging in an inn until I could obtain more decent quarters. I spent the day resting and experienced how much more delightful and salutary it is sleeping on land than at sea, where one always goes to bed dreading that some disaster may strike. The following day was set aside for fulfilling the vow we made during the tremendous storm. So all those from our ship who had gone ashore, including myself, readied themselves at the pier. From those remaining on board came the chaplain with the captain, pilot, and others carrying the foremast sail with them. We set out barefoot in a procession to the Church of the Divine Shepherdess, where mass was sung by the aforementioned chaplain. After the foresail was deposited, everyone went about their business.

Going about the city, I met a Spaniard who told me that in Veracruz there was another Capuchin father, who lived at the hospital. I promptly went to see him and learned how for nearly ten years he had been an alms-gatherer in Mexico for Propaganda Fide. Now he was waiting for some ships sailing to Spain because he had to return to his province of Andalusia. His name was Father Jerónimo de Jerez.[1] He arranged lodging for me in the monastery of Bethlehemite fathers (about whom I will provide a brief notice later on).[2] I was affectionately received by these fathers and well treated. I stayed a week with them, rested, put my affairs in order, and at the same time went out to observe the city—for me a novelty—of which I will provide a brief description:

Santa Veracruz la Nueva—at 19 degrees, 16 minutes of northern latitude, 273 degrees and 15 minutes of longitude [96.10]—is a town of the province of Tlascala, under the spiritual jurisdiction of the bishop of Puebla, who maintains a vicar there. It is a small city.[3] There are various monasteries, one of the Observant fathers, another of the Dominicans. There are Augustinians and Bethlehemites. The Jesuits were there, too, and a few nuns. This city's climate is quite bad, particularly for Europeans. Beginning in March, the dryness and heat are so extreme that the country becomes unlivable. Aside from that, there is a great abundance of mosquitoes, which torment those who sleep out in the open at night.

The city is poorly fortified because the landward section has walls not much higher than a man, on top of which timbers are set like a rack. When the north winds blow, they are so powerful that in some places they cover the low wall with sand, so that prisoners have to be employed to carry it away. On the side facing the sea there are some batteries with a small castle. Because this is the primary port for so wealthy a kingdom as Mexico, it struck me as not being properly garrisoned. However, about a mile away, planted on top of a reef facing the port, there is a fine castle called San Juan de Ulúa. It is completely surrounded by the sea. Indeed, this is the primary fortress for defending the city and harbor. This castle has the name "de Ulúa" from the time when Cortés, the conqueror of these lands, dropped anchor near this reef. The inhabitants were Indians, possibly fishermen. Having never seen ships or people looking so alien to them, they loudly cried out "Ulúa" in their language, and this term left a lasting impression on the Spaniards. I do not know what it means.[4]

The churches are not very fine or well maintained. Because of the foul air, the people are pallid; and Europeans especially languish in this place, as I have noted above. No sooner have many disembarked than they come down with the *vómito negro* [yellow fever] and die within a few days. This is what happened to Father Filippo Portogruaro, a Capuchin from the province of Venice, who, like me, was invited to Mexico in 1767 by Propaganda Fide to serve as alms-gatherer. Having arrived in Veracruz, he stayed with the Bethlehemites and was immediately afflicted with the *vómito negro* and died a few days later.[5] He was interred in the church of the Observant fathers. This Father Filippo had embarked in Cádiz with the new viceroy of Mexico, who was entrusted with transporting items for the use of this Father Filippo in Mexico City, where he faithfully handed everything over to Father Paolo Maria da Ferrara.[6]

A governor and other royal officials—i.e., treasurer, accountant, and others—with a modest number of militia reside in Veracruz. The city is situated on a plain but has a rather irregular formation. There is nothing of value there other than lots of watermelons, or *sandías* as the Spaniards call them, which provide some refreshment during intensely hot periods. There are still other fruits and abundant fish. During the week I was lodging with the Bethlehemite fathers, every evening, for supper, I received a generous helping of large fish cooked in a special way, something I really enjoyed.

From the very first day I arrived in Veracruz, I was told about the very bad climate there. For that reason I hurriedly put my affairs in order to transfer to Mexico City as soon as possible. Although other people and I had been looking for a horse for hire, we were unable to find one. For that reason I decided to depart on foot, despite advice to the contrary by the Bethlehemite fathers. But because I had made up my mind to travel the same way as in Italy, I paid no heed to their warnings. Before long, though, I regretted this decision. I consigned my trunks and other items to a merchant, with instructions to send everything to me in Mexico City. I changed about two hundred Spanish coins I had into gold. I bade farewell to the Bethlehemite fathers; and with my basket provisioned with bread, cheese, and a bottle of brandy and my walking stick in hand, I departed Veracruz on my own, as soon as the gates opened on May 17, and headed toward old Veracruz, popularly called La Antigua.[7]

Before relating my journey, I will display a small geographic map including part of the Mexican kingdom. This I diligently copied from another one in copper.

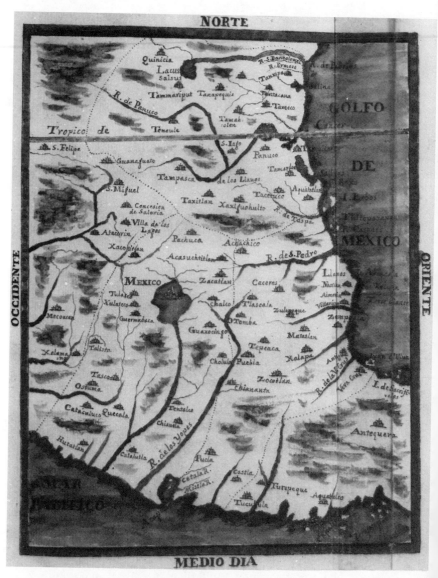

Central New Spain (Mexico).

I traveled many miles, always along the seashore—rather enjoyable so long as the sun's heat was bearable. Toward noon, though, the heat became so intense that I sensed from above and from below, at my feet, that the sand was blazing hot. I could no longer continue my journey because I felt like I was burning up— all the more so after drinking brandy to summon energy for traveling. So, burning up from within and without, I was half fried. When it pleased God and I discovered along the route a little river, which emptied into the sea, I immediately thought about refreshing myself. After gazing intently all along the horizon, I saw no one. So I undressed and sprawled out in the water. Leaving this after a while, I had a bite to eat and resumed my journey. Such, in brief, was the debility that overcame me. Because of the intense heat I could no longer walk. Truly, I suffered considerable torment, not only from fatigue but also from the tremendous thirst that afflicted me because I had not found other fresh water since passing the little river. Had I found a hut of any kind, I certainly would have stopped. Thus I had no choice but to continue the journey ever so slowly, with so much weariness and torment that it felt like I had a severe fever.

After a while the route began moving away from the sea. Having already left that blazing sand that scalded my feet so badly, I began moving inland. After traveling a while, I entered a meadow where some *arrieros* or muleteers were standing around. I asked them for water. They politely gave me some, but it was quite warm. In return I offered them some brandy. They pointed out the route to me, and I realized there was still a long way to go before reaching La Antigua. For that reason I redoubled my efforts, as best I could, to move on. No sooner, though, did I encounter my first tree (because up to now I had not seen a single one) than I stretched out in its shade, even though I was reposing on swampland, and slept awhile. Upon awakening I moved on, though quite slowly.

Eventually I encountered a small Indian house made of reeds and covered with thatch. When I entered, there were only a few Indian women there. I asked them for something to eat (they understood Spanish) and said I would pay for everything. They promptly cooked some eggs, and this helped me recoup somewhat. Having regained some of my energy, I continued my journey, though the Indian women tried to dissuade me and invited me to stay in their house until the following day. I paid for what they had given me. Continuing my journey with somewhat more vigor, I reached La Antigua that evening.

Before commenting about old Veracruz, I will mention the immense diversion I had in that short stretch of road, that is, from the home of the Indian women to La Antigua. Although I was sapped by fatigue, the novelty of the countryside and the variety of birds and plants nevertheless made me feel like I was in a new world—as, indeed, I was. If I wanted to reach my destination that evening, though, I did not have time to pause and mull over everything. I will only say that I was utterly astounded by the tremendous size and multitude of trees, which no longer had fruits; and from this alone I realized the country was very fertile. Among the other trees that struck me as rather amazing were several from a species in which the primary trunk not only rose to the height of two men but had other trunks as well, descending vertically from the branches into the ground, almost like roots. All this appears around the primary trunk, which looks like a palisade. It produces no fruits and is called *mangle* [mangrove, *Rhizophora mangle*]. Here is an illustration:

Mangrove tree.

Arriving at La Antigua around evening, I found lodging in the home of Indian folk, as there are no Spanish inhabitants. I spent the worst possible night because there was nowhere to sleep except on certain items resembling mats for silkworms, made of woven reeds, just like the houses. There was nothing to protect me from the mosquitoes and no bedding, as there was no need for anything to keep out the cold, with the climate still being warm.

The next day I halted to rest as well as to observe the area (this being the site where the conqueror Cortés landed). I saw that there was not much land and few stone houses, most being made of reeds and all of them inhabited by Indian folk. The location is 18 degrees, 40 minutes [19 degrees, 18 minutes] north latitude. In the middle of this territory flows a river, once navigable from the ocean as far as La Antigua. Heading toward Mexico City, one crosses it with a well-made, sturdy carriage because the river here is wide and swift. All around this area I observed many uncultivated lemon trees bearing fruit; otherwise I noted nothing special.

On the 19th I left La Antigua, heading alone toward Jalapa. I did not note anything of consequence, except for the variety of birds far different from our own, about which I will have something to say in due course. Because I encountered some small houses of Indian folk now and then, I had the chance to refresh myself whenever I needed to, for all these people have chickens, and thus eggs. These were the only things I ate until reaching Jalapa because I had not yet developed a taste for those foods seasoned according to their custom, especially meat with chili or pepper. They were too piquant (though in time I got used to all of these things). I also found another way to assuage my thirst; watermelons, several of which I ate, turned up in various places and in the gardens of these Indians.

But along with the diversion of my journey, I suffered a discomfort, unforeseen, as I had not yet been forewarned about it. Whenever I walked underneath those trees, I felt a stinging sensation all through my body. I was continually scratching myself while walking—now here, now there, almost as though I had mange. At first I attributed this to heat but, to investigate, I looked at my arms and legs and saw that many very minute creatures had intruded beneath my skin. They have a special name. Though I do not recall it now, I do know that they are not the same thing as the niguas of Puerto Rico.[8] So vigorous was their assault that only with great difficulty could I extract a few, not quite totally buried, with my fingernails. So, retiring to a woods, I undressed, and with the point of a knife I removed whatever I could. The rest I had to leave for another time and occasion.

As I was now traveling alone and was exhausted, it pleased the Lord that I should encounter muleteers, who, moved to compassion, offered me a mule to ride to Jalapa, my destination. I accepted this considerate offer, and in two days, that is, on May 21, I successfully reached Jalapa, where I lodged at an inn. The following day being the solemn day of Pentecost, I headed early on to the monastery of the Observant fathers, which was located there, to perform my devotions. It should be noted that, as in Veracruz, I made a friendship—with a local Italian merchant named Don Bartolomeo Borxa, a wealthy man and a good Christian, whom I met on my way back from church. He wanted to take me to his home for chocolate. Not only that, but he obliged me to stay in his house until there was an opportunity to continue my journey to Mexico City in greater comfort.

Jalapa is called a city by its inhabitants but is nothing more than a big village, inhabited in large part by Indian folk and located along a mountain slope.[9] This locale has a somewhat more temperate climate, and it is a district of the province of Tlascala. The purgative root bearing the name of the town is collected here.[10] There was nothing else, in particular, that I observed.

I stayed a week in this village. Eventually I had the opportunity to travel with a Mexican merchant, who had been in Veracruz making purchases for his business. Heading back to Mexico City, he thoughtfully welcomed me into his group, providing me, at his own expense, with a fine horse and something to eat all the way to Mexico City. We left Jalapa on May 28 and in the evening arrived at a little town called Perote. This day's journey was largely exhausting because it was nearly always through mountains and valleys. But upon arrival at the just-mentioned village, there was an almost level route ahead. So here the aforementioned merchant was outfitted with a *forlone*,[11] or, as they say in Italy, with a calash; and with this we arrived in the city of Mexico four days later.

During these four days of traveling, I was unable to note anything of significance, as the forlone we were traveling in was always closed because of the sun and dust, and also because we halted only at nightfall, spending the night in places where we arrived around evening. Thus we arrived in Mexico City on the evening of June 1, 1763. That night the merchant who brought me there put me up in his home, and the next morning I went to lodge in a mesón or inn. That year the festival of Corpus Domini [Christi] fell on this day, so I headed to the cathedral to view the very solemn procession taking place—but I will discuss that elsewhere.[12]

After two days I succeeded in locating another Capuchin, Father Lorenzo da Brà, a Piedmontese. Although he was an alms-gatherer for Propaganda Fide, I did not know where he lived; and because the city was huge, it was quite a problem locating him. Eventually, after considerable searching, I found him—he was living in the home of a very devout lady, a benefactress of the Capuchins. She welcomed me into her home too.

Two or three days later I introduced myself to monsignor the archbishop, and I handed over my credentials from Propaganda Fide. I was received with great cordiality and affection by the archbishop, whose name was Monsignor Don Manuel Rubio y Salinas.[13] He invited me to dine with him the following day. I went there, and during the meal this prelate greatly enjoyed my discourse about various matters regarding Italy and my journey. Because I still was not well-versed in the Spanish language, I frequently uttered gross malapropisms, at which he laughed heartily; and the pages, too, who were serving at our table nearly laughed their guts out (as they are wont to say here).

Archbishop Manuel Rubio y Salinas. Courtesy of the Bancroft Library.

I also visited the viceroy, the Marqués de Cruillas, who had previously traveled in Italy.[14] So he was delighted to discuss various
matters with me in my native language.

Viceroy Marquess of Cruillas. Courtesy of the Bancroft Library.

CHAPTER SEVEN

DESCRIPTION OF THE CAPITAL

Now it is time to provide a brief description of Mexico City. I will do so very summarily in order not to repeat the more systematic accounts of other authors and not to be prolix either. Readers looking for more extensive information about Mexico City and the entire realm should consult Gemelli's *Journey around the World*; the reports by the conquistadors to the king of Spain; Solís, the author of the history of the conquest of this realm;[1] and the abundant writings of other authors.

Mexico City, which in the Mexican language was called Temistitán—Tenochtitlán by others—had its origins in 1325, the year it was founded.[2] It is the capital of New Spain and bears the rank of imperial court because its last king, who succumbed to the forces of the conquistadors, had the title of emperor. It was subjugated by the celebrated captain Hernán Cortés on behalf of the king of Spain, who was [also] the [Holy Roman] Emperor Charles V. That occurred during the year of our salvation 1521, in the month of August, on the day of St. Hippolytus. That day is still celebrated today, too, in commemoration of the Spaniards' taking possession of the city.[3]

There is some disagreement among various authorities regarding its location. Buffier places it at 19 degrees and 53 minutes northern latitude, and 273 of longitude. Lieutaud situates it at 20 degrees of latitude, De Lahire at 20 and 10 minutes, and others at 20 degrees and 40 minutes.[4] It is eighty leagues from Veracruz, and there are a hundred from Mexico City to the port of Acapulco.

The entire kingdom of Mexico, or New Spain, is in the torrid zone.[5] It is bounded on the north by New Mexico, to the east partly by the Gulf of Mexico and partly by the Sea of the North [Atlantic Ocean], to the south partly by South America and partly by the South Seas [i.e., the Pacific]. The capital is ensconced on an immense lake in the middle of a plain, fourteen Spanish leagues in length from south to north, seven in width, and forty in circumference. The lake is thirty leagues in circuit, half of which has fresh water and the other half salt water.[6] From the two different maps I include in this work, one can see the shape of the lake, the rivers, and nearby towns.

The principal provinces or governments subordinate to the Viceroyalty of Mexico are from north to south: Sinaloa, Nueva Vizcaya, Nuevo León, Culiacán, Huasteca or Pánuco, Chiametlán, Guadalajara, Jalisco, Michoacán, Tlascala, Oaxaca, Tabasco, Chiapas, Soconusco, Yucatán, Verapaz, Guatemala, Honduras, Nicaragua, Costa Rica, Veragua, and Panamá. But for many years now the aforementioned provinces or governments over here are limited to three royal *audiencias* [administrative-judicial courts]: Mexico, the primary one, where the viceroy resides and to which appeals come from the other two—that is, Guadalajara and Guatemala, which, owing to the distance of the regions and multitude of affairs, could not replace the single audiencia at Mexico City.[7] These audiencias decide not only civil but also criminal cases, when there is not a matter requiring a decision from the court of Madrid.

The city of Mexico is three leagues in circumference and two miles in diameter. The city, with neither walls nor gates, is entered by five *calzadas* or causeways, high and sturdy because of the water. The calzadas are those of La Piedad, San Antonio, Guadalupe, San Cosme, and Chapultepec—the Calzada del Peñón, through which

Villages around Mexico City.

Cortés entered when he captured the city, is no longer in existence. The plan of the city is similar to the Bergamo market—that is, with straight streets from east to west and from south to north. These streets are moderately wide so that four coaches can comfortably pass side by side.

Nothing is swept, and rubbish of every kind is cast into the streets, though it is true that a little water runs in a channel, concave in shape, through the middle of everything. Every week certain men assigned to this task go into all the streets to scoop the refuse out of the water, most often leaving it for one or two days along the bank of the ditch, allowing it to dry. Then they cart it out of the city. So, whenever they carry out such operations in that part of the country, people traveling past encounter such a stench that they have to plug their nostrils. Indeed, this is most out of keeping with the other amenities of this city.

In the houses they do not use "common areas" [latrines], as in Italy, but pots instead, because every morning nothing else can be seen but women moving through the streets emptying the previous night's filth into the channels in the middle of the street. Moreover, there is another very indecent abuse: in the streets, plazas, and wherever else, when the need arises for a person, be it man or woman, to have a bowel movement or merely make water, they do their business in total liberty wherever they happen to be—even if others are present (which is not the practice in Italy, nor in many other countries).

The city of Mexico has more than one hundred and thirty thousand inhabitants.[8] Moreover, such is the daily concourse of other people from the city and other surrounding towns that there is a continual ebb and flow of people in the streets and plazas, providing the semblance of a continual fair. There are numerous plazas, and in practically all of them there is a fountain in the middle spurting water. The principal plaza, though, is the one with the cathedral and viceroy's palace, where people primarily gather to carry on their trade. And the immense variety of things sold here—

for food, clothing, and every other human use—and the mechanic
arts are a sight to behold. Indeed, any kind of item for whatever
use a person might deem necessary can be found here. This huge
plaza is filled with shops made of boards, which, if need be, can be
quickly lifted [and removed]. In the middle of this plaza is a very
lovely fountain, with jets of water soaring to a considerable height.
Here, too, a gallows consisting of four columns is invariably
erected off to the side. There are various districts with their arcades
all lined with stores full of merchandise. Various canals from the
lake, which they call *acequias*, enter the city. Through them the
Indian folk from nearby places convey in their canoes items of all
kinds like vegetables, lumber, wheat, flour, charcoal, fruits, and
many other things, which are consumed daily in Mexico City.

In the districts where there is no canal or acequia there are
subterranean water conduits, which perennially supply not only
public fountains but many houses as well, these benefiting from a
well-constructed receptacle in their courtyard. This water, which
fills the need of the entire city, is conveyed in a canal [i.e., an aque-
duct] seven leagues from the city, built entirely of arches and rather
elevated in some places.

The viceroy's palace, though of minimal height, has a better
outward appearance than any other building. It is off by itself and
more spread-out than most buildings of this country, because, in
addition to the apartments of the viceroy and his family, there are
also all the agencies with their special offices.[9] The main ones are
the viceroy's secretary; royal audiencia; royal hall of crime; fiscal
agents; civil attorneys; criminal attorneys; secretaries of the civil
chamber; secretaries of the criminal chamber; lawyers for the indigent; Indians' lawyers; general interpreter for the royal audiencia;
advocates for the Indians; tribunal and royal audiencia accounts;
accountant of accounts; budget accountants; ordering accountants;
organizing accountants of provisions; bookkeepers; royal officials;
tributes; tolls; private land judges; general probate judges; general
judge for the Indies; *media anata;*[10] mercury [monopoly]; and a few

others. The number of officials for all the aforementioned functions reaches 152. In addition, there are prisons in the small towers at the four corners of this palace, which, as I have noted before, is not very high but quite spread-out.

The viceroy receives a stipend of one hundred thousand pesos a year, and his term of office lasts five years. Ordinarily, though, he is confirmed for another tour. The king maintains a company of soldiers to serve as his guard.

Independent of the viceroy there is another court called the Acordada,[11] created for dealing with thieves and murderers, in which the countryside abounds. This tribunal has certain horrific and terrible prisons, and few who fall under this judge's sway ever leave as free men because practically every week the malefactors are hanged.[12]

I should not move on without mentioning the illumination that takes place every evening in all the districts of the city. Based on laws enacted by the viceroy, at the Ave Maria [dusk] each house must light a *farol* or lantern above the door or one of the windows until three or four at night. What a lovely sight—standing at the head of a district, where everything is illuminated with so many lights [all the way] to the other end since [the streets in] the districts run in a straight line. This law was enacted to deter the great evils resulting from robbery, murder, and violation of women because there it is customary, even for those who are young and alone, to wander about at night. Even so, this is not an adequate remedy because every day evil deeds occur in the aforementioned places and in no small measure.

For the quality of its buildings, ornaments, and wealth of its churches, it [the capital] can be said to vie with the finest cities of Italy. It is true that there are no grand palaces, as in Rome and its outskirts, because they cannot erect massive buildings since the foundations are not completely solid. But in their interior, perhaps, they are richer for the sumptuousness of their ornamentation. All the houses of this city are of stone and brick and whitewashed.

Viewed in perspective, they are of fine architecture, with well-ordered balconies, windows and soffits in Chinese style, magnificent gates, courtyards with marble columns, and spacious and commodious entrance stairways painted between one step and the next in checkered fashion so that, viewed from a certain distance, the entire stairwell looks as though it were covered with cloth. The only defect the houses have is that they are not proportionate in height, though I have seen various ones five stories high. Most, though, have three. The rooms located on the floor by the door are where the serving people dwell. Above them are the rooms they call *entresuelo*, where there are stores of merchandise, because here practically everyone is a merchant. Finally, there are the masters' quarters. Though not very wealthy, all have their forloni or coaches because these Mexican gentlemen are so dainty that they would not go on any outing unless they went by coach.

And as for the coaches, I recall having read that in Mexico there are four fine though rare items, which are: fine churches, fine streets, fine ladies, and fine carriages. As for the latter, there are quite a few, but they are all rather ordinary, i.e., of minimal value. No one uses a coachman as in Italy. Instead there are one or two outriders, but only the viceroy is permitted to travel with a team of six. Apart from that, everyone uses mules rather than horses. I have made mention of the streets above; the churches I will discuss elsewhere.

As for the women, it is true that they are very beautiful and of a fine disposition, spirited, pretty, and with considerable rhetorical talent, so that they far surpass our Italian women. But they are ambitious (as in every other country), proud, dainty, and indolent. Many favor the Europeans (who are called *gachupines*), and they more willingly marry them, even though impoverished, than their own compatriots called creoles, even though wealthy. They view them—that is, the creoles—as lovers of mulatto women, from whom they have imbibed bad customs with their milk.[13] Consequently, the creole men hate the Europeans.

The women adopt the Spanish style of dress—that is, the ladies as well as the merchant and artisan women who can [afford to]. The rest are attired as their status permits. Because there are different castes of people, each person thus dresses not only on a level with her wealth but also according to her caste. If a woman is an Indian, though wealthy, she dresses in accordance with Indian custom, however opulently; if she is mulatta, according to mulatto custom, etc. I regret having lacked familiarity with the design so that I could provide an illustration of those women's dresses, which certainly are a matter of curiosity in some cases, perhaps more so than in the case of Greek women.

The mulattos are born of whites and blacks and vice versa. The mestizos are those who are born of Spaniards with Indian or creole women and vice versa, so that they have a varied physiognomy. Thus, there are six castes of people in this realm: Europeans, creoles, mulattos, mestizos, Indians, and blacks.[14]

It would not be out of place to describe the chronological succession of kings of Mexico, the last of whom was the unfortunate emperor Moctezuma; but in order not to bog down in a narrative that would turn into an overly long digression, I refer the reader to Gemelli's *Journey around the World* and to Solís, author of the history of the conquest of Mexico, which provides a detailed treatment. Even though somewhat partial to the Spanish nation, this second author certainly deserves to be read by those curious [about these matters]; for the stratagems, violence, artifices, and methods adopted by both sides to defend themselves—that is, by the Spaniards to take control of Mexico and by Moctezuma to drive them out—form a plot of considerable interest and erudition.

They [Mexican Aztecs] adored many idols—the principal one being Viztzilliputzli,[15] signifying the god of war—for whom they regularly sacrificed men captured during their wars. According to tradition, his temple was where the cathedral is located today.[16] Moctezuma, after having been put in chains by Hernán Cortés, was accidentally struck in the head by a stone from his own vassals, who had come to the palace in a huge throng to rescue him. He had stepped out onto an elevated area, where he could be seen, to calm these tumultuous Indians who were hurling stones at the Spaniards escorting him. He was struck, as I have noted, and died an idolater.[17] A few descendants of that emperor still survive. When I left Mexico in 1768, a canon of the cathedral, who was a descendant from the direct masculine line of the aforementioned Moctezuma, was still alive. The aforementioned descendants have always enjoyed great privileges, honors, and titles granted by the king of Spain.[18] A small part of the palace of Moctezuma, which I went to see, still remains standing. It is somewhat distant from the city. For that reason I thought it might be some pleasure palace and not one of his regular residences, or that the city after its conquest had been rebuilt anew and located in a different site. In that palace fine architecture is not to be seen. Its main gate is very low, and the entire construction, though sturdy, is still quite crude.[19]

I will pass on to other matters and, first of all, I will discuss the Mexican language [Nahuatl], which scholars say is a very refined language with a rich vocabulary. I cannot confirm this, though, because I never learned this language. I had no need to, because Spanish is widely spoken and also because it seemed difficult to learn. To provide a sample here, I will insert the Paternoster [Our Father], the Ave Maria, and the [Apostles'] Creed in this Mexican language:

Izcatqui in Tolarzin e
Totatzin e, ynilhuicac timoyeztica, majectenehualo
inmotocatzin, mahualauh inmotlatocayotzin, machihualo
intlalticpac inmotlanequilitzin
in yuchihualo inilhuic, intotlaxcalmomoztla e
totech monequi maaxcan xitechmomaquili
maxitechmotlapopolhuili intotlatlacol, in iuh
tiquintla popolhuia intechtla tlacalhuia,
macamomoxitechmomacahuili, inicamo ipan,

tihuetzizque in teneyeyecoltiliztli: çanye
xitechmomaquixtili inyhuicpa in amoqualli.
Maiuhmochihua

Izcatqui in Santa Maria e.

Maximopaquiltitie Santa Maria e, timotemiltitica
inçenquizca yectiliztica gracia,
monahuactizincomoyeztica intheotlatoani Dios;
çencatiyectenehualoni intlan inixquichtinçihua, ihuan
çenca yectenehualoni in itlaquilo moxilantzin Iesus.
Santa Maria e mochipa huelnelli ichpochtzintle Dios
inantzin e, matopan ximotlatolti in titlatlacoanime,
in axcan ihuan in iquac ye tomiquiliz tempan
Maiuhmochihua.

Izcatqui in Neltoconi.
Nic moneltoquitia inçenhuelitini Dios Tetatzin, in
oquiyocox, oquimochihuili in ilhui
catl, ihuan intlalticpatli. Nonicmoneltoquitia
in Jesu-Christo inçanhueltiçeltzin Ypiltzin
ihuan totlatocatzin, omonacayotitzino itlama
huiçoltica Espiritu Santo, auh itech omotlaca
tilitzino in Santa Maria mochipa huel nelli
ichpochtzintli. Auh omotlaihyohuilti itlatoca
yopan in Poncio Pilato, Cruz titech quauh
nepanoltitech omamaçoaltiloc, omomiquili,
ihuan otocac, auh omotemohui mictlan, eiil
huitica omoizcalitzino intlan inmimique,
omotlecahui ilhuicac imayec campatzinco
mehuititica inçenhuelitini Dio Tetatzin
Auh icompa hualmehuitiz inquinmotlatzonte
quililiquiuh inyolque, ihuan in mimque.
Nonicmoneltoquitia in Dios Espiritu Santo,
ihuan nicnelctoca camoyeztica Santa Iglesia

Catholica Romana. Nonicnelctoca caonca
inneçepan icneliliz in Santome.
Nonicnelctoca caonca tlatlacopolihuiliztlli, ihuan
nicneltoca camochihuaz ininezcaliliz intonacayo,
ihuan nicneltoca caonca çemicac yoliliztli. Amen.[20]

Besides the aforementioned, there are two other principal languages in the realm, which are Ottomita [Otomí] and Mequa [Maya]. These three languages are subdivided into many others, which are not understood except with difficulty—as is the case in Italy.[21] In Mexico City, however, and in the surrounding area the Indian folk use only Mexican or Otomí since few understand Maya. And in all the dioceses of the realm, which are eight or nine in number, Holy Orders are given to many clergy only after they have learned some of these languages. Priests are examined in them and without other endowment are ordained and sent to some Indian village as curates.

Though in the torrid zone, Mexico has a mild climate. Over the course of the year there is neither excessive heat nor severe cold, the harshness of which would be comparable to the month of October here in Italy. In the mountains, though, it [the cold] is somewhat more palpable. For all that, neither snow, nor ice, nor frost can be seen there, except in a high mountain between Mexico City and Puebla, which is always covered with snow. The summit of this mountain is a volcano, which sometimes expels flames.[22] This is called the Mountain of Orizaba.[23]

This volcano proved a blessing for the conquistadors because, while they were exploring the country, they discovered in the mouth of this volcano plenty of saltpeter with which they made the gunpowder needed for their artillery.[24] Having depleted their supply, they were unable to provide themselves with any more elsewhere because Captain Cortés had scuttled the ships at the port of Veracruz so that his soldiers, constrained by their inability to flee, had to conquer or perish. Certainly this was a providential occurrence; for if there had not been powder to charge the field cannons with their cartridges and withstand the tremendous number of Indians who resisted their advance into their country, and (according to the history [of Solís]) nearly darkened the sky with the immense quantity of arrows launched against the aggressors, they would not have been able to decimate them as they did. Based on the accounts of the conquistadors, the author of the history of the conquest of Mexico has calculated that for every Spanish soldier there were more than a thousand Indian foes to vanquish (and what a massacre that must have been).[25]

These wretched Indians had all the more reason to claim that the Spaniards manipulated lightning when they heard the noise and saw the fire from the artillery and, at the same time, countless numbers of their own people dropping dead. At the beginning of the war, that race [the Spanish] had the reputation of being immortal because they [the Indians] had not seen a single dead Spaniard, whether from a natural or violent causes. They also said that the Spaniards were children of the sun, and they thought the cavalryman was a single body of both horse and rider.

CHAPTER EIGHT

FOODS AND PLANTS
OF NEW SPAIN

Enough of these digressions. Let me return to the climate, in particular, which varies greatly during the same season and over very short distances. One need only cross over a minor mountain to pass from a hot climate to one almost chilly. It could be said that in this country winter begins roughly halfway through the month of June or, at the latest, toward the end of that month. During that period it is nearly always raining all the way through the month of October, with just a short pause in the month of August. At this time the sun is rarely seen, and rainfall is nearly constant, especially in the mountains. In Mexico City, though, it is not so incessant that one cannot go outside, particularly in the morning, to carry on one's business.

By the beginning of January spring has already set in, so that by March it is quite hot. Wheat is harvested at the end of this month and in the beginning of April. They plant a considerable quantity of this grain, which they call *trigo*. Compared to that of Italy, it is cheap, and they produce a very fine bread. In the fields where wheat has been mowed, they plant nothing else for two or three years because there is plenty of other land already lying fallow. Those lands by themselves are quite fertile, and they do not require the same toil and industry to cultivate them as in Lombardy; for they neither fertilize, irrigate in time of drought, till the soil, nor perform other labors, as in other countries. Only when the grass, which grows among the stubble, is ripe and dry do they take advantage of the opportunity afforded by a strong wind and set it ablaze. In this way these rather vast fields remain fertilized and clear, especially of animals. Nor do they mow hay in the meadows there, because horses as well as mules eat straw, and some people reward them in the evening with a little barley or oats.

They still harvest plenty of corn, which is the daily bread for Indian folk. Nowhere in America is it the practice to grind corn for making bread as in Italy—to say nothing of making polenta, something they are unaware of. To make their bread from this, they instead soak the grain in water with a little lime inside a vessel they call a *comal* [tecomate].[1] They leave it there two days. Then they thoroughly rinse it, and between two stones made for this purpose—one of which they call the *metate*, the other the *mano*—they mash it up to such an extent that it is shaped into a mass similar to what the women of our country prepare when they make bread from maize. Then they take some of this mass, and pound it between their hands, shaping it into a round, thin pancake, which they place on top of a special thin, round, and flat earthenware instrument, which they call *tecomal* [comal]. Under this they light a fire and, after turning these pancakes just once, prepare their bread, which they call tortillas. This type of bread is in such widespread use that not just the Indian folk and other poor people eat them out of necessity, but well-to-do people, and even the upper classes, put those tortillas on their table along with wheat bread. In particular, the well-to-do eat them for lunch, which they call *almuerzo*. Between two tortillas they mix pork, *jamón* or ham, and *chorizos*, which are a kind of small sausages,[2] with broth and a quantity of chile or red pepper. In this way this whole concoction turns out red and so piquant that it is rather difficult for a person not accustomed to it to eat this combination [an enchilada].

This dish enjoys the same esteem among them as polenta with fowl does in Bergamask territory. After eating the above-mentioned item, most of them also drink pulque,[3] but afterward many drink brandy as well, and in such an amount and way that it is quite beneficial for those thus habituated. Many times I have eaten this food out of necessity, finding myself in regions where there was no other type of bread; but many times I also ate them out of choice, particularly those made with chile—that is, in the manner described above—and I found them quite delectable. The Indian women bring these tortillas to the plaza to sell just as Bergamask women do eggs. In the travel narratives of Pietro Della Valle, I recall having read that in Persia they make bread in the same manner described above, i.e., like tortillas, but there is no explanation regarding the type of flour.[4]

Apart from that, in this country they prepare a beverage from corn that they call *atole*.[5] To avoid bogging down in details, I will briefly mention that essentially this atole differs not at all from the broth that comes from boiling polenta here in Italy, except that the former is whiter and they pass it through a strainer and it has practically the consistency of curdled milk. Poor people imbibe the hot beverage early in the morning. Some of them mix in a little chocolate, other poorer people do not—and that is their breakfast.

To put the matter in proper perspective, one should be aware that all over the kingdom of Mexico it is the practice to drink chocolate twice a day (because coffee is very little used, and during the approximately five years of my sojourn in that kingdom I drank it only once—in the home of a gentleman friend of mine). The first [time] is early in the morning—many times they drink it in bed. The second time it is taken is around 21 hours, Italian time [4 P.M.].[6] But because there are so many poor people who cannot afford to have pure chocolate for breakfast, and it is customary at the same time for everyone to take something warm in the morning, they replace it with the aforementioned atole alone or mixed with a little chocolate, which they then call *champurrado*.

And as for chocolate, I read in some history, [whose title] I do not recall, that this concoction (chocolate) originated in Mexico and in the Mexican language is called *choco-atle*.[7] And it should be noted, too, that in these lands it is customary for people from all classes to drink something warm in the morning. So, if some poor man or woman should happen to go without chocolate, champurrado, or atole for just one morning, he or she would be regarded as a most unfortunate person, wretched, and on the verge of desperation.

The chocolate that is used throughout the realm has very little in common with ours in Italy, though there is cacao in this country,[8] at least in the provinces of Yucatán or Campeche, Caracas, and Cartagena. From there it is transported partly by sea, partly overland to Mexico City. Nevertheless, they do not drink chocolate there as they do in Italy because they do not know how to combine it. That was demonstrated when I returned to my homeland and I brought some Mexican chocolate with me, but the brothers who sampled it made light of my chocolate. Even though vanilla is collected in the kingdom of Mexico, they are not accustomed to combining it with chocolate.

Inadvertently, I have passed from corn to chocolate, though the digression certainly has not been out of place because I had the opportunity to discuss how corn is put to use in this country. Here I would still need to describe tamales,[9] which they make from corn (and this item, which they make considerable use of, is also part of their diet); but because this is a matter of minor import, I will pass it up. So I will likewise pass over in silence other products derived from corn by the Indians' industry, so as to avoid digressing in matters of lesser importance.

In references above to tortillas, I have noted that many people drink pulque with them. To explain what this pulque is, I must first note that throughout the entire kingdom of Mexico wine is not produced because the laws of Spain prohibit planting vines in this realm. In my opinion the intent of this law was to sell Spanish wine in this country, because all the wine consumed over there, for mass

as well as by people desirous of drinking it, is imported from
Spain. For that reason it is quite expensive.

Now the industry of those Indian folk or, better put, Divine
Providence has provided that country with another beverage
practically equivalent to wine, though nowadays they abuse it in
the same way that wine is abused in Italy because it is just as
intoxicating as wine. Everyone is aware of that plant called aloe[10]
(an illustration of which I am providing here). There are two or
three kinds [of *Agave*] here, which are planted in fields the same
way cornfields are planted in Italy. They let these plants grow for
three years. Then, with a special cutting iron made for this
purpose, they slice the inside leaves of this plant, and at its base
they hollow out an area that they cover with a stone. The next
morning the aforementioned hollow area is nearly full of a very
sweet liquor, which the Indians call *agua miel* [honey water]. They
call this plant maguey.[11] They extract the liquor, then make a fresh

Maguey plants.

abrasion in the hollow area so that fresh liquor seeps out the following day. They do this every day until November, which is about when the above-mentioned plants, which have provided liquor for four months and longer, die. The collection of agua miel never ceases, though, because at various times they make their incisions or hollow areas in magueys in different fields.

The Indians bring leather bags full of the liquor collected to their homes. They place it in a huge wooden receptacle like our vats, where they mix in a substantial amount of water. In one or two days fermentation occurs, and the color changes from that of water to milky white. Once that occurs, they put it in special, rather large, leather bags, which they send by mule to the city and primary towns.

Today consumption of this beverage [pulque] is so widespread that everyone drinks it. There are public *pulquerías*, which are like our public wineshops. A few years ago it was not proper for people with any kind of [social] standing to go into them because entering a place frequented only by drunks and by rabble of every ilk seemed to undercut their respectability. Now people of every rank frequent them; and during the time of my stay in Mexico, I observed many carriages and coaches of gentlemen, ladies, merchants, and other respectable people heading to these places.

This is a beverage that is especially intoxicating when it has taken on a somewhat more sour flavor, which would be the case, for instance, if it were produced in two days because it is supposed to take one day to make it. It is very diuretic and quite beneficial in quenching thirst for anyone who travels in this country. It is invigorating and nourishing. It also serves as a remedy for various maladies, especially diarrhea, for which it seems to be the specific remedy; and doctors frequently prescribe it for their patients. In sum, used with due moderation, it is a quite useful beverage. As for myself, in the roughly five years I resided in that country, I could not get used to drinking that liquor because of its foul odor, even though Europeans, after drinking it for two or three days, become even more keen on it than the local population itself.

In Mexico City there are twenty-eight to thirty pulquerías, which open about two hours before noon to dispense pulque and continue until twenty-two hours Italian time [i.e., 5 P.M.]. Every morning one can find a large number of mules loaded with pulque waiting at the gateways to the city to pay the duty on it. So the customs officials weigh all the pulque entering the city, and the duty on pulque alone provides the Royal Treasury of Mexico two hundred thousand pesos a year. Now, though, it will be considerably more because of the much greater use or abuse, which is increasing from day to day.

In addition to the product pulque, they also extract from the aloe or maguey plant a variety of brandy called mescal, a considerable amount of which I consumed because it is light and salubrious. But they also make a refined variety that is stronger, and they call it *mescal resecado*.[12] *Tepache* is another beverage they extract from the aforementioned plant,[13] which also provides a kind of linen from which they make very thin handkerchiefs. They make sewing thread, which they call *pita*, and I still have some, unbleached and dyed, as well as non-spun linen. From this plant they also make a large number of ropes and bags, which they call *costales*, and miners use them for transporting ore. From this plant they derive various other items, which for brevity's sake I will pass over. All are products obtained exclusively from the maguey plant by the industry of those Indians.

This plant is also held in special esteem by the Most Blessed Virgin Mary, because in the year 1540 she appeared to an Indian named Juan de Aguila on the hill of Totoltepec, which is not far from Mexico City, and told him that he should look for her image in that very same place. After initial efforts he found, in the middle of one of these plants, a small statue of the Blessed Virgin with her babe in her arms, though it is not known from what material it is made. A very fine church, celebrated for its important and recurrent miracles, was then constructed on this site. They call it Nuestra Señora de los Remedios. Every year they bear this statue into the cathedral of Mexico City in a very solemn procession. In a huge throng all the regular and secular clergy head some distance outside the city to welcome it with great pomp. For three months it remains inside the cathedral. Then, with the same solemnity, they carry it [back] to its church. The Mexicans show great faith and devotion to this, and in time of greatest need they have special recourse to it through public prayers. I keep a small paper image of this statue, which I viewed and adored one day in the cathedral. It is more than roughly three hand spans in height, yet very rich in ornamentation.[14]

I still have to mention briefly some other beverages consumed in Mexico. First of all there is *mistela*,[15] which in essence is nothing but some kind of *rosolio*.[16] [Then there are] English *pung* [punch], which consists of pure water, brandy, lemon juice, sugar, and a little cinnamon or cloves; rum; and finally *cañeta*, which is brandy extracted from sugarcane. After having crushed the sugarcane in the press, they set the crushed cane aside to ferment, distill it, and from this extract the aforementioned brandy, with which they usually mix another liquor, also distilled. I do not know what it consists of. They call this *chinguirito*.[17] This liquor is prohibited because those who drink nothing else become quite offensive. Even so, they consume plenty of it on the sly.

Such are the beverages consumed in this country, where every day numerous drunks can be seen, perhaps on a worse scale than in Italy. It can be difficult adapting to that way of life because in whatever home one dines, among gentlemen too, drinking is not customary during the course of the dinner or supper; one has to wait instead until it is all over. Then they bring to the table some preserve or other sweet, which they consume in huge amounts. At the same time they put drinking water, the universal beverage for dinner and supper, on the table.

Now let us move on to see how and what they eat. The commonplace dish is *olla* [stew], Spanish in origin. This consists of mutton, ham, chickpeas, cabbage, onions, turnips, garlic, and every other kind of vegetable in season, with saffron and spices. This medley is the dish they generally eat in all Spanish territories, and, to tell the truth, it is quite good because there is food for various tastes. In Mexico they do not consume soup; instead of that, they offer a cup of broth and eventually the side dish, which ordinarily is meat with chile. Then it is an inviolable custom of sorts to offer at the end of dinner and supper, all year long, a small plate of beans prepared in a thick soup, similar to what we have in Italy. As they put it, these are served to set the stage for drinking water. So they do not injure the stomach. After the beans they offer some preserve or sweet, as I have noted above, and then drinking water—and thus the most commonplace dinner comes to an end.

In the evening there is usually a salad and *clemole* or roast. The clemole is a meat gravy with a great deal of broth, heavily laden with chile, or pepper, which, like cancer, gnaws at the innards of one not accustomed to it.[18] They prepare foods of various other kinds with vegetables and other items, the description of which I will pass up for the sake of brevity.

Besides the abundance of wheat and corn, they harvest products from the country like sugar, tobacco, cacao, sorrel, wood of Campeche for dyeing, vanilla, cochineal, *xialapa*[19] and *mechioacan*[20] (both medicinal roots), [and] abundant special fruits from the country. Farther on, I will provide an illustration of some of these as well as some plants and flowers. In addition, there are legumes of every variety, numerous vegetables or greens in whatever amount. What a sight to behold—the immense quantity of these things that the Indians bring into Mexico City by canoe. I noted something special about the vegetables as well: that in those plazas all kinds of vegetables, which in Europe appear only in season, were available throughout the year. So all year long there are cabbages, lettuce, endive, beans, peas, artichokes, onions, parsley, garlic, and other items—always fresh and green. Thanks to the industry of those Indians, the temperate climate, and the fertility of the soil, they have come to enjoy wondrous benefits. Besides these things, there are a large number of fowl of all kinds, sheep, cattle, mules, horses, donkeys, pigs, etc. For the moment, I will not mention the gold—to say nothing of the silver—mines, the reason for the immense wealth in that country. Later on, I will take the opportunity to refer to these mines.[21]

Practically all year long, canoes filled with fresh flowers of various kinds enter the city, and they are all sold in the plazas as well. Accordingly, in certain areas of the immense lake I have noticed a curious sight—something like small floating gardens, which are formed from tightly linked platforms. On top of them they place earth an arm's length[22] in depth, or somewhat more, and there they plant a variety of flowers, which, once they emerge, are taken from one place to another on the lake by the Indians in row-boats.[23] Because the entire shoreline is covered with villages, the ultimate effect is a gorgeous view.

The plant illustrated here is commonly called *nopal* [prickly-pear cactus], and its fruit is called *tuna*. There are various species. They are quite tasty, very succulent, and invigorating. When the red tunas are eaten, one's urine takes on the same color, not at all dissimilar to blood. Once I was nearly startled by a [possible] mishap, not real-izing the effect of these fruits, of which I had one day eaten a large amount. I noticed that my urine looked more like blood, and I thought I had some fatal malady. But after consulting with a few people, I was assured that this was the effect of the tunas I had eaten. The tunas *joconoztles* are only good for making preserves. In January and February, when the nopales sprout, their tender leaves are eaten. The women who cook them call them *nopalitos*. I found them quite delectable.

Nopal or prickly-pear cactus.

From this plant is collected the insect called cochineal, so renowned in earlier times, from which they dye [cloth] in cochineal color and, if I am not mistaken, in scarlet. These insects are collected particularly in the diocese of Antequera [Oaxaca]—a rather hot region. To avoid getting bogged down in descriptions of the method of reproducing and collecting these insects, which would be quite lengthy, I will simply note that they apply equal and perhaps greater care and diligence here than is the case for silkworms in Lombardy.[24]

Mexican rose.

The trees that produce the *zapotes* [including the zapote negro, the zapote boracho, and the chicozapote] are called cochiczapotle by the Indians, and [the fruits] are large like walnuts. They are very fine fruits, but the *chicozapote*, which is exquisitely sweet, surpasses all the others. All of them quickly rot, though.[25]

Peanuts grow underground. They plant them every year like legumes, and their roots produce various pods, which contain two, three, four, or even more seeds the size of a chickpea, but with an irregular shape.[26] When they are ripe, they are scooped up and dried in the sun. Then they are lightly toasted over the fire with a tecomal [comal], without being removed from the pod. Some people are of the opinion that it is impermissible, or at least risky, for anyone who is not married to eat these fruits: a ludicrous opinion. They taste like our hazelnuts. Huge quantities of them are brought to the plazas, and I have eaten a large number of them.

The *chirimoya* has a most delectable flavor and is held in high regard by the local inhabitants as well. It is very white in the middle and ordinarily is eaten with a spoon because it has the consistency of coagulated milk. The plant producing this fruit is the size of our walnut tree. There is also another variety that they call anona, and it has a shape quite similar to the aforementioned one. This one is even more special—i.e., it tastes better, and it is more highly regarded too. Few can be seen, however.[27]

The guava has a very unpleasant odor, resembling that of a pigsty. Even so, they do eat it. For the most part, though, it is only useful for making preserves.[28]

[The Chinese pomegranate (*Punica granatum*) and *ciriguelas* (*ciruelas*; *Spondias purpurea*), rather sour fruits, are also part of their diet.][29] The camote is a root that is eaten cooked and has the flavor and consistency of chestnuts.[30] The *chilacayote* is a kind of gourd and, because of its singular character, serves no other purpose than being made into preserves.[31] The *cero peruviano* is called *órgano* by the Mexicans because of its resemblance to an organ. It is very abundant in this country. It produces two species of fruit called *pitahaya*.[32]

The avocado is a very delicate fruit, but not much is edible because of its enormous seed. They have various colors and shapes, like figs in Italy, but they all have the same flavor. [There is] also a species of avocado, though they call it by another name that I do not recall. It cannot be eaten raw, just cooked. P.S.: Now I recall the actual name of the fruit, which they call *pagua*.[33]

Chiles are essentially nothing more than peppers. They are widely used all over America. There is not a city, villa, or town, however small it may be, where they do not bring huge quantities into their plazas to sell, especially the ones called *ancho* and *pasilla*. They use the former especially in clemole and tortillas with chile, and they add the second variety to practically every type of food. They place the green chile *meco* on the table, and ordinarily it is eaten with soup, into which they also squeeze lemon or orange. They put the elongated one [i.e., the pasilla] into vinegar so they can then blend it into their salads. The *chile manso* or *chiltepín* and the *chilito redondo* are also eaten green, but they are seldom used because they have little bite.[34]

By itself the grass depicted below is nothing special; I depicted it only because of its clearly specious name [maiden's flesh]. Boys chew it, like garden sorrel in Italy, since it has a very tasty sour flavor.[35]

Carne de doncella (maiden's flesh).

The *Perú* is quite abundant all over America, both in the mountains and in the plains. It is a species of pepper because it resembles true pepper in the shape of its seeds as well as in its piquant flavor. They do not use it, however, not only because of the foul odor, which stays in one's mouth after chewing it, but also because it is said to be harmful to one's health with frequent use.[36]

Chayotes are somewhat odd because of their shape and use. They lack flavor. They are eaten cooked and are almost like boiled turnips.[37]

I have no idea why the Americans have given this fruit the name "apple of death" because it is not one of those things that, when eaten, can cause death by poisoning. On the outside it is quite lovely, and inside, when it is fully ripened and opened, contains a black substance, which is transformed into smoke in the form of soot. I believe this is the veritable apple of Sodom, even if it is true that such apples can be found in the province of Pentapoli, or five cities,[38] located along the Dead Sea, which also has the name Asphalt Lake. It seems I have read somewhere that these are exactly like the apples described, lovely on the outside but containing nothing inside except a black soot. But how was the seed from this plant brought from the Dead Sea to America?[39] Whatever the case may be, the Americans have no other use for them than putting them in their homes as lovely ornaments.

There are still various other fruits I have seen in this country that I might describe; but because I do not have a solid conception of them, I will refrain from depicting them and, instead, resume the thread of my narrative.

Manzana de la muerte (apple of death).

CHAPTER NINE

MEXICAN OCCUPATIONS AND AMUSEMENTS

Nearly every kind of mechanical art can be found here, but, generally speaking, the people are not as industrious as Europeans. In my opinion the sole reason for this is the surfeit of money. Hence they have no need to challenge their ingenuity to improve on their labors or devise new inventions. As for clothmaking, in Mexico there are only very few weavers who weave certain commonplace items.[1] Of those, I have seen only one making damasks—and he was a Frenchman. All the linen goods, silk cloth, fine fabrics, and every other item making up one's attire come from Europe and China.

The most common occupation throughout that realm, not just in the cities but in every small village, is the *cigarrero* [cigar maker], owing to the widespread use of cigars among both men and women—and even children. Hence in every district of Mexico there are two, three, and even four cigar factories. In each one of these shops there are ten or twelve men and women who do nothing all day long except make cigars, which are nothing more than tiny scraps of paper containing a small amount of smoking tobacco.[2]

Everyone indulges in these scraps of paper. Both men and women offer them with considerable gallantry; and it is not proper to turn them down because that would be impolite. In a bag people carry the flint, steel, and tinder for lighting the cigar, wherever one may be. Practically all of them carry something like a small silver box where they put their cigars, but the women keep them attached to the belt of their petticoats—*naguas* in Spanish. Gentlemen carry a gold watch suspended on their left side and a cigar case of pure gold on the right. In whatever home you visit or store you enter, or whenever you encounter someone you know on the street, the first thing you do is take out the case of cigars and offer one, as is customary in Italy with the tin of tobacco, little of which is consumed in this country. The Genoans have grown wealthy from these cigars because of the huge commerce in paper they carry on with Mexican merchants.

There are other kinds of smokers, or *chupadores* [suckers] in Spanish, who put on a big show of affluence. For that reason they smoke the cigar in a different manner. They take a whole tobacco leaf, shaping it into a long roll for the whole length of the leaf. Then they light it at one end and put the other end in their mouth. However, this method of smoking soon proves intoxicating for the person not accustomed to it because these tobaccos are strong by their very nature. This type of cigar they give the name of *puros*, and they are used in private or in public only in the Windward Islands like Puerto Rico and Havana [Cuba].

From tobacco, I will move on to provide a brief account of popular customs, mainly involving the Indian folk[, who] are more industrious and sharpwitted than the creoles because they readily imitate whatever they observe.

Generally speaking, the creoles, Indians, and mestizos, along with mulattos, are sluggards, drunkards, thieves, swindlers, and lechers—and that is also true of the women. Nevertheless, it cannot be denied that there are people of every status, sex, and condition who are very good Christians, are generally charitable, and give alms. They are cordial, though somewhat averse to foreigners. Though they have an inherent esteem for the Spaniards, they confuse them with other Europeans, whom they all call gachupines, using another term for the others. In view of the affection and esteem for them, it is generally appropriate to pass as gachupín, but not particularly as Italian, French, or German, et cetera.

Ordinarily their songs are quite shameless, but still worse are their dances, which include rather indecent gestures. Three kinds of fiestas are conventional in the realm. The first is the festivity, properly speaking, where they dance French-style. Here aristocratic and polite society is involved, and there are no disorders or scandals. The second they call *saraos* [i.e., *soirées*], in which there is a medley of songs, music, dancing, drunkenness, and other ills. The third, finally, is the so-called *fandango*,[3] which is the most universal one among the common people and where, for the most part, they perform the dances they call the *chuchumbe, bamba,* and *guesito*, which are all quite indecent.[4]

The climate of this country is more hot than temperate. Brandy consumption, foods heavily seasoned with pepper, and popular custom (introduced, in my opinion, by the first conquistadors, as the historical accounts make clear) have resulted in a universal epidemic as far as women are concerned. For it has been attested to me many times by various people of probity that the majority of young people who marry (referring here to the common people) are not virgins. The main evidence of this is the great abuse prevalent in those lands of living *amancebao* [i.e., *amancebado*], as they put it, which in Italian means living in concubinage. Great are the numbers of those who pass through life in such a wretched state, including quite decent people, too, whom their superiors, both spiritual and temporal, are unable to reform. And very frequently these people, wretched in spirit after having been together awhile, separate, not out of a sense of obligation but due to a change in fortune or inclination. And thus so many women marry having children without having had a husband, and hence the country is rife with illegitimate progeny.[5]

. . . to some extent public locales are available for such purposes, and thus a means of making it easier for many men and many women to go and do as they please using different pretexts. First of all, in Mexico City, there are various public bathing places where men and women enter freely. [Men and women bathe together,][6] and one need only pay the custodian of the baths the usual amount with a bit more for a gratuity so that he will pay no heed to whatever might transpire. So one can well imagine the consequences. I was invited various times to see those baths, but I never went there and hence will not describe them. And because I have mentioned baths, I will be permitted a minor digression. In those lands every Saturday, or at least on holidays, there is the indispensable practice of [deleted word or words: probably "bathing"] or at least the head. Many women do this in their own homes, but most of them head for the river in those places where such an opportunity is available.

As the second example of the aforementioned subject of public places, or locales convenient for [deleted word], with specific reference to the city of Mexico, there is the Alameda (because in the villages they eventually head for the woods). This is nothing more than a kind of woods, similar to the woods of our Bergamo monastery, located in one quarter of the city. It is rectangular in shape and about an eighth of a mile across. It is filled with trees and pathways; and in the middle there is a very lovely fountain, which spurts water very high, which then circulates within these woods through various brooks. During the day many carriages arrive with gentlemen out for a promenade because it is a cool, shady place.[7] During the night, though, it serves as a lair for many infamous wolves. Although this Alameda is surrounded by a ditch and the four main gates are closed at night, they find a way of staying hidden there. Or, at nighttime, they cross the ditch by means of a plank, allowing them to roam in total liberty.

There is another place, too, which they call Xamajca.[8] This is like the Posilipo of Naples[9]—that is, nothing more than a passage outside the city approximately two miles long. One travels there by land and also by water in canoes on the acequia [canal]. I went there two or three times, always by water, and returned by land.

Each time I went there with respectable, upstanding people. I observed both banks of the river, all green, with meadows, flower gardens, fruit trees, and many country cottages. An everlasting spring seemed to shed its beneficent smile upon the region because of the benign climate, the fresh air, and the abundance of refreshing and flavorful beverages, as well as foods, encountered from time to time. What is most delightful, though, is the music, which can be enjoyed in various places—that is to say, in the gardens and meadows. With instruments they accompany the song of those Mexican sirens, whose singing is not unpleasant—the same being true for other productions or talents of theirs. For that reason, here I would deem it befitting to apply to this pleasant locale two excerpts from Tasso, which seem quite appropriate to me:

> Cool breezes, ever fragrant, ever sweet,
> were blowing in a steady, soothing way;
> and there the sun, as in no other place,
> fell on that coolness with its circling rays,
> without dispensing, as it elsewhere does,
> now ice now heat, now fair now cloudy time.
> Forever luminous, forever white
> the sky was there, and knew no summer flame
> nor wintry frost, and to the mead gave grass,
> to the grass buds, to the buds scent, and shade
> to the trees. . . .[10]

Now I will move on to describe the most commonplace games of theirs, which include billiards, ball games, bullfights, and cockfights. Cards and dice are clandestine amusements. In 1771 Charles III, monarch of all the Spanish dominions, prohibited bullfighting throughout his realm.[11] And truly that was the right decision because these spectacles with bulls are nothing more than relics of ancient cruelty, which tyrants resorted to against the holy martyrs when they set wild beasts upon them, or of the ancient gladiators.

Because the Spaniards are so keen on these spectacles with bulls—hence reckless—many deaths occur. In Cádiz, not only every summer, but also whenever there were public celebrations, the amphitheater was set up for bullfights. The same was true in Mexico City and other principal cities of America.

Hence a wooden amphitheater, like the ones where comedies are performed, is set up in a spacious plaza, with boxes for gentlemen and bleachers for the common people. When the day of combat is set, ten or twelve toreadors (as they are called) are waiting in the wings. They are very agile on horseback and each trained accordingly with a pike or very long lance in hand, not at all unlike ancient warriors. They enter into the arena, just two at a time. When a bull is released, they goad it, wounding it with their lances. What is impressive, in first viewing this, is the agility of horse and horseman in evading the deadly lunges from the enraged bull, which with its horns tries not only to defend but to avenge itself as well. The spectators do not always witness a joyous spectacle, though: with my own eyes I watched a horse, which was being ridden, hurled to the ground by an enraged bull after being disemboweled by its horns. This is a matter of no great importance, though, as only the horse suffers. Later on, one will witness worse things. If the bull continues to display vigor and the horses of the first two toreadors are exhausted, and if they have shown sufficient proof of their skill to leave the arena with some glory, then two others enter. If the bull is then listless from exhaustion and spilt blood, they kill it on the spot and have another one enter.

Now comes the choice part of the farce. When the spectators are weary of watching combat on horseback, the men on foot enter, more audacious and foolhardy than the horsemen. Armed with some barbed shaft, and with a good blade, they enter the plaza, one or two at a time, holding cloaks, with that habitual Spanish air of indifference to life. (What is most distressing concerns their souls, because excommunication awaits these people, both men on horseback and men on foot, as it does so many duelists. For they are exposed to a clear peril of life because deaths do, in fact, occur; and I have been witness to some. That zealous bishop of Cádiz, Don Tomás del Valle, a Dominican, fulminated [threats of] excommunication for clergy too, both secular and regular, who did nothing more than watch.) Then, I would imagine, with horses exhausted and the bull still brimming with vigor, these footmen enter and, one at a time, display their cloaks to the bull, which furiously lunges toward its adversary. Turning very rapidly, they avoid being struck, and the bull remains thwarted in its lunge.

After amusing themselves for a while in this fashion, they grasp the arrows [*banderillas*]. These toreador-footmen are of two sorts: some are truly in love, others are interested only in themselves. When it is time for them to deal a *coup de grâce* in honor of their beloved, the former have a rather perilous task facing them because the arrows are not shot from a bow but must be lodged into the bull's neck by hand. Because these ladies are always onlookers of their heroes, being already predisposed to them, the bold lover, before dealing his blow, brings himself with his arrow in hand before his mistress and, hat in hand, virtually dedicating his own life to her, presents her the arrow. The lady responds with some sign of approval. Puffed up with daring and foolhardiness, ambitious for honor and applause, he then stations himself in front of the enraged bull. If he succeeds in planting the arrow into its neck, he will enjoy universal applause from clapping hands, and particularly from his mistress. Deemed a man of valor, he will grow immeasurably in her love and esteem.

The second type of horsemen, with pikes, present their shafts to some gentleman or lady, from whom they are hoping for recompense of some kind. When they have succeeded in dealing their coup, they return to the person for whose sake they risked their lives and receive ample acknowledgment.

These spectacles ordinarily last three months, and during that time they are performed one and even two times a week. But in the villages, where there is no opportunity or possibility for setting up the arena or plaza, they amuse themselves with bulls they butcher every Friday at the slaughterhouses. With a very long rope, they lead them into some spacious area, where all kinds of people entertain themselves all day long, making them run and inflicting wounds on them until they are nearly dead from exhaustion and loss of blood. In a large village called Tolenzingo, I saw a man conveyed by an enraged bull on top of its horns all through the plaza of the arena, which was spattered with blood and intestines, and where he died with no one to commend his soul. A similar case occurred in another village called Actopán, where the bull caught on its horns a toreador, who died in the arena without sacraments.

Here is how the bullfight ends: when the final hour has arrived, the most intrepid and audacious person (for there is no other word to describe him) places himself in the middle of the plaza, blade in hand, waiting for the bull to come to him. Seeing no other adversary nearby, the bull dashes swiftly toward that sole person, who awaits him in the middle of the arena with one leg free.[12] If, during the frenzied and perilous encounter, the gladiator succeeds in planting the blade in the middle of its chest, the bull drops dead and the killer walks away with applause and rewards. But if the wound is not on target, on which the fall of the beast depends, normally the person who sets out to kill is himself killed.

After having briefly described the inhuman bullfight, I will now provide a short account of the truly ludicrous cockfight, the tendency of which is not the ruination of the players' lives but of their property instead.

In Mexico and in all the cities and villages, however small, throughout America there is the so-called *plaza de los gallos* [cockpit]. This, too, is shaped like an amphitheater, but it has little space in the middle because they do not need a great deal of room for two roosters, who fight each other while all the spectators sit around on the bleachers and boxes. So widespread is the Mexicans' propensity for this amusement that few are the homes where roosters are not raised for this sport. They import them from far-away lands, but the most highly prized are those coming from the Philippine Islands (a sign that in those countries, too, the aforementioned pastime is widespread). I have seen people paying twelve, fifteen, twenty, and even more Spanish pesos for each rooster, even domestic ones. Walking through those villages, one can hear nothing but crowing roosters. If you spend the night in one of those homes, you will have to endure that cacophony practically all night long; for the person not accustomed, this can be quite aggravating.

From the time they [the roosters] are little, they tie them by one leg, as fowlers do with decoys, to one of four corners of a room, with four to six in each one, far enough apart from each other that they cannot come into contact. They do not let them mate with chickens. They are well fed. Every day they leave them out in the sun, tied down for two or three hours, and they prepare them in other ways, which would be long and tedious to describe. When they reach an age and size where they are capable of fighting, they carry them to the plaza or to the cockpit. Each of two owners makes his own selection, and a *gamautto*[13] or curved blade is fastened to the left leg of both [roosters]. It is designed for only one purpose and is quite sharp.

But before setting them on the ground where they will fight, they place their bets—and that is the gist of the game. Gentlemen, merchants, priests, and monks, with numerous riffraff of all kinds, attend this variety of theater (and in Mexico City I have even seen judges, who look like the *pantaloni*[14] of Venice). They all place bets, large and small, that the rooster of this or that color will win. During my stay there, there were wealthy merchants who wagered a thousand pesos on each fight. This done, a hush descends so that it seems like no one is even breathing. In the middle of the plaza, they set down the two roosters, who immediately lunge at each other feet first after their own fashion because they have never been acquainted with each other. They do this over and over again, wounding each other with the blade fastened to their legs. For that reason, they shed blood in amounts proportionate to the wounds received. If one of them falls lifeless to the ground or scurries away, all bets are lost. What sold a few moments before for ten to twenty pesos or more they now dispose of for a pittance, while the person who won the wager picks up his money, which always is customarily entrusted to the keeping of a third party.

There is also another type of cockfight they call *tapada*, but it differs little in substance from the one described above.[15] To avoid being tedious, I have left out various minutiae about this sport, and again I reiterate that such is the propensity of this people for cockfighting that one hears nothing else spoken about—in the same way that fowlers in the Bergamask region talk about birds during autumn.

CHAPTER TEN

MEDICINE IN COLONIAL MEXICO

I will now move on to provide a brief overview of various other matters, relating everything I have seen and something of what I heard regarding the city of Mexico. It has a university, which I cannot describe, though, because I have no information about the chairs that comprise it.[1] The material edifice is huge with a fine façade, and it has a very fine plaza in front. Based on accounts from men of intelligence and experience, I can, however, attest that Mexico has attained a high level of civilization because practically all the schools were managed and governed by the Jesuit fathers, who practiced and taught the sciences in the great seminary of San Ildefonso.[2] They occupied the principal chairs of the university and provided various other staff for schools that now have all come under the control of other orders.[3]

There is the Hospital Mayor, where they have established a kind of medical university.[4] There are, indeed, fine physicians in Mexico who treat their patients virtually in accordance with European practice, making allowance for the peculiar characteristics of prevailing illnesses in the country and the climate. In general, they amply prescribe emetics and clysters. Bloodletting is infrequent, cupping quite rare, quinine scarcely heard of. The most widespread illnesses prevalent in this part of the world are syphilis,[5] lung ailments, malign fevers, and some, though just a few, [resulting] from stagnation of the blood.

There is another hospital in which only syphilitics, men and women, are treated; another one for invalids; another for the insane.[6] Aside from that, there is the Hospital of San Juan de Dios,[7] as well as the infirmary of the Bethlehemite friars where patients who leave San Juan de Dios go to convalesce. In addition, they also take in some sick people, and many times I have seen the aforementioned friars going about the city with a stretcher, bearing the patients on their own shoulders and carrying them to their monastery.

As for patients, I must recount two odd practices in those lands:

The first involves women in labor, nearly all of whom take the *temazcal* (particularly in mountainous regions) about the eighth day after delivery.[8] In my opinion this is nothing more than stimulation of some kind because the temazcal consists of an oven made specifically for this purpose, though similar to those used for baking bread. When a woman wants to take the temazcal, they bring this stove up to a mild heat, to a level that can be endured. The woman convalescing from childbirth enters the oven totally nude and in a short time is completely bathed in sweat. Now the women attending her sprinkle her entire body with cold water, causing the patient to feel considerable pain because it feels like hot embers are being tossed on her (as various women who have tried it have attested to me). She starts sweating again, and the attendants again sprinkle her with water; and they go on doing this as long as the patient can stand it. Then she leaves the oven, or temazcal, so exhausted and weak that she can stay on her feet only with great effort. They put her to bed, giving her some refreshment, and the treatment is over. They do this with each regimen, just as in Italy they are accustomed to very scrupulous observance of the quarantine.

And because we are discussing women in childbirth, I will add that in those lands it is not usual to swaddle children, nor envelop them in small feather quilts. Cradles or other implements providing comfort and shelter for them are not to be seen. In countries where the hammock or net is used, they place them inside it, and they rest there quite comfortably. Where the hammock is not in use, they carry them awhile wrapped in a piece of cloth. Then they deliver them to the *pilmama* [nanny], a girl who carries the child wrapped in a cloth behind her back all day long. And despite all that, it would be extremely rare to see a cripple, lame person, or hunchback in this part of the world. In whatever home, even minimally affluent, each newborn child is immediately provided with a *cicigua* [chichihua], who is the wet-nurse, and with a pilmama.

The other odd practice is the method of drawing blood adopted by the Indian folk in lands remote from Mexico City. (I do not know whether they are the Otomís or the Chichimecs.)[9] The practice is as follows: If the doctor knows that he must draw blood from the patient, he has him stretch out in the sun on a straw mat completely nude, even though he actually has a high fever. There he leaves him for three or four hours. Then the same doctor sits on the poor patient's belly, thereby making the veins of the head swell, from which he draws the blood. I do not know in which vein, nor with what instrument the operation is performed. Accordingly, one witnesses an operation worse than [those carried out] on brute animals.

CHAPTER ELEVEN

ANIMALS OF NEW SPAIN

This city ought to be well supplied with fresh fish because it is located on top of a huge lake—to say nothing of others not very far away. The opposite is the case, however: these lakes yield nothing but certain small fish, which they call *pescadito blanco*, and in minimal quantity. They are slightly less than a hand-span in length and quite good. The Indians also bring to the plaza certain tiny little fish, which they call *mesclapites*, wrapped in corn leaves, already cooked in maize flour.[1] Sometimes a certain large fish that they call *bobo*, quite highly prized and similar to the Italian trout, reaches Mexico City from the interior. In a journey I made to Nueva Galicia,[2] I found many fine fish of varying quality, all freshwater and inexpensive. For that reason they caught my fancy.

The birds of those lands are many and varied, but people make no use of them, except for the wild ducks, large numbers of which they bring to the plazas to sell. They also eat some partridges. As for all the others, especially little ones, not only are they not accustomed to eating them, but they find them repugnant, as I observed on one occasion when I had captured three or four small birds, somewhat larger than our sparrow, which are so abundant in the country. They are almost human in the way they go bounding about, quite tamely, through the streets and everywhere else with a rather familiar air. In a house where I felt at ease, I came upon one of the birds, which was dead. In jest I picked it up and fondled it, but those present were flabbergasted and, acting nauseated, wanted me to throw it away. Furthermore, they told me that they would rather have fondled rats than those birds. By way of experiment, though, I cooked it, and it struck me as not inferior to what we have in Italy. Nor are they accustomed to keeping birds in cages, apart from some turtledoves, cardinals, parakeets, and *loros*, or parrots.

There are four species of crows. The first, larger in size than all other species, they call *zopilotes*.[3] These normally perch on top of the *tacamaniles*, that is, on top of the roofs of small wooden houses. The second species resemble our own [crows], but there they are quite abundant.[4] In this connection, I would not want to omit a brief story, ludicrous but amusing.

One day, while I was traveling on horseback close to the city of Mexico, near the road I was crossing there was a herd of grazing horses. Another flock of the aforementioned crows was scattered among them as well. Now some of these horses had sores. So, while the poor sore-ridden creatures were grazing on the grass, the crows were also trying to graze on their flesh, flying onto their backs now and then to peck away at their sores. In their midst, though, I observed one of these crows, possibly more famished and audacious than the others, which had one of these sore-ridden creatures in its sights and was incessantly on top of its back. The poor creature defended itself with its tail and head as best it could and suffered the crow's insolence for a while. But seeing that it could not save itself that way and relying upon its supposed common sense, it devised a remedy, which did not help either: setting out at a rapid gallop for some distance across the countryside. But the crow was upon it again, having also accompanied it on the wing. It was prodding it anew by pecking at its sores, from which blood was flowing profusely. Having suffered the ravenous cruelty of the crow for quite some time, the wretched creature thought of another remedy since the first one had been to no avail. This was to hurl itself on the ground, belly up as much as possible. Now the crow went after its eyes, for them the most delectable fare. Seeing that something worse could befall it, the poor horse got back on its feet again and ran off to mingle among its companions. Then I resumed my journey, weary from laughter over the comic episode.[5]

The third species [of crows] are a little smaller than the afore-mentioned, but fly in unison in such numbers that when they alight on plants these look like they are covered by a black cloth.[6] The last species are the size of our hen sparrows and usually linger around water.[7]

There is a bird, the name of which I do not recall, whose whole garb is azure in color, and it is a fine sight when in flight.[8] The cardinal is of a vivid, wholly red color. There are ossifrages; parrots; a number of loros (a species of parrot), which, when taught prop-erly, do the best talking of all and which are commonly called "parrots" in Europe. The parakeets, the fourth species of parrot, have very fine plumage but do nothing more than stretch out and put on a display of irritation. [There is] a fifth species of the above, though quite scarce, which is called *rara*. Like the parakeet it has no attractive features other than fine plumage, and it is larger than all the aforementioned.[9]

There is a little bird, too, which because of its rarity, beauty, and fine plumage—and also for its smallness and slenderness—is, in my judgment, the most estimable bird of America. It is much smaller than a wren and has a very long, slender beak. It feeds exclusively on the honey [i.e., nectar] it extracts from flowers—not unlike bees. It also collects it in the same manner because, just like the bee, it moves from flower to flower, supporting itself by con-tinually flapping its wings with such rapidity that they cannot be seen, and draws out its sustenance, slipping its beak into the flower. When it is finished with a tree or plant, it flies to another one with a swiftness surpassing thought. The Indians call it *guachichil*; it is called *chupaflores* [flower sucker] by the Spanish, *colibrí* by others, and hummingbird as well.[10]

Game animals include a large number of hares and wild rabbits, deer, and female chamois,[11] a considerable number of which the Indians kill with arrows. There are wild beasts, too, but I have not seen any.

And as for arrows, the ancient custom of the Indian folk of walking about armed with bow and arrow persists because they do not have firearms. Because these Indians are accustomed to traveling in bands, though for no great distance, each individual carries his own bow and a few arrows. They are skilled in using them because they freely bring down birds in flight, and in one village I witnessed an apple placed on top of a man's head being lifted off with the first shot of an arrow from another Indian about forty paces away.[12]

I will finish up the details about animals of that realm, in which—besides the ones known in Europe such as vipers, scorpions, spiders of extraordinary size, and others I do not recall—there is also another creature, very horrid to look at. Essentially this is nothing more than a lizard. It is hairy with many blotches on its back, somewhat slow of movement, and at first sight horrific. It somewhat resembles our aquatic salamanders,[13] but they are larger. This animal is not poisonous. Indeed, in the province of Guatemala, Indian folk eat them; and in the history of these countries written by Girolamo Benzoni, one can read that in the province of [blank] they were eaten for lack of other food.[14]

CHAPTER TWELVE

MISCELLANEOUS TOPICS
AND DISASTERS

From one topic I will pass on to a totally different one, so as not to fail to mention all the matters that strike me as worthy of note. Thus I will provide a very brief description of *tequesquite*. In my opinion this is nothing more than a saponaceous salt, because it is very salty to the taste. After being mixed with water, it forms a soft, mucilaginous material like soap. The women of the country use it for washing their linen or doing the laundry. In addition, they use it for cooking beans and other hard items; then they rinse them with fresh water to remove the dirt they carry with them. This tequesquite is collected in the area around the lake when it settles, following dry spells or after some rainfall along the shores of this lake, where the sun condenses those acid and saline particles, forming something like a crust over the surface of the soil. The Indians then collect it and convey it throughout the realm, where it serves a variety of uses.[1]

Among the other curiosities of Mexico, the coinage house, or the mint, should not be overlooked because of the huge size of the building, and the multitude of officials and offices, but even more because of the amount of gold and silver minted here. I will not pause to describe in detail all I have observed in this mint—that would take considerable time; I will just say that two million marks of silver, of eight ounces each, are minted here or issued from one year to the next, in addition to that which slips through or is converted into contraband. Of this quantity, each year seven hundred thousand marks of eight pesos per mark are coined in pieces of eight [or pesos, each weighing one ounce]. Gemelli notes that in his day sixteen thousand pesos were coined per day, a sum that to my mind seems somewhat exaggerated. At the present time they no longer produce those poorly minted pieces, the so-called *tacones* [i.e., *patacones*], though some are still seen, particularly in the [Caribbean] islands. Besides pesos they coin half, quarter, eighth, and half-eighth pesos, which are the only coins used in the realm, all of the very finest silver.[2] Here any other foreign coinage has no worth apart from the value of the metal composing it.

The lowest coinage of those lands is the half-real, or half of an eighth of a peso. Because they cannot divide it up and there are no copper coins, they have devised the method of further dividing this into four parts, using certain small pieces of round wood, like counters in the game of backgammon—pieces they call *clacos* [i.e., *tlacos*]. In every store they have a number of these clacos, all of them with the store's special mark. Whenever a customer goes to a store like this with his own clacos, the storekeeper is obliged to accept them. They have, as well, another method of dividing the real or the half-real—with cacao beans, sixty and even eighty of which they offer for a real. But this number increases and diminishes depending on whether there is a greater or lesser abundance of cacao in the city, and consequently its price remains relatively high. With these beans they can make purchases in any store and in the plazas, where everyone accepts them in exchange for coins, but always at a rate more favorable to the seller.

This vast emporium of North America, which is the city of Mexico, is prey to two calamities: floods, caused by overflowing of the lakes, and earthquakes.

As for the first of these, practically every year, in July or at the beginning of August, the city faces the imminent peril of being submerged under the multitude of torrents coming down from the mountains surrounding the lakes—this being precisely the season of the heaviest and most widespread rainfall. In 1764 practically the whole city was inundated with water, so that in various sections it was necessary to ferry across from one district to another with canoes. Moreover, all the patients of the Hospital of San Lázaro were transported to another part [of the city], and many residents of the neighborhoods were in grave distress and peril. It pleased God to deliver them promptly thanks to public prayers, and primarily intercession from the powerful Virgin of Guadalupe, the patroness and special protectress of the realm (about whom I will provide some brief information later on).[3] The last flood registered in the chronicles of Mexico City occurred in 1636. I believe it had fatal consequences for them because it figures among what I would call one of the epochal events of the realm.[4]

After Spain acquired Mexico, it tried in every way possible, at enormous expense, to channel the waters of the lakes, sending in the most renowned French, English, and other foreign engineers. They have employed an enormous multitude of Indians to build dikes and other works, but always with little or no success. The work, which would have been most helpful if it could have been maintained, was the *desagüe* [drainage], as they refer to it. This is a huge underground tunnel, very deep and sufficiently wide that it begins in a section of Lake Zumpango, where practically all the waters of the other lakes flow together: for those from Chalco empty into that of Mexico [Texcoco], this into San Cristóbal and Xaltocán, and these into Zumpango, like the new lake as well.[5] On the hydrographic map on page 103 [of the MS] one can clearly see all these lakes, as well as their drainage, the desagüe and its route. This desagüe, or subterranean conduit, has been of little benefit, though, because the quantity of water flowing into it brought stones, dirt, and wood—items that obstructed the tunnel, causing damage besides. So it served little purpose despite the almost continuous labors invested in it. I went to see this desagüe. It is truly a grandiose work, and it seemed virtually impossible to me that these huge walls should succumb to the force of water, had I not also viewed the damage.[6]

The second kind of calamity to which the kingdom of Mexico is often exposed is earthquakes. Indeed, in five years of my stay in this realm, I experienced tremors just one time, these occurring on April 4, 1768, the second day of Easter, when I was in Real del Monte, two days[' journey] from the city of Mexico. It happened early in the morning when I was in church attending mass, but no damage took place there. It merely frightened the people when they felt the shock and saw lamps swaying, but no one budged from his spot.

That is not how it was in Mexico City. Even though it [the quake] lasted just six minutes, various houses collapsed. Many people perished in the ruins. The churches, palaces, and every other structure of any considerable bulk were quite badly damaged, with the walls cracking open from top to bottom. In various places, such as the monastery of Bethlehemites and the Sagrario of the cathedral (both large structures), and in other places, I myself inserted my hand inside the fissures of the walls caused by the shock from the earthquake.[7] The monastery of the Philippine fathers suffered greater damage. Part of the monastery collapsed, along with the dome from the church's choir. Some repairs were made with props, but because the fathers' safety could not be assured, they were transported to the Jesuit house of La Casa Profesa since its former owners had been evicted.[8]

Moreover, because the districts of Mexico City have many underground conduits for water, not only for the public fountains but for the many private houses as well, all these aqueducts broke, and water could be seen escaping all over the streets. Repairing that damage would have required a truly vast sum of money. Fear and destruction gripped all the towns surrounding Mexico City, particularly at Puebla, where it was known that damage had likewise been done; and the carnage eventually reached Veracruz, eighty leagues away from Mexico City.

A week later, while I was alone in Mexico City in the house of our Capuchins on the so-called Relojeros Street, as the Ave Maria was nigh, a new tremor was felt, which left me in a state approaching bewilderment.[9] Barely aware of what I was doing, I lunged down the stairs and exited through the doorway, landing in the middle of the street, which was already filled with people kneeling, crying out to God for mercy, and loudly proclaiming their sins. It [the earthquake] subsided and at the same time everyone sang the "Alabado," which is a prayer of thanksgiving. When I returned home after about an hour, my legs were still trembling from past fear. Behold—still more tremors, though somewhat less severe. Again I ran into the middle of the street, where, as before, people were weeping and yelling. Great indeed was the terror because various all-but-naked people were still there. I spent the night without going to bed, fearful of other recurrences.

In 1769, when I was in Bergamo, I received a letter from a Mexican gentleman, my good friend, a sincere and truthful man named Don Pedro González Méndez. In this letter, dated December 25, 1768, he provided me an account of another earthquake, which occurred in the city of Havana, on the island of Cuba, on the day of Santa Theresa that same year, in which he claims 4,789 houses collapsed. With their cables broken, all the ships anchored in that port were dashed to pieces, one against the other. Moreover, the sea moved a league and a half inland and thus flooded the entire city because of its low-lying location. He does not inform me about the death toll among the people, but surely it must have been very high. He says that many churches collapsed, along with the campanile or towers. The walls cracked open. Great, too, was the damage that occurred in the famous castle El Morro, especially in the subterranean chambers. All around, the trees fell to the ground. And at the end of the letter he says that the dead were many, and great was the number of injured.[10]

CHAPTER THIRTEEN

RELIGIOUS LIFE IN NEW SPAIN

And now it is time for a few remarks about clergy and religious affairs. This I will do with considerable brevity, noting only the most essential matters, because so far it has been my practice to avoid needless prolixity that comes from relating too many minutiae, tedious for all concerned.

Let me begin with the Metropolitan [church] of the realm—that is, with the Cathedral of Mexico City.[1] This is a huge building of fine architecture, consisting of three naves with fine marble columns as well as balustrades leading from the choir to the main altar. (For in all the cathedrals of Spain and America the choir where the canons stand is located right inside the main door of the church, with organs and orchestra pits above them.) I do not know why it is done differently there than in Italy. There is no question that this detracts considerably from the beauty and spaciousness of the churches because, upon entering through the main door, one cannot see the building from its vantage point in the middle; for there are only a few paces from the door to the wall of the choir, which rises toward the dome and in sheer bulk occupies the entire center nave. Being square in shape, it manages to take up no small part of the church.

Cathedral of Mexico City. Courtesy of the Bancroft Library.

Now, from the choir, as described, to the steps of the main altar there are balustrades of white marble on each side, and during days of solemnity they completely cover its railings with silver plaques. The floor of the entire church is made from large marble squares of various colors. All the rest of the church is well maintained with great cleanliness. There are some fine paintings. There is no stinting on any expense, for the cornices, carvings, and other related items are gilded.

For me, however, the most splendid feature of this church was the architecture and opulence of the main altar. It has four façades, and in every one there are altars, quite similar to one another, for celebrating sacred services. It [the main altar] is elevated by some marble steps with balustrades. Above them are solid columns of very fine marble, which support something resembling a huge imperial crown, also of marble, in which there are various recesses and bas-reliefs of floral designs and other items in lapis lazuli and other fine marbles. Similarly, two kinds of cornucopia with silver leaves and flowers gilded on top are suspended between one column and another. I cannot properly describe the tabernacle. In my opinion, the silver and gold used in it must yield the place of honor to the exquisite marbles and precious stones. The architecture of this tabernacle is equally admirable, being made of various orders of small columns, with an elegant and consummate skill and a taste not inferior to that of the Italians. On various occasions I observed the Blessed Sacrament displayed [in] a very large monstrance with stones glittering all over it. All the other ornaments, like the chalices, et cetera, and priestly vestments are of comparable character.

To avoid the appearance of competition with the viceroy, the archbishop of Mexico does not have a baldachin in the cathedral; in accordance with royal ordinances, he sits in the choir.

Parallel to the cathedral façade there are two towers, not very high, which jut out from the church somewhat.[2] They have eight fine bells each. The sound of the largest one very closely resembles the main bell of the city of Bergamo, the so-called Campanone.

Joined to the cathedral, there is another very large church, recently built. They finished erecting it during the time of my stay in Mexico—that is, around the year 1765. They call it the Sagrario.[3] It is utterly resplendent with gold, which they use without stinting as ornamentation for its many plaster figures and wood carvings, or retablos as they call them. This building was seriously damaged by the earthquake noted above. In front of these two churches— that is, the cathedral and the Sagrario—there is a very fine court-yard completely paved with stones and surrounded by tall stone pillars with gates.

Close to the cathedral there is a small church of octagonal struc-ture with a single altar, which is reached by climbing a few steps. This church, so they say, was the first one, built on orders from Hernán Cortés, the conqueror of Mexico. Every day several masses are celebrated there.[4] According to some traditions, on the site where the cathedral is located today there once stood that vast temple of the idol Huitzilopochtli, held in such awe by Moctezuma and by all the Mexicans, where so many thousands of people were sacrificed.[5] The archbishop's palace is of average size, but it has no noteworthy features, except for the hallway leading up to the rooms occupied by the archbishop and members of his household. These are truly regal, as is the audience hall, which is huge and richly ornamented, the floor covered with carpets.[6]

This archbishop has as suffragans the bishops of Tlascala or Angelopolis [Puebla de los Angeles], Michoacán, Nueva Galicia or Guadalajara, Chiapas, Yucatán, Guatemala, Vera Paz or Oaxaca, Honduras, and Nueva Vizcaya or Valladolid.[7] The cathedral sup-ports nine canons, plus another one for the king; five *dignidades*: deacon, archdeacon, schoolmaster, choirmaster, and treasurer; six *racioneros* and six *medio-racioneros*;[8] a major sacristan; four curates chosen by the viceroy; twelve royal chaplains nominated by the [cathedral] chapter; and eight others who are called *de Lorenzana*[9]— these also elected by the chapter, all the others being royal posi-tions. From common assets the archbishop receives 60,000 pesos a year; the deacon 11,000; the four dignidades 8,000 each; the canons 6,000; the racioneros 5,000; the medio-racioneros 3,000; each curate 4,000; each chaplain 300 or less. The remaining assistants and clergy number three hundred all told. From this calculation it can be determined that the metropolitan church of Mexico has a budget exceeding three hundred thousand pesos. To the prebends must be added the expenses required for the building, candles, vestments, and other items intended for sacred rites.

Outside the city to the north in a small village a league distant is the celebrated sanctuary of Our Lady of Guadalupe, elevated to a collegiate church in the year 1750. They call it a renowned and royal ecclesiastical college. It has its canons, but I do not know how many; and they are independent of the archbishop, directly subordinated instead to the Holy See, I believe.[10] The edifice of this church vies with the cathedral for the opulence and pricelessness of ornaments and, in the case of sacred vessels, surpasses it.

Leaving the city, one proceeds along a very lovely calzada or causeway, which begins at the *garita* or toll house and continues in a straight line to Guadalupe, which, as I have noted, is three miles distant. On both sides of the calzada there is a lagoon, nearly always full of water. For this reason the aforementioned road is high and completely paved, with sturdy lateral walls that sustain and protect it. Here and there some stone plaques have been erected with the fifteen mysteries of the Holy Rosary carved on them.[11] In the middle of this road there are three fine gateways in the shape of a triumphal arch, on top of which can be seen the marble bust of Emperor Charles V, who was the conqueror of this vast realm with Cortés as his instrument.

Upon reaching the end of the calzada, one enters a large plaza, in the middle of which there is a very beautiful fountain with various statues, with water spouting upward from several sides. The church has four towers of equal height in four corners, and in each one six fine bells. It is wealthy, and well maintained, and holds many masses, for great is the devotion to this most miraculous

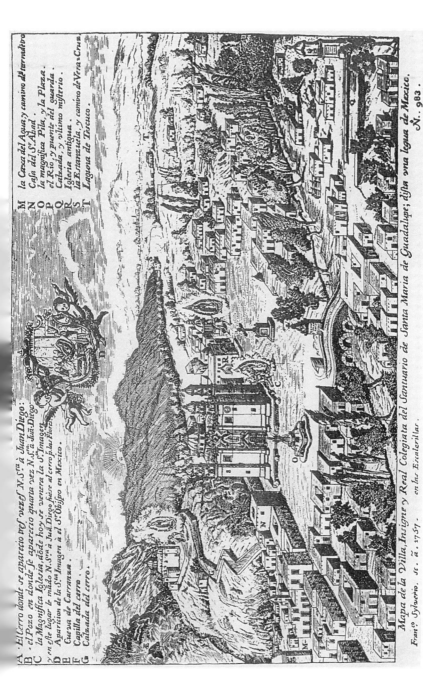

View of the shrine of Guadalupe. Courtesy of the Real Academia de la Historia, Madrid.

Virgin displayed by all inhabitants of the realm—not just the Spaniards and the creoles but the Indians of the entire realm to an even greater degree. There is no home here, rich or poor, that does not have an image of this Most Blessed Virgin. I also carried with me two pictures made of paper, which I still have. Every time I came to Mexico City from the interior to attend to my business, I usually went one or two times to Guadalupe to perform my devotions, depending on the time available.

What an immense pleasure to view every morning the many carriages heading to this sanctuary from Mexico City and, even more, the people on foot reciting the rosary aloud along the route. On Saturdays and every festival day there are always solemn celebrations. The *ayate*[12] on which the image of Most Sacred Virgin is imprinted is kept on the main altar. It is not unveiled except during the most significant solemn occasions dedicated to the Most Blessed Virgin and on the day of her appearance, which is celebrated on December 12 and occurred in 1531, ten years after the conquest of Mexico.[13]

The concourse of Indian folk, especially, is so immense that it is a source of wonderment. The eight consecutive days leading to the apparition turn into a fair. The jubilee occurs on this day in the aforementioned church. So abundant are the alms collected that they exceed one hundred thousand pesos; for on that day every Indian man and woman, great and small, gives some alms in [the form of] money. I have been assured of this several times by various trustworthy individuals.

It is cause for considerable mirth watching those bands of Indian men and women, hand in hand, who, as they approach the sanctuary, dance, making various jubilant pirouettes, some of them also playing their rustic instruments.

During my stay in Mexico, I read about the history of this [miraculous] appearance, though without recalling all its minute details. Nevertheless, I will briefly summarize the essential elements. One day, when a Mexican Indian named Juan Diego was crossing a little hill, at the foot of which the sanctuary has been erected, the Most Blessed Virgin appeared to him in the same form that remains imprinted on the ayate. As the story is usually told, she instructed him to go to the archbishop of Mexico (who was Fray Juan Summarica [Zumárraga], an Observant, the first archbishop of the city of Mexico) and tell him on her behalf that she wanted a church built in her honor in that same place where she was standing and speaking to him. The Indian left to carry out his mission, but no one believed him, or rather they would not allow him to speak to the archbishop.

Juan Diego returned to the spot where the Most Blessed Virgin appeared to him. And behold—once again she revealed herself in the same form as before. The Indian explained to her how events had turned out badly because no one believed him. So the Most Blessed Virgin instructed him to pick the roses from a nearby bush and present them to the archbishop as a sign of the authenticity of his mission. The Indian was greatly amazed as he gathered the roses because it was the month of December and they had never been seen in this spot. With the roses in his ayate, he headed toward Mexico City. (The ayate is a cloth of fiber that the Indians here wear in the form of a tunic. It has an opening in the middle where they insert their heads. Half of this ayate covers them in back, and the other half hangs over in front.)

Juan Diego resumed his mission on behalf of the Most Blessed Virgin and as a sign of authenticity showed them the roses. When the pages saw the miraculous roses, they believed him; and he was presented to the archbishop, to whom he explained the reason for his coming, showing him the roses as evidence for the genuineness of his mission. But not content [with this alone], the Most Blessed Virgin of the miraculous roses provided another, even greater miracle: on the same ayate containing the roses they found imprinted the image of the Most Blessed Virgin, in the same form as she had appeared to the Indian. This ayate is the same one that is venerated in this church, mounted in the shape of a picture with very ornate frame and glass. Indeed, the Most Blessed Virgin appeared to Juan Diego three times, but, as I have noted above, my recollection of the story is incomplete.[14]

Three churches have been built in three distinct locations where the appearances took place. The main one is the Collegiate Church, which stands at the foot of the small hill. Another small chapel, a short distance from the first, where there is also a miraculous spring, was built in commemoration of the second appearance. The third is built partway up the hill where the Indian gathered the roses.[15] In sum, throughout the realm tremendous devotion is professed for this most miraculous Virgin, and in the year 1737 she was chosen as the principal patroness for all Spanish North America.[16]

As regards this sanctuary, I would like to recount an amusing little incident that occurred on the same hill, at the foot of which stands the church of Guadalupe. On that hill certain hermits had set up various abodes in the form of hermitages. Under the guise of sanctity, cult practice, and veneration for the sanctuary, they received generous alms from the overly credulous people who gathered there. But their real aim was improving their own livelihood, and with choice hypocrisy they feigned an austere way of life, spinning off revelations and miraculous apparitions. Thus they lived comfortably, honorably, respectably—and gainfully.

Now it so happened that Archbishop Monsignor Rubio y Salinas (the same person I met upon arriving in Mexico City) received trustworthy reports that at night these hermits were all keeping their women friends. To find out for himself, the archbishop one night sent constables, or *alguaciles* as they are called, to these hermitages. In the course of their investigations, they knocked on the door of one of them, receiving from inside the response: who dares disturb the servant of God? Because he was unwilling to let them in, the constables broke down the door. When they entered, they found the "holy" hermit with a female companion. Both were taken into the city. I was told that the same thing occurred in all the other hermitages. This happened just shortly before I arrived in this country. For that reason all these hermitages were permanently closed.

In Mexico City there are twenty-nine monasteries of regular clergy and twenty-two with nuns—besides all the other churches, which, all told, reach the number of eighty-six to eighty-seven—just within city limits.[17] Generally speaking, they are all well maintained, have fine ornamentation, and hold frequent services, particularly the parish churches and those of the regular clergy for both men and women. There are numerous priests but even more friars.

To provide a few details about these matters in an orderly fashion, I will start with the Dominican fathers from the huge monastery where 180 friars dwell. This monastery is practically in the center of the city. They have a very beautiful large church with forty altars, fine organs, and a bell tower with sixteen bells. In another location these fathers have a hospice with the Ara Coeli [Porta Coeli or Gate of Heaven] church, with some friars always dwelling there. This has been made into a place where those priestly passengers headed for the missions of the Philippines, China, and other regions can stay. In addition, there is another small monastery called San Jacinto, where students dwell with some other fathers, thirty friars in all.[18]

Next is San Francisco la Grande of the Observant fathers, who are quite numerous.[19] They all wear the dark-blue habit. In their church, which is rather large, are interred the remains of the conqueror of Mexico, Hernán Cortés.[20] In this monastery reside not only their father provincial but the most reverend father general commissary as well, to whom all the Franciscan friars of the entire realm are subordinated, even those from a different branch. This father commissary enjoys better entrée than the archbishop himself and is nearly the equal of the viceroy.[21] He has his own carriage with livery. Furthermore, these fathers have two other monasteries in Mexico City—one the so-called Santiago Tlatelolco, the other I do not recall.[22]

The Augustinians and the Mercedarians have two other sizable monasteries with their large, well-maintained churches holding frequent services. Within the city these two orders also have other lesser monasteries devoted to study.[23]

There is a large monastery of the Reformed [Franciscan] fathers. [There is also] one for the Cosmites, so-named for the titular of their church, San Cosme.[24] They are nothing more than a minor branch stemming from the Observant fathers, and they cannot be found except in the kingdom of Mexico. There is a monastery of Fernandinos, who are named after the titular of their church, i.e., San Fernando. There are only four of these monasteries in the entire realm, all of them taking the name of the titular of their respective church— who are the Fernandinos, as I have noted.[25] [In addition to the college in Mexico City, there are the] cross-bearers of the Holy Cross of the city of Querétaro, the Guadalupans of our Lady of Guadalupe in the Bishopric of Valladolid, if I am not mistaken, and the fourth I do not recall. Like the Franciscans they are also under the charge of the Royal Commissary, but I should state that they do not form a complete entity by themselves because they do not have a provincial, just a local superior. For this reason each monastery is self-governing, apart from some exceptional disposition from the most reverend commissary. Their goal is to undertake perpetual missions.

There are the Philippine fathers, the cross-bearers, or those of San Camillo de Lellis; but here they do not serve in hospitals, as is their wont. There are Discalced Carmelites, who are quite wealthy and great alms-collectors. The friars of Saint Anthony the Abbot, who are like regular priests, have their own monastery and church as well. They go about the city seeking alms for Saint Anthony. They enter every gateway on horseback and, without uttering a word, ask for alms while ringing a bell, which they carry in hand. There is the monastery of Saint Pius of God with a very fine church. They maintain an infirmary for the indigent. The priests of Saint Hippolytus also have an infirmary of sorts and take under their care all demented clerics from every institution still [serving] as priests. These priests are directly subordinated to the archbishop of Mexico, who presides over their chapter.[26]

The Bethlehemites, who have a very large monastery in Mexico City, are all lay brothers, like those from San Juan de Dios, and have a rule about not taking in priests, save one per monastery who can serve as chaplain. Therefore, because of their rule, no priest has ever been elevated to the duties of a superior. Nevertheless, it is not true that there are no men of immense talent and learning in this order. They are attired almost like Capuchins, bearded and barefoot, and the only thing that distinguishes them is that affixed to their cloaks they wear a fairly large medallion depicting the birth of Our Lord, from which they take their name. Like the Augustinians they gird themselves with a leather belt. Their cowl is somewhat smaller than that of the Capuchins. The founder of this religious order was the V[enerable] F[ather] José Betancur, a native of the province of Guatemala, whose beatification is expected shortly.[27] This religious order received its sanction from Pope Innocent XI and exists only in the two Americas. Their order takes in and cares for the sick; they also receive convalescents coming from other hospitals. In addition, they provide schooling for children. They are mendicants, yet they have a decent income.

Finally, a word needs to be said about the Jesuit fathers, who, in addition to the Casa Profesa, had four other colleges: San Ildefonso Seminary, San Andrés, Loreto, and Espíritu Santo. The latter served the Indian folk, so the Jesuit fathers preached, catechized, and confessed in the Mexican and Otomí languages.[28] And because this is an appropriate moment, I will briefly recount their expulsion from those lands and from all of Spain, which occurred on June 26, 1767.[29] Some of the motives for this expulsion can be read in the Royal Decree issued from El Pardo [a Spanish royal palace] on April 2 that same year, and some the Catholic king, Charles III, kept to himself. I could append the same royal decree in its entirety, but because it is a rather long item and was published that same year, I will forego this.[30]

67

-(:✝:)-

DON CARLOS FRANCISCO

DE CROIX, Marqués de Croix, Cavallero del Orden de Ca-
trava, Comendador de Molinos, y Laguna Rota en la mifma Orden, Theniente General de los Reales Exercitos de S. M. Vi-
rey, Governador, y Capitan General del Reyno de Nueva-Efpaña, Prefidente de fu Real Audiencia, Superintendente general de Real Hazienda, y Ramo del Tabaco de él, Prefidente de
la Junta, y Juez Confervador de efte Ramo, Subdelegado general del Eftablecimiento de Correos Maritimos en el mifmo
Reyno.

Hago faber à todos los habitantes de efte Imperio, que el Rey nuef-
tro Señor por refultas de las ocurrencias paffadas, y para cumplir fu
primitiva obligacion con que Dios le concedió la Corona de con-
var ilefos los Soberanos refpetos de ella, y de mantener fus leales
amados Pueblos en fubordinacion, tranquilidad, y Jufticia, à de
de otras graviffimas caufas que referva en fu Real animo; fe ha dig-
do mandar à Confulta de fu Real Confejo, y por Decreto expedido el veinte y
de Febrero ultimo, *fe extrañen de todos fus Dominios de Efpaña, è Indias, Islas Phi-
n..s, y demas adyacentes à los Religiofos de la Compañia, affi Sacerdotes, como Coadjut
ò Legos, que hayan hecho la primera Profeffion, y à los Novicios que quifieren fegu:
y que fe ocupen todas las temporalidades de la Compañia en fus Dominios.* Y havie
S. M. para la execucion uniforme en todos ellos, autorizado privativamente al Ex
Señor Conde de Aranda, Prefidente de Caftilla, y cometidome fu cumplimiento
efte Reyno con la mifma plenitud de facultades, afigné el dia de hoy para la
macion de la Suprema Sentencia à los Expulfos en fus Colegios, y Cafas de I
dencia de efta Nueva-Efpaña, y tambien para anunciarla à los Pueblos de ella,
la prevencion de que, eftando eftrechamente obligados todos los Vaffallos de
quiera dignidad, clafe, y condicion que fean, à refpetar, y obedecer las fiempre
tas refoluciones de fu Soverano, deben venerar, auxiliar, y cumplir efta con la
yor exactitud, y fidelidad; porque S. M. declara incurfos en fu Real indignacic
los inobedientes, ò remiffos en coadyuvar à fu cumplimiento, y me verè precif
à ufar del ultimo rigor, y de execucion Militar contra los que en publico, ò fec
hizieren, con efte motivo, converfaciones, juntas, afambléas, corrillos, ò difc:
de palabra, ò por efcrito; pues de una vez para lo venidero deben faber los Su
tos de el gran Monarca que ocupa el Trono de Efpaña, que nacieron para calla:
obedecer, y no para difcurrir, ni opinar en los altos affumptos del Govierno. Me
veinte y cinco de Junio de mil fetecientos fefenta y fiete.

El Marqués de Croix.

Por mándado de fu Exà.

Viceroy's decree expelling the Jesuits. Courtesy of the Bancroft Library.

So, on the aforementioned day of June 26, 1767, the viceroy of Mexico, through some judges, publicized the royal decree to all the fathers of the Company [of Jesus], enjoining them to depart immediately from all the king of Spain's territories. This decree was posted in various locations of the city. In essence, His Catholic Majesty ordered the banishment forthwith of all the aforementioned fathers from all his territories for motives long public and for other motives he did not deem appropriate to explain.[31]

How remarkable that on the same day the ban of these fathers was implemented in Mexico it was also carried out in Lima, capital of the Kingdom of Peru in South America, and in all the nearby areas of the two kingdoms where houses of these fathers were located. Either this had been planned beforehand by the viceroy or else he had orders from the court to do so (which is more likely). To this end, the militia had been called up some time before, and during this entire period merchants could be seen wearing the [militia] uniform, or rather the livery, of the king. So on these days the Baratillo (which is like a daily fairground of Mexico City) did not open. Also closed were all the shops of the Portal, Monterilia [Monterería], and other places of commerce.[32] Now on the same day of June 26, very early in the morning, the Casa Profesa and the colleges of San Andrés, San Ildefonso, San Gregorio, and San Pedro y San Pablo were all surrounded by soldiers with bayonets fixed to the barrels of their guns; and there were sentinels on all the main streets because the gates of all the aforementioned [religious] houses were closed. No one was allowed to enter or leave, and day and night various pickets made the rounds on every street and particularly along the acequias or canals, where canoes from the city enter and leave.

During daytime on the 28th, standing alone in the house on Relojeros Street where we resided, I heard a tremendous clamor. I went to the window, which looked out onto the street, and saw an immense multitude of people of every age, sex, and social class, who were all weeping and shouting loudly. I then saw four forloni, or coaches, in each of which were four Jesuit fathers from the company of the college of San Gregorio. They were being escorted by a company of soldiers on horseback and another on foot with bayonets attached to the barrels of their guns to stifle somewhat the shouting and weeping of the people facing the gates and the windows. They came to blows with anyone [who got in their way] and made no exceptions for age, social class, sex, and condition (such was their fury). To tell the truth, I was moved at the sight of this spectacle: and I could not hold back my tears, especially after seeing the sorrowful demeanor of these fathers as they entered their coaches, their eyes streaming with tears. They were sent to Veracruz, where two seagoing ships were waiting to transport them to Spain. All the other fathers from Mexico City, as well as the others who came in from the interior day by day, were then dispatched from Mexico City to Veracruz at nighttime for fear of possible revolt.[33]

Here I could recount particular details about this matter, but I will pass them up to avoid prolixity. Let me just say that, on the day following the banishment of these fathers, the archbishop ordered the closing of the churches. For two days divine services were not celebrated publicly, except in the cathedral, and the bells were not rung, as though it were Good Friday.

Neither in Mexico City, nor anywhere in the realm, nor in the two Americas are there the various special religious orders encountered in Europe. For that reason one does not see there Camaldolese, Carthusians, calced Carmelites, Minims, Capuchins, and various others who have not ventured to enter this part of the world. In truth, it is not suitable for various religious orders because they would not be able to abide by their own institutional rules.

Nuns are also quite numerous, not just members of orders but other women attending them as well, with all of them living inside the cloister. It is well known that in all those convents each nun lives and supports herself from her own [resources]. (The only exception is the Capuchin nuns, for whom there is just one convent, and they are maintained on a lavish scale.) Nearly every nun has her own servant, and some even two, all of them young and in secular garb. Each nun has her servant prepare meals for her.[34] For that reason at the gate of these convents it looks like a perpetual fair is going on from morning until night because there are hawkers of every kind. One person is carrying vegetables, another fruits, another meat, another mats, another blackbirds, another ribbons and fabrics, so that the two gates of the convent stay open practically all day long and are packed with nuns and servants. The same thing even goes on at the grilled windows. One person calls out for one item, and some other person for something else, and those whose faces cannot be seen because of the crowd raise their arms. In sum, there is a clamor unlike any you have heard before. I could add sundry odd details about these matters, but I will pass them by because of the brevity I imposed upon myself at the outset.

Close to the huge monastery of Santo Domingo, there is a palace of no middling size, which houses the Holy Tribunal of the Inquisition, the members of whom are some Dominican fathers, canons, and other priests.[35] It meets there on specified days. The system of this Inquisition for interrogating and sentencing the accused is not unlike that of Lisbon, capital of Portugal, faithfully described in volume XII, p. [blank] of Salmon's work,[36] to which I refer the reader so as to avoid repeating what the aforementioned author has written on this subject.

In this regard I do not want to overlook a minor episode, which occurred in March 1768. On a certain predetermined day, in the church of Santo Domingo eight live relics were exposed, not to communal veneration but to public derision. They were a heretical blasphemer, an obdurate Calvinist, an idolatrous Indian woman, a witch, a bigamist, a secular cleric with only minor orders[37] who had celebrated some masses, a lay brother of a certain order who had said mass, and an obdurate Jew. All of them were then exposed all day long to public view in the presbytery of the spacious church of Santo Domingo. To this end, the main altar with some other

accessories had been removed to allow a good view of these cul-
prits. The reason for their condemnation was publicized by a placard
on their chests. All day long they suffered the scorn, derision, and
gossiping of the people. Nevertheless, some of them endured this
with great composure, as though it meant nothing. Moreover, such
were the alcoholic drinks administered to them (because on such
occasion they are given all they ask for) that some of them were
partially intoxicated.

The following day they were all led through the open streets of
the city, accompanied by police and escorted by soldiers and all
the officials of the Inquisition, both priests and regular clergy, and
laypersons, too, all of them on horseback. The throng of people
was beyond number. Riding a young donkey, each culprit was
wearing on his or her head a long cap shaped like a horn, formed
of cardboard, except for the two who had celebrated mass, who
went with their heads uncovered. On his chest each one wore a
sign listing his or her offense. Around the neck of the idolatrous
woman they hung a tiny idol, and each person was accompanied
by an Indian in the guise of an executioner, who, with a wooden
stick in hand, dealt each one light blows on the back from time to
time. After this event they were all returned to the prisons of the
Inquisition. I do not know what happened afterward because a few
days later I left Mexico City for Italy. According to the laws of
Spain, some of them ought to have been burned alive.[38]

CHAPTER FOURTEEN

THE MINES OF REAL DEL MONTE

There are many other things I might mention regarding this metropolis, but already I am weary of discussing it and eager to move on to other tales. Nevertheless, to apply the final brushstroke to this miniature portrait of North America, and its capital in particular, I will state that nothing caused me greater consternation when I first arrived here—and even more after I had settled in— than to see, in the midst of such wealth, the vast multitude of poor people, both men and women. Many of them went about the streets like beggars with hardly anything to clad their private parts, while others remained almost entirely nude.[1]

Idleness and vices are the primary reason for this. That is why there are so many thieves and swindlers and so many bad women, who earn their livelihood attempting to beguile whomever they can by whatever means available. In short, this city is a wondrous composite of wealth and poverty, abundance and scarcity, fidelity and cunning, little faith, larceny and many frauds. It has many churches and public gaming houses too, much outward integrity but a great many prostitutes as well, though not brazen ones. In the end, the thrifty person has the opportunity to succeed and in time will become wealthy. On the other hand, people who never let themselves profit from the stream of wealth grow poor in body and spirit, becoming the fount of every vice.

Let me provide one small example: In Mexico City I knew a man, the son of a great Cádiz merchant who had moved his entire family to Lisbon, where his wealth grew considerably. From there he sent his son to Mexico with a capital of 600,000 pesos to carry on business. The poor wretch became mired in the vast Mexican lagoon filled with sirens, enchanting as they were alluring, as beautiful as they were cunning. In a short time he depleted all his capital, so that he was reduced to being a toll collector to earn his livelihood. He had a wife and three daughters of marriageable age who, together with their mother, now and then came to the house where I lived to ask me for some alms in the form of food or garments—such was their poverty. They admitted to me that their father spent everything he earned on drink or women. I could cite various other cases, but I will refrain from doing so.

Now that I have provided a brief sketch of this vast theater of North America—though quite imperfect because of its brevity—I will move on to relate what happened to me during the course of my stay in the city. For the first three months after my arrival, I lived in a house with only the aforementioned Father Lorenzo da Brà, a Piedmontese. He left Mexico City at the beginning of September 1762 for the city of Guadalajara, 160 leagues distant from Mexico [City]. Remaining by myself, I took a young man into my service and carried on with my task of collecting alms in the city for Propaganda Fide.

On November 16 that same year Father Paolo Maria da Ferrara, a Capuchin priest and alms-gatherer for Propaganda Fide, arrived in the capital. He was returning from Ciguagua [Chihuahua], a region quite far from Mexico City. My association with this father lasted a short time because, once the archbishop appointed him as our president, he directed me to head for Real del Monte or Pachuca, where there are silver mines, to solicit alms.[2] I provided myself with a good riding mule, with all the remaining items needed, and departed by myself from Mexico City on December 20.

After two days of travel I arrived at the town called Pachuca, near Real del Monte, where I stayed a few days in a gentleman's home. I walked through the town of Pachuca once. At the present time, however, it is nothing more than a small, somewhat decaying village. Nevertheless, a monastery of the Reformed fathers, or Franciscan friars, and another one of San Juan de Dios can be found there. There are royal officials too: an *alcalde mayor*,[3] accountant, and treasurer, because the *insaje*, or smelter, where they purify the silver of every other admixture, is here. After having taken the king's fifth,[4] they mark the bars or *piastres*, because piastres that have not been marked cannot enter Mexico City, to say nothing of the mint, because they would be contraband. The piastres are pieces of silver that ordinarily contain a thousand Spanish pesos, of eight reales each.

The gentleman in whose home I was lodging persuaded me to go with him to a large village called Tolenzingo [Tulancingo], a good day's journey from Pachuca, where they perform certain festivals on the solemn day of Christmas. Due to the throng of people, I would be able to collect sizable alms. I decided to go there, lured by the hope of good takings, as indeed was the case because there was a cockfight in the morning, the *plaza de toros* [bullfights] in the afternoon, and processions and other church functions in the evening. I stayed ten days in Tolenzingo, returning from there to Pachuca. After a few days there, I headed to Real del Monte, the town that was my destination. I rented a small house where I lived alone, cooking my own meals. I could not continue doing this for any length of time, though, because of my occupations, and thus I had to hire a neighbor woman to prepare them.

I visited the mines, familiarized myself with the countryside, and obtained information about everything under my purview. A few days later, I paid a visit on Señor Don Pedro Romero de Terreros, a very wealthy gentleman and owner of all the principal mines of Real del Monte.[5] From him I obtained permission to solicit alms at his mines. So I began my work. Every day, evening, and night I went to the mines to gather rocks and earth from where they were digging for silver and then sold them; and sometimes they also rendered them for my account.

It would not be out of place to provide a brief account about the mines and how silver is extracted. However, I will do so very briefly, referring the reader to Gemelli, who, in his *Giro del mondo*, provides a more detailed description of these same mines, namely Real del Monte, where I spent a few years. He calls it the Trinidad Mine.[6] I have been there many times; I was living not far from this mine.

Real del Monte has a circumference of roughly five or six leagues. The countryside is entirely mountainous with barren soil. Within this area there were three hundred or more apertures for mines, some of which are being worked at the present time and some of which are abandoned. The apex or main branch of these mines starts at the east and heads toward the west; then it forms a cross of sorts with another primary lode running from south to north. Generally, it is called the *veta Biscaina* [Viscayan lode], and it has always been prolific—as it would be today, too, if it were worked as it ought to be. Unfortunately it has huge quantities of water in every section. For that reason it is not possible to burrow into the bowels of those mountains in search of good veins, which are frequently encountered, without running into a huge spring, just when one is on the verge of extracting rich ore. For that reason the enterprise sometimes has to be abandoned.

Real del Monte has about twelve thousand people, and the greater part are employed in the mines and in metalworking. Gemelli wrote that with nine hundred and more people working there every day, forty million [pesos] were extracted in Real in ten years.[7]

The chief mines found in the principal lode, which runs from east to west, are Santa Teresa, San Cayetano, La Joya, Los Dolores, and La Palma. From south to north are Todos Santos, Trinidad, Sacramento, and various others whose names I do not recall. All

View of Real del Monte. Courtesy of the Bancroft Library.

the aforementioned mines belong to Señor Romero de Terreros. There are many others there as well, with various owners, such as La Compagna [Campaña], Il Reschisio [El Resquicio?], L'Avagnil [El Albañil?], La Blanca, Morán, La Manzanera, and many others, which I will omit for brevity's sake. Now I went collecting alms in all these mines every day, and it was no mean feat having to pass from one to another, even during periods of rain, intense heat, and other discomforts brought on by hunger, thirst, fatigue, sweat, and the like.

The mines are essentially deep shafts, some having eighty or more stations. Each station has two [horizontal] arms plus a third one. The opening of the mine is completely framed on all four sides, or supported by large beams and other cross timbers so that the ground does not cave in. From this opening they are constantly drawing water day and night and on holidays and Sundays too. From the same openings they also remove bags of metal [i.e., ore].[8] All this is done with the labor of horses and mules, which turn a machine called a *malacate*,[9] of which there are three or four for each mine. Every six hours they switch the four horses required for turning each malacate. Thus every day at least sixteen horses are working there continuously. They do not last long because of the tremendous labor they perform.

The miners of the ore then descend into the interior of the mine through another shaft with special ladders made of a single huge tree trunk. They are provided with lamps, a good hammer, and other tools for cutting stone, along with powder for sapping should the need arise. Their work lasts six hours. For this, the owner gives them four reales, or one-half peso, in payment, along with a certain portion of ore. Due to avarice they labor more willingly for the ore than for the salary because sometimes (if there is good ore) their portion from a single six-hour day will yield fifteen to twenty, or even more, pesos of eight reales. These six-hour days are sometimes shorter and sometimes longer because it should be understood that the mine-owner distributes to each *baratero* (that is what

the diggers of ore are called) three, and sometimes four, bags to fill;
and they must do this to receive their salary of four reales. Now, if
the laborers encounter soft material, they hasten to bring their
workday to a close; if they encounter live rock, they face a more
difficult task. After they have filled the costales, or owners' sacks,
they fill another one, which is divided up—i.e., half for the owner,
half for themselves. From their portion they gave alms daily, not
just to me but to various other alms-gatherers as well. Because
there are many workers in various mines, they spend the whole
week collecting this ore, and eventually they sell it to those able to
resell it, and at times they credited it to my account, as I have noted
above.

Once the ore is extracted and leaves with the workers, certain
men called *pepenadores* enter the so-called gallery. Their job is to
smash the rock with hammers and separate the ore into three groups
depending on quality: the first, and the best, for the *chacuacuo*,[10] the
second for the *plancha*, and the third for the *azogue* [mercury]. The
chacuacuo is a furnace where silver is extracted from ore in a few
hours by means of fire. It [the ore] is blended with lead, *temesquitate*,[11] and clay. Similarly, the plancha is another type of furnace,
which refines a larger quantity of metal of lower quality than the
aforementioned. The operation lasts several days; but when the ore
is of such quality that it can be subjected to fire, it is always better
to refine it by plancha than by chacuacuo or *cendradas*[12] because in
this second process [i.e., plancha] a proportionally greater amount
of silver is extracted.

The third method of refining the metal is by means of azogue,
or mercury. This is done in the following way: After the pepenadores have inspected the ore and separated what is suitable for the
chacuacuo, for the plancha, and for azogue from the *tepetate* (the
worthless part, which they throw on the ground or leave behind),
the arrieros or muleteers arrive and load the ore onto mules and
take it to the mill and refinery. These buildings are all located above
rivers, where the ore is refined in three ways: here it is crushed; or

all the ore is finely ground separately with mortars, which are run by water power; then it is passed through a sieve.

To refine it with mercury, they take a heap of about a hundred-weight from this powder. They soak it with ordinary water, giving it a puddle-like form. Then they blend it with a specific quantity of mercury, salt, another blend of earth salt,[13] and another material they call *magistral*.[14] To blend the aforementioned items well, they have six or eight men tromping for two or three hours in their bare feet over this form of mud smeared across the tightly fitted [floor] slabs. Then they heap it up and every third day carry out the same procedure of thorough treading until roughly the end of a month. Then they pass water through all this mud, carrying off all the worthless material. The silver, combined with mercury, remains at the bottom of those receptacles designed for this separation [process]. From there they extract this material, which is nothing more than minute particles of silver united with mercury.

To separate the two, they mold this blend into certain chunks like bricks, but with a somewhat different shape. Then they place them over an iron grating inside a pit beneath which a small channel of water passes. After forming a little pyramid of this silver [amalgam], they put something like a bronze bell on top, plugging every tiny airhole it may contain. They surround this bell with a considerable quantity of burning charcoal, and they keep it there for six or seven hours straight. Now, while heating up the mercury combined with silver, everyone knows that it [the mercury] will vaporize and, finding nowhere to escape after having circulated along every side of the bell, it must drop down into the water. There it resumes its former shape because of the water's cool temperature and its own weight. They lose very little mercury this way.

Any person can exploit the mines, whether gold or silver, by paying the quinto to the king. If a mine is abandoned for three months by the initial discoverer, it reverts to the king. Then, after notification of the first owner, it belongs to whoever decides to mine there. If he objects and offers a good reason why he has not maintained workers, the royal audiencia decides whether the objection should be sustained or not. The king grants sixty Spanish *varas* of land, which roughly amount to the same number of Italian braccia,[15] in all directions from the mouth of the mine or all on one side, depending on the miner's wishes.[16] Beyond this interval, another person may, in fact, open another mine, leaving five varas of solid ground as a dividing wall. For the sake of brevity, there are many other factors I will omit, but these can be found in the mining legislation.

I will conclude the subject of mining with a brief account of an uprising that occurred in 1766 in Real del Monte, where I was living. There were some dissensions, the reason for which I do not know, that erupted between the mineworkers and officials acting on behalf of the owner, Don Pedro Romero de Terreros. Before long, on a certain day, a large number of Indians gathered in this mining camp. All of them were mine workers, not just from this location but from other nearby areas as well. The intention of these people (as was later determined) was to kill the owner, i.e., Señor Terreros, and all of his officials and burn down the mines. Had this occurred, it would have been their own ruination and that of the whole country as well. But God did not permit such ravaging to occur.

So, on August 15, [1766,] the day set by that rabble for the total destruction of Real del Monte, many of them gathered in the mine of San Cayetano. There, after some quarrels between them and a miner, or mine official, they stoned him so that he died a few hours later. When the alcalde mayor or *podestà*[17] of Pachuca, a young man recently arrived from Spain who happened to be there, attempted to bring these people to a halt by drawing his sword, they flung themselves on him with such ferocity and cruelty that they left him there dead, completely crushed by stones.

Señor Terreros, having heard about the uprising and the two fatalities that had already occurred, hid in a room where he kept plenty of fodder for the horses, burying himself up to his neck in this. However much the rebel Indians tried to hunt him down and kill him, they could not find him. It was necessary for the parish priest to lead a procession with the Blessed Sacrament, which I also accompanied, so as to convey Señor Romero de Terreros from his hiding place and guide him into the church, underneath the balda-chin, as a sanctuary for himself and his general foreman. It was a gratifying sight arriving in certain places with the Blessed Sacra-ment. There were many women and children, [and] listening to their wailing and weeping one would have thought it was the final day [of judgment].

While all this was going on, other women, enraged like their husbands, were going about tossing lighted embers onto the piles of straw of the mines to set them ablaze. There was no damage, thanks to the diligence of a few individuals. The insurgents moved on to a house where they believed a certain mine official was hidden, whom they had vowed to kill. They smashed in the door and windows and went inside, but they did not find the one they were looking for. They moved on to the jails, ecclesiastical as well as secular, forced them open, and removed all the prisoners, their accomplices.

Then they passed on to Pachuca, where they did the same thing, i.e., forcibly liberate all the prisoners. They then headed to the home of the foreman of the mines to burn it down. Those enraged individuals only desisted from their design because some Reformed fathers, who have a monastery in that town, had promptly arrived on the scene, loudly threatening to bring down the wrath of God, while hoisting a crucifix above their heads.

The matter ended with the mines being closed down for some time, and the first to experience the devastation were the insti-gators of the uprising. As day laborers in the mines with no other means of livelihood, they were compelled to suffer from the damage they themselves had wrought.

Some troops were sent up from Mexico City with orders to put down the revolt. Some [instigators] were hanged in Mexico City; others less culpable were sent to labor in the garrison.[18] And finally

I made my little rounds, not finding alms at this time except by happenstance.

I have mentioned a few things about the mines, but there is a lot more that could be written about them. I refer the reader to Gemelli, who treats these matters in greater detail.[19] I will only say that, after these lands were conquered by the Spaniards, such was the quantity of gold, silver, and other precious articles coming from there that all Europe has felt the effects and still feels the benefit.[20]

CHAPTER FIFTEEN

EXPULSION FROM MEXICO

In the beginning of the year 1764, if I am not mistaken, the archbishop of Mexico, Monsignor Rubio y Salinas, died, much to our regret, because our prelate had been kindly and devout and was otherwise very well disposed to the work of Propaganda Fide.[1] That same year two Capuchin friars, also sent by Propaganda Fide, arrived from Spain to carry on with alms-gathering. One was a priest named Father Francisco de Ajofrín, the other a lay brother from the same [order], Fray Fermín de Olite. Both were from the province of Castile.[2] At the outset there was some disagreement between them and Father Paolo Maria da Ferrara, our president—with Father Ajofrín claiming precedence over Father Ferrara and the administration of alms, as well as all other affairs affecting the interests of Propaganda Fide under the president's area of responsibility. But because Father Ferrara had been entrusted with this task by none other than Cardinal Spinelli [Spinola], now prefect of Propaganda Fide, and [this had been] confirmed by the late archbishop, Father Ajofrín thus lacked sufficient authority to strip him of his functions. That is why, in their heart of hearts, the two Spaniards nurtured a certain ill-will toward us three Italians, which, as will be noted, later came to the fore.

In 1765 [July 1766] the new archbishop, Monsignor Francisco Lorenzana y Buitrón, arrived with the new viceroy, the marqués de Croix.[3] They were also accompanied by a certain Father Filippo da Portogruaro from the province of Venice, sent by Propaganda Fide as our president because Father Paolo da Ferrara had repeatedly pleaded with Propaganda to return to his province of Bologna. No sooner had the aforementioned Father Filippo da Portogruaro arrived in Veracruz than he died there a few days later in the hospice of the Bethlehemites. He is buried in the church of the Observant fathers in Veracruz.[4] For that reason Father Ferrara had decided to stay behind in Mexico City and manage the affairs of Propaganda Fide until it sent a new person to replace Father Portogruaro, whose death had been promptly reported to Rome.

The two Castilian friars had strong friendships with the principal notables of Mexico and had formed an influential party on their behalf. Because the initial discord prevented them from achieving their aims, they got their revenge by maligning us three Italians, and particularly Father Paolo da Ferrara as president for the others.

Having now learned of the arrival at Veracruz of the archbishop and the viceroy, these two friars, along with various Mexican notables, went to greet them in a town called Cholula. There they had the opportunity to sway the archbishop with all the unfavorable opinions they were aware of and could use against us. When Monsignor Lorenzana arrived in Mexico City, Father Paolo, in keeping with his obligation, promptly went to visit him because he was the only one [i.e., Italian Capuchin] in Mexico City. The reception he received from the archbishop was the recommendation that he leave America for Italy as soon as a vessel was available. There is no explanation for this precipitate decision by the archbishop other than the unfavorable impression created by the insinuations of the two Castilian monks against Father Paolo and his own hostility toward Italians and the interests of Propaganda Fide.[5] I lived only two days away from Mexico City, and because I had

harmonious relations with Father Paolo, I received detailed information by letter about everything [that had happened] from the
time of the two friars' arrival to his own departure for Europe.

Archbishop Francisco Lorenzana y Buitrón. Courtesy of the Bancroft
Library.

One day, when I happened to be in Mexico City, I also paid a visit to monsignor the archbishop, but there were no new developments. He merely instructed me to write to Father Lorenzo da Brà to have him come to Mexico City as soon as possible. At that time the aforementioned father was in the city of Guadalajara, more than a hundred leagues from Mexico City.[6] No sooner had he arrived and presented himself to the archbishop than it was proposed he depart for Italy and that, while awaiting the opportunity to embark, he should withdraw to a monastery—which he did.

Because Father Brà, in handing over his accounts to the archbishop, left him a note for five thousand pesos deposited in the hands of a gentleman from Guadalajara, the prelate therefore entrusted me with the mission of going to collect this money. Under no circumstances did he want Father Brà to go there himself, even though he made a case in a memorandum for going there in person. The archbishop paid no heed, however, and wanted me to carry out this inquiry, having formed a somewhat better impression of me than of the two [other] Italian priests, i.e., Father Brà and Father Ferrara.

While these events were going on, it was the month of July [1767] and hence the rainy season. It was therefore an inopportune time for traveling because such a journey would entail crossing many rivers and streams, which are swollen more than usual during that period. For this reason I obtained the archbishop's permission to wait until the rains subsided.

Meanwhile, I headed back to Real del Monte to continue my alms-gathering. For a year now I had been living in the home of Señor Don Bernardino Díaz, a man of moderate means but an upright individual, as was his numerous family. He provided me free board, and I lived contentedly in his company because I was free to dine at their table when I chose. Or if I wished to dine alone, they brought me my meal in the room assigned as my habitation, and I promptly received every kind of service. So great was the love we felt for each other while I lived in this home that I was considered by the parents as their son and by their children as a brother, and we used nicknames in our relations with each other. When we finally had to part, we both wept profusely. I still retain some tokens of their affection expressed in some letters, [from] which anyone versed in the Spanish language could readily appreciate the esteem, affection, respect, and love that everyone in that house professed for me.

A little while after I had returned to Real del Monte, monsignor the archbishop also arrived there to pay a visit. Once again he entrusted me with the aforementioned collection and treated me in a very affable manner. When an opportunity came to make the journey, I provided myself with three good mules—one for myself, another for a man whom I brought with me as a servant, and a third to carry some items essential for the journey and as a replacement, should that prove necessary. I also provided myself with some firearms for self-defense against murderers lingering about the roads, if the need should arise, because there were a goodly number of them in those regions.

I left Real del Monte around the middle of December 1767 and headed to Mexico City, where I stayed a few days to make the necessary arrangements for my excursion. From the viceroy I obtained a dispatch with which I could recover the money with assistance from the judiciary (if it came to that). I also had some letters of recommendation for certain prominent gentlemen of Guadalajara. I left one afternoon from Mexico City, and after walking six leagues I arrived that evening in a little village called Cuautitlán. In this village there was a novitiate of the Jesuit fathers. The next day I covered twelve leagues and spent the night in another village called Tepozotlán.[7] Then, after walking eight leagues, I arrived at Tepex [Jilotepec]. I headed to another large village called Tepex del Río [Tepejí del Río] with twelve leagues of highway. Then, after traveling twelve leagues across a vast terrain, I arrived in San Juan del Río. Here I found accommodation in the home of the parish priest, a very upstanding cleric, much devoted to the Capuchins.

I covered another ten leagues and arrived in the city of Querétaro, where I rested a whole day. A special attraction of this medium-size city is the church of the Observant fathers, justly renowned throughout the kingdom of Mexico. It is large, even though it has only one nave, and is a fine work of architecture. It has good paintings with many gilded carvings, and, all in all, is so ornate and resplendent that it is evocative of paradise.[8]

From Querétaro I proceeded to the town of Celaya, four or five leagues distant. Here there is also a very fine monastery and church of the Observant fathers mentioned above. In the plaza of this city I saw a man placed in the pillory. From Celaya I went to Salamanca, across vast [expanses of] land, on a six-league stretch of road. Then I reached Irapuato, a medium-sized village, arriving on Christmas Eve. Because there was no place between there and Guadalajara where I could hear mass, I had to stay for all the Christmas festivities. In this town I ate good, big freshwater fish, quite inexpensive.

On the Day of Holy Innocents [December 28] I departed. After covering fourteen leagues, I arrived at a hacienda or property called "La Concepción"; it is also called "La Mariscala" because it belongs to the *mariscal*[9] marqués del Valle, a descendant of Cortés the conqueror. From there it is just two leagues to San Pedro, a tiny village, whence it is six leagues to Carisso [Carizo?]. This Carisso is nothing more than a small house with Indian folk. Besides the family living there, it also accommodates passengers who stop. That accounts for a wretched meal and a sleepless night. It is four leagues from Carisso to Saos [Sauz?], which amounts to nothing more than a few Indian huts.

It is six leagues from Saos to Cerro Gordo, a hacienda of a gentleman from Guadalajara, where I was received most ungraciously by the administrator. It is eight leagues from Cerro Gordo to Puentezuela, six from there to Zapotlán. I spent the night in that small town. They told me that the day before, not far from the terrain along the main road where I had also been traveling, they found

two poor passengers tied to two trees and clubbed to death by murderers. I received practically the same news from the parish priest
of San Juan del Río: that just a few days before, he had buried two
other people murdered by robbers. It is eight leagues from Zapotlán
to Puente Barania or the San Jacobo [Santiago] River, and six from
there to Guadalajara, so that there are approximately one hundred
and thirty-two leagues from Mexico City to this city, besides the
additional twenty-two from Real del Monte to Mexico City.

I arrived in Guadalajara on January 2, 1768, having spent eighteen
days on this trip, including the three I stayed in Irapuato. A great
part of this journey is extremely uncomfortable and exhausting—
along rocky roads, across mountains and cliffs, to the swampy
plain. There are numerous rivers and streams, and it was easy to
lose one's way because in many places there are very few signs of
the road, especially from Irapuato to Puente [Puentezuela], because
very few people pass through here. In addition, during nearly the
entire journey, I was accompanied by strong winds, which caused
me no little annoyance, all the more so because they swept up huge
amounts of dust. When the wind subsided, I was seared by the
intense sun. Ordinarily I arrived at my accommodation so exhausted
from spending all day on horseback that many times, after taking
a little refreshment, I lay down to sleep on a table, using the saddle
as my cushion, without even removing my boots or shoes. Nevertheless, the bottle of brandy, which always supplied me throughout the journey, kept me hale and hearty.

Guadalajara is a medium-sized city[10] situated along a gentle
slope—though nearly level, in fact. In outline it resembles Mexico
City; but since the streets are not paved with stones, as in Mexico
City, the considerable dust, whipped up by wind and carriages,
causes great discomfort. There are fine buildings—houses, churches,
and monasteries. A bishop resides there. It was founded by Nuño
[de] Guzmán in 1531.[11]

Despite its location at 21 degrees [of northern latitude] and 272
degrees of longitude, this city has a very warm climate—i.e., it is

one degree farther from the equator than Mexico City. Nevertheless, the degree away from the equator is offset by closer proximity to the Tropic of Cancer.[12] This would hardly have seemed possible had I not seen it with my own eyes.

As already stated above, I arrived in this city on January 2. After a few days of rest, I began to move about through its various sections and *barrios*, or suburbs, at the foot of which flows a little river.[13] Here I saw people bathing completely nude, as they might do in Lombardy during the month of July, were there such a custom. Certainly the heat of this climate during the month of January nearly equals that of Lombardy in the months of July and August. As for bathing, in particular, there is considerable license, because the women bathe themselves in this river utterly without restraint, even though there are no sheltered areas or remote locations; and in this regard I have at times seen things that are better left unmentioned. Many times, indeed, has that zealous bishop fulminated threats of excommunication against those who bathe without heeding the necessary precautions. But they pay the same heed to excommunication that they do in Rome.[14] What is also reprehensible is that they allow both male and female children (though from the common people) to walk stark naked through public streets at the age of three or four, or perhaps even older—even white children.

Guadalajara is the capital of Nueva Galicia. It [the territory] is bounded on the east and the northeast by the Puerto de la Natividad and swamp of Chapala,[15] which divides it from Nueva España, toward the west [by] the Gulf of California, and toward the northwest and the north it extends toward a vast tract of unknown lands. The government of this Nueva Galicia embraces many provinces, of which the primary ones are Guadalajara, Jalisco, Zacatecas, Chiametlán, Culiacán, Sinaloa, and Nueva Vizcaya. It has an audiencia with seven judges, including the president; but, if need be, appeals from this audiencia, as well as those from Guatemala, go to Mexico City.

I will not dwell on a detailed description of this country, nor on disputes encountered in recovering the money, which after a month of struggle was eventually delivered to me in the form of a promissory note for Mexico City. I visited monsignor the bishop, who received me with a show of affection.[16] He was aware of my purpose thanks to Judge Becerra. This gentleman gave me a very cordial welcome when I first visited him, offering me his assistance and guidance in the arduous task ahead of me. Every day he invited me out to dine with him, but I limited myself to going just a few times. Eventually, when I had taken care of all my business, I made preparations for my departure to Mexico City, which took place around the middle of February.

On the last day of Carnival[17] I arrived in Puentezuela. This is on a small plain where there are a few thatched houses with Indian folk. It was necessary to spend the night in this place even though we arrived about 21 hours by the Italian clock [at 4 P.M.]. After I placed my effects and animals in one of these houses, men and women on horseback began arriving, so that in a short time a not inconsiderable number of purely Indian folk had gathered in this small but agreeable place.

The reason for their arrival was to celebrate, after their fashion, the final evening of Carnival. So, with the women lined up in a certain fashion, the men began horse-racing. To tell the truth, I was amazed at how swiftly they came, after a certain determined signal. Moreover, they played a variety of games. For example, two men, each on his own horse, would embrace each other and ride off at rapid speed while maintaining this embrace. Others rode while standing on the bareback horse. Then they performed two or three minuets on horseback, with four standing on each side, but with such skill and agility that I was astonished to observe the swiftness of those horses at the movement of the reins. Finally, they fought a mock battle—one side playing Turks, the other Christians—during which some of the latter made prisoners of some of the former, whom they then presented as an offering to some of the women spectators, their friends.

At nightfall, each person retired into the few available houses, and in the one I had already picked there was practically no space until the wee hours. They passed the whole night in music, song, and dancing, and everything ended in drunkenness. I had my man keep watch all night long so that none of my mules would be stolen (what usually happens in such situations). Somehow I made it through that night, for the house was filled with men and women milling around, devoid of either modesty or respect (but anyone who travels must endure many things in silence). In the morning I departed, returning [to the capital] by the same route I had come.

After arriving safely in Mexico City, I delivered the promissory note to monsignor the archbishop, along with all my accounts. I should explain that one year after the expulsion of the Jesuits from all the king of Spain's states, a royal decree arrived in Mexico banning all foreign clergy, whether secular or regular, from his American states.[18] This was posted in places customarily for public viewing, and I was not unaware of it. Nevertheless, I was not convinced that this would apply to me as well. I was, after all, residing in Mexico with the king's special permission, obtained by monsignor the nuncio, at the request of Propaganda Fide. Furthermore, a ten-year sojourn had been planned by Propaganda, and so far only five years of my stay had elapsed. So I was confident there would be no surprises.

But the outcome turned out to be exactly the opposite: After all the documentation and account books concerning the alms-gathering and other interests of Propaganda Fide had been delivered to Monsignor Lorenzana, he submitted the royal order to me. Here it should be noted that this archbishop was motivated solely by the interests of his monarch, and not at all by Propaganda Fide. Now that he could see what considerable sums of money were being transferred to Rome, he also revealed to me on various occasions his total opposition to our alms-gathering. If his predecessor, Monsignor Rubio, had still been alive, he would have ignored this royal order; and nothing would have changed because not only was he devoted to the Capuchins, but he was also quite partial to Propaganda Fide's interests. I should not fail to mention, though, that while the current archbishop opposed alms-gathering, he did not have the same attitude toward those who carried it out, i.e., the Capuchins. This he publicly demonstrated in his circular issued in print a short while after assuming office. Here he stated, for reasons unknown to me, that it would be desirable if all the priests were like regular clergy and the regular clergy like the Capuchins.[19]

For my own well-founded reasons I asked the prelate to give me the royal order in writing. At first he balked at the request, but on my insistence he eventually had his secretary provide me an honorific document, which I am pleased to insert here, faithfully translated from the Spanish:

> We, Don Francisco Antonio Lorenzana, by the grace of God and the Holy See, Archbishop of Mexico, of the Council of his Majesty, et cetera.
>
> Upon the entreaty of the Reverend Father Brother Lorenzo da Brà, a priest, and Fra Ilarione da Bergamo, a lay brother, Italian Capuchins sent by the Sacred Congregation of Propaganda Fide to collect alms in these realms of New Spain for the missions of Tibet in Asia, we provided them with our testimonial letters and the means to return to their homelands and monasteries, pursuant to royal decrees, and particularly the most recent one from October 18 of the previous year (1767), in which His Royal Majesty, bearing in mind the grave inconveniences (i.e., the misinformation from our adversaries) that ensue from the passage of foreign clergy into his American kingdoms, commands and enjoins respectively the higher authorities of the various territories of America (monastic orders and secular clergy, and particularly the archbishop of Mexico and the viceroy) that they promptly remove from his

dominions all foreign secular clergy and friars who there abide.

Complying with such a just request, and also bearing in mind that the two aforementioned clergy have presented and delivered to us the account books and other instruments with the amount of alms they have collected, and which in accordance with our instruction are deposited in the nearby commercial Banco de Plata of Don Manuel de Aldaco of this city, we, for our part, give them our leave that they may return to their homeland. For this purpose, and so that this may be effected with the decorum appropriate to their status, we enjoin that, from the funds they have deposited, they be given the amount necessary for their needs, sustenance, and passage.

So that no impediment will be put in the way of their journey until arrival at their respective destinations, we certify to the Most Illustrious Señor Don Franco Fabian y Fuero, bishop of Puebla de Los Angeles, and to all the most illustrious archbishops and bishops of Spain and their just provisors[20] that the above-mentioned Reverend Father Lorenzo da Brà and Fra Ilarione da Bergamo leave this realm solely in compliance with the royal orders cited above, and that they do not leave as fugitives, suspects, or under interdiction. Nor is there any irregularity with the first of them, nor any other obstacle that would impede him in the use and exercise of his orders and permission to preach and confess, which he definitely has. For this reason we urge you, illustrious and honorable sirs (bishops and provisors), that in your respective dioceses, where they will be passing through, you will receive them kindly and charitably, and that we will do the same each time whenever comparable letters are presented.

Mexico City, March 22, 1768
Francisco, archbishop of Mexico
On the command of my archbishop, Señor Don Andrés Marin Campillo, secretary

In fulfillment of the uncompromising royal orders in this particular matter, the viceroy also had all monasteries with friars account for each foreign individual. I do not know what the outcome was.

I returned to Real del Monte for a few days to bring to an end my alms-gathering, which was going on despite my absence. With the deepest regret I took leave of my friends, and particularly from the Díaz family, in whose home I had lived in the way described above.

I returned to Mexico City with my effects. Here I had to make hasty arrangements for the journey and embarkation. Because Father Brà, in whose company I was to return to Italy, had become half-witted and thus incapable of doing anything due to his advanced age and customary indispositions, I had to carry out all the preparations deemed necessary for the journey by land and sea. From the archbishop I obtained a letter for a merchant of Veracruz, whom he obliged to make arrangements for the embarkation, or rather to pay with Propaganda Fide's funds for the transportation of both of us to Cádiz on one of the three ships about to depart from the port of Veracruz. He also gave each of us fifty pesos for the journey from Mexico City to Veracruz. Beyond that, I had about eighty pesos, which I carried from Real del Monte the last time I was there, which he also allowed me to use for incidental expenses of the journey.

I hoped to pass through Puebla solely from the desire to see that city, which was once the episcopal see of the venerable Palafox,[21] but for various reasons I was unable to go there. Puebla de Los Angeles is in the audiencia of Mexico City, and in the *gobierno* of Tlascala, about twenty leagues distant from Mexico City. It was established in 1530.[22] It is twenty-seven leagues from Puebla to the mines of Alchichica, where for four months the aforementioned venerable [bishop] was hidden to elude the fatal persecutions of the reverend Jesuit fathers.[23]

Each day the pressure to leave, in order to reach Veracruz on time, grew more urgent because the ships were getting ready to sail soon. For that reason I had no time to gather some rare items from those lands to transport them to Italy. We took care of all our affairs then and departed from the great city of Mexico on April 18, 1768, with two men and some mules to carry our things. Truly, a malefactor condemned to the galleys or the guardhouse does not leave for his place of torment with such pain and regret as I was now experiencing on departing from Mexico, never to return. I had come to feel completely at home with the climate, the food, my work, the cordiality of the inhabitants, and, in the end, everything else. And then reflecting about how I must expose myself anew to the perils of an ocean voyage, I had greater apprehensions than when I arrived.

I was also wrapped up in other reflections, as a result of which I made that voyage with a reluctance and weariness that are beyond explanation. On May 4 we arrived in Veracruz, and on the 10th we boarded a war frigate named *Pallas* with thirty-six cannons. We paid six hundred pesos for our transportation to Cádiz in the aft cabin with meals.

CHAPTER SIXTEEN

RETURN VOYAGE TO EUROPE

We set sail that same day and plunged into the vast Gulf of Mexico, where the heat was so intense that no one could sleep either day or night. On May 29 [1768] we dropped anchor in the port of Havana after spending nineteen days at sea. It is three hundred leagues following a straight course from Veracruz to Havana. Until coming within sight of the Florida cape, our pilot followed the coastline almost the entire length of the Gulf to avoid the reefs and shoals one may encounter. For that reason we covered more than four hundred leagues. According to my calculations, we covered about a hundred miles a day, averaging out one day against the other because one does not travel at a uniform rate.

The pilot showed me the site in this ocean where, around 1744, practically the entire Spanish fleet, heading from Veracruz to Spain with vast treasures, was lost, save one ship. The fleet consisted of eighteen vessels, large and small, and it was lost one night—not because of a storm but because of a mysterious current, which dragged all these ships toward the coast, where they ran aground.[1]

During our passage through the Gulf of Mexico there were no exceptional events, apart from the death of our chaplain. He was a young priest from the city of Málaga, and this was the first voyage he had made to America. He came down with the malign fever the second day we were at sea. The inexpert ship's physician did what he could to cure him (which was not very much). Eventually he died, two days before our arrival in Havana. They tossed all his effects into the sea, and, after that, he went too, encased in a box, with the customary obsequies of a cannon shot as he was cast overboard. On May 29, the same day that we dropped anchor, we went ashore.

Father Brà carried a letter of recommendation from the father president of the Bethlehemites in Mexico City for the [corresponding] one in Havana. So the two of us went to their monastery, hoping they would provide us shelter while the ship lingered in that port inasmuch as it was not customary for ships to provide food to passengers while at anchor. The aforementioned father presented his letter to the president of the Bethlehemites and entreated him to take us into his monastery for a few days. This father started mumbling and with great discourtesy told us they had little to offer in the way of comfort. If we wished to remain nevertheless, we could do so but would fare poorly. Faced with this display of bad manners, I preferred not to stay; but to avoid spending money, Father Brá dissembled whatever way he could and stayed with them.

I went around the city to try my luck and by fortunate happenstance entered a shop to drink brandy. The shopkeeper struck me as a solid, upstanding person. I asked him where I could find a house with decent people who would provide me lodging. He promised me that in a few hours he would speak with some of his neighbors. So I returned that afternoon for his response, and he told me he would be delighted to take me into his home. I went to see the house, and we came to an agreement on how much I should pay each day for room and board. I stayed in this house three weeks, which was exactly the time that our ship remained at anchor in that port with its other two companions, one of which was a seafaring vessel, *La Castilla*, and the other a merchant frigate, *El Rosario*.

The city of Havana is the capital of the island of Cuba, or Fernandina. According to Vallemont and others, it is situated at 23 degrees and 20 minutes [north latitude], even though M. de l'Isle puts it at 22 degrees and 30 minutes, as is clearly evident from his geographic maps.[2] It is little more than a half-league in circumference and round in configuration. There is a governor with the title of captain-general of the island. The bishop for the entire island normally resides in this city, even though his episcopal see is the city of Santiago, located at the other, or eastern, tip of the island. This is one of the Greater Antilles or Barlovento—that is, Windward Islands.[3] It is 230 leagues long—others say 220—and 60 or 65 at its greatest width. It is 15 to 20 in the more narrow stretches.

Cuba is no farther than eighty miles from the island of Santo Domingo.[4] Its eastern tip is situated at $20\,^1/_2$ degrees and the southern at 19 degrees, or a little more on our side of the Arctic pole [northern latitude]. The point or Cape of San Antonio, which is the westernmost part of the island, is situated at $21\,^1/_2$ degrees. This island was discovered by Christopher Columbus in 1493.[5] Part of it was conquered by Captain Don Diego Velasco [Velázquez], a captain of the Second Admiral, Don Diego Columbus, and the last remnant was conquered and subjugated to the crown of Spain by Captain Pánfilo de Narváez.[6]

The climate of this island, and especially in the city of Havana, is quite hot. We also arrived during an extremely hot season, which, as I have noted, was the end of May. Blacks inhabit the greater part of this city. Because it is a port, though, and the principal stopping point in America, many Europeans pass through and others stay there because of the modest trade.

In setting foot in this city, I was greatly astonished to see the blacks, men and women, walking through its plazas and districts almost completely unclad. Some of the men wear a small pair of trousers; others barely cover their private parts with some sort of rag, with everything else quite bare. The women wear a simple petticoat of very thin, nearly transparent, fabric, leaving everything else exposed. It is true that the youngest, and especially those who are not married, cover their breasts with a scarf, which they knot around their neck. Yet these Negresses, particularly those somewhat along in age, are so ugly that they are hardly in any danger.[7] Ordinarily they have hideous-looking faces because when they are young they cut [i.e., scarify] their cheeks to beautify their appearance, as I have noted when I referred to the ones in Puerto Rico. So they always retain those scars, which render them utterly hideous. They have a small forehead, a big, blunt nose, and lips turned outward—especially the lower one, thanks to the prodigious amounts of tobacco consumed beginning in childhood. I was flabbergasted to see these blacks, men as well as women, at noon and at all hours with such a scorching sun searing their backs, walk through those streets smoking tobacco and spewing forth such quantities of smoke that it almost looked to me like they were on fire. All these black men and women are slaves.[8] In addition, there are a large number of mulatto men and women who have finer features. They wear shirts, but these afford few advantages because they let them droop down on all sides, the women especially letting them [sag] from their necks for a considerable length.

There are white women, too, and they generally have lovely features and at least go outdoors more fully clad. The ladies of this city, along with their other lofty and ostentatious manners, are still accustomed to the following [practice]: that when they go to church, some of their slaves or slave women walk behind them with a fine rug, which they spread out in the church in the place where they want to station themselves and on top of which they kneel. The blacks and mulattos, men as well as women, are all branded on their backs because they are all slaves. They are heavy brandy drinkers, thievish, and licentious.

All over the island cassava bread is customary fare, as in Puerto Rico. Wheat bread is seldom consumed, even in the masters' homes. There are numerous American fruits, especially coconuts. I ate fine seafood there. In this city I found inexpensive red wine from Catalonia. Because it had been six years since I drank quality wine,

I purchased a few bottles, which cost me no more than two reales apiece. There is an abundance of brandies and many other items, which I would have enjoyed immensely had not the season and this country's intensely hot climate caused me grief. I felt the scorching heat from this sun. Ordinarily, I did not go outside except early in the morning to hear mass in the church of the Augustinian fathers, near the house where I lived, and in the evening to take a short stroll along the seashore. Both at home and outdoors, I had not experienced such a sweltering climate until now. And, as they say, how true is the proverb: "One must experience evil to understand it." Maybe I had experienced hotter climes than this, but because the distress was now past, I had no recollection except of the present. I do recall, though, having suffered tremendous drowsiness because the intense heat during the day made it impossible to sleep. At night, to revivify myself somewhat, I stayed in the middle of the courtyard under the open sky until nearly midnight. Because I went to bed with just one garment (though of rather light material and which I could not take off), falling asleep was out of the question.[9] To make matters worse, the mosquitoes, which abound, stung me cruelly; and when I went on board, my face, hands, and legs were all swollen from the inflammation caused by bites from these creatures.

Nevertheless, I was not without some diversions in this city because the wife of the governor of Veracruz was on board our ship. A young, appealing, and lovely woman, she was heading to Madrid. So, to honor and entertain her at the same time, the governor of Havana ordered not only the entire garrison of veteran soldiers, both foot soldiers and horsemen, but the militia, too, to perform firing exercises—one day for each regiment. The cavalry began by performing military maneuvers, which, after the firing rifles and pistols, consisted of brandishing sabers. The blacks, who looked like a demonic host, came last. There were also cannonades with balls.

Praiseworthy, too, was the procession of Corpus Domini,[10] a solemnity observed [on June 2, 1768,] at the time of our stay in Havana. There was a huge throng of people, heavy artillery fire from both the castles and the ships, and immense wealth in the many statues of the saints that the regular clergy are accustomed to carrying, particularly the founding saint of each religious order. Once the Corpus solemnity is over, each successive Sunday there is a procession for each order in this city: that is, the first Sunday for the Franciscans, the second for the Dominicans, then the Augustinians, and so on. Because each order vies with the others in putting on the biggest display in ornate garments for the statues of their respective saints, I thus had the opportunity to view the ornaments. Never would I have thought such immense wealth existed in this city's churches.

As for processions of Corpus Domini, I recall finding myself in a Mexican village called Actopán,[11] where I had gone to collect some alms at the time this procession was to take place. As I was lodged in the home of the alcalde mayor, or podestà, an Indian chief entered the hall where I was talking with the alcalde a short time before the procession took place. I then learned that he was the governor of the local Indians. He was accompanied by other Indians, less impressive in appearance, who were carrying various bouquets of green flowers, with some long garlands of these flowers threaded with yarn. The principal Indian made a deep bow, then made a fine compliment in Spanish to the alcalde, and, taking one of these flower necklaces from one of his companions, he placed it around the alcalde's neck and also placed in his hands a small bouquet of flowers he was carrying. I observed that the alcalde received all these things with signs of pleasure. Fortunately for me, I noted everything because the Indian did the same with me as he had done with the alcalde. But later, when I wanted to remove the garland of flowers from my neck, I was dissuaded—indeed entreated to keep it on—because the Indians would have interpreted this action as a gesture of contempt and would have been offended and scandalized. For that reason, I decided to enter the church in the alcalde's company and accompany the procession with my flowers in hand and around my neck.

In Spain, as well as America, I have seen processions of Corpus Domini being performed with great solemnity. Over there they commingle certain features that strike me as disrespectful. For example, two or three days before this solemn occasion, some young men, dressed somewhat like valets, can be seen in the streets. They go about dancing beneath the windows. Some do this to entertain the women and others out of self-interest, because coins are tossed their way. Then, on the morning of Corpus, these young men are brought to church, where the Blessed Sacrament is displayed in full view. There they dance on and off before the main altar. To be sure, they maintain that in doing this they symbolize and imitate the exultation and gladness of heart of revered King David, when he, too, danced before the Ark of the Covenant, figure of this divine sacrament.[12] But ordinarily this is accompanied by curiosity-seekers, indecency, drunkenness, and other ills. At the time of the procession, they go forth, now in one group, now in another, always dancing before the baldachin. Then, in the afternoon, they go dancing through the streets, as on previous days. Ordinarily these dancers bring some fatal malady on themselves because of their tremendous exhaustion. Another prank customary to this festivity is that from cardboard or other light-weight material they fashion various statues of giants and giantesses, signifying the four corners of the earth, and they also go dancing with them at the head of the procession. But some of these figures of giantesses they design in such indecent fashion that they cause scandal more than anything else.[13]

To omit nothing of what I have observed, and because this touches on the subject of processions, I will briefly say a few things about the ones I witnessed during Holy Week in Real del Monte and other places. Every day of this week they have a procession, but until Thursday there is nothing particularly worthy of note. Then on Holy Thursday, early in the morning, they display the Blessed Sacrament to public adoration with pomp and a moderate number of candles. In the afternoon, after the washing of the feet of twelve poor people, the procession, composed entirely of Indians coming together from small districts and *rancherías* [settlements] nearby, leaves the church. Accordingly, those from each district bear a huge crucifix, and all the inhabitants of this district march under their own huge crucifix, which serves as their standard. In his hand each person carries another crucifix—some medium-sized, some small—and the entire procession consists of crucifixes. There are no women marchers except two or three for each large crucifix, who march in front, holding in their hands special clay braziers into which they place incense from time to time. They are crude folk, who lift their arms as much as they can because the crucifix supposedly senses the odor of incense. Besides these fatuous women, a boy marches ahead of each large crucifix, exclaiming now and then in Spanish: *Quien se hincare delante de este divino Señor y rezare un Credo gana 40 dias de Indulgencias.*[14]

On the morning of Good Friday, the procession of the so-called three falls takes place. In the plaza they set up a pulpit that a preacher mounts. While the preacher recounts the passion, the procession comes out of the church carrying a statue of Jesus bearing the cross. Once it arrives close to the plaza, they suddenly reenact the first fall, so that the preacher accompanies this sign with his words. The statue is made in such a way that they can raise and lower it with some small cords. They move forward a few paces and reenact the second fall.

Meanwhile, out of the other chapel comes a procession of women with a statue of Mary, the Virgin of Sorrows, who goes to meet the statue of Jesus. When they are quite close, it falls a third time. Now the bearers of the statues approach the pulpit, where the preacher, with intense fervor, reenacts the deeply felt sorrows of Jesus and Mary for each other, especially when faced with such a troubled parting. Having brought the two statues together with his own hands, as though in an act of embracing and kissing, he moves the listeners to such tearful contrition that it is a source of wonderment; for there, among the people, the sounds of weeping and beating the chest well up, so that all of them seem truly contrite—but this contrition of theirs passes before long. When the sermon is over, the procession continues with the statue of Jesus in front and that of the Blessed Virgin right behind.

On the evening of the same day, the best of all the processions is performed because in it certain barefoot men, dressed like flagellants, each with his own container, carry all the instruments of our Lord's Passion—various boys, very finely dressed as angels, being interspersed among them. In these processions there are also a large number of penitents, some of whom are quite unusual. Certain individuals flagellate themselves, as in Italy. A great many go to the charnel house or cemetery, and each person snatches from the dead those bones that most strike his fancy. Some form a cross from the tibia of arms and legs and, with that cross and a crown in hand, walk barefoot in procession, wearing the habit of flagellants and with their faces covered. Others—the larger group—carry a skull, engaged in the act of gazing continually at it and meditating on death. Others bear very heavy crosses. Some bind their feet with huge chains and walk along dragging these chains behind them. Some put logs on their feet, and some carry huge chains around their necks. Some bind their arms with a wooden crosspiece over their back, like a cross. Some have other people strike them, and [there are] thousands of other contrivances.

Once I saw someone who wrapped his entire body with a rope in such a way that he had not covered anything except his private parts, and everything else—i.e., chest, abdomen, arms, thighs, and legs—was tightly bound with a cord. He turned completely black from blocked circulation. There are various people who ride on top of spirited horses, dressed in armor and carrying some kind of device as though it were a flag, the inscription placed on the cross, the lance, and other items. But the main personage among them is the one whom they call "Robeno,"[15] who bears the death sentence of the Savior, inscribed on a placard placed on top of a pole. Like the others, he is dressed in armor and rides a very fine horse, which is specially trained. It takes such small strides and rears up stiffly so that it looks like it is continuing to dance, and it makes other motions that draw the spectators' attention. On Holy Saturday they undertake the procession of Soledad, i.e., solitude, for they carry a statue of the Blessed Virgin dressed in mourning for the death of Her Most Holy Son. Only women participate in this procession.

Now I will return to the city and port of Havana, which has three fine castles: i.e., El Morro, which is the main one; the castle of the promontory, [so-named] because it is located on a promontory at the entrance to the bay facing El Morro; and another castle called La Fuerza. They are, as a matter of fact, the oldest castles. But after Havana was restored by the English to its original owners, i.e., the Spanish, they rebuilt El Morro practically from its foundations, and on the landward side they have even created a new one. When I passed through, they were building alongside El Morro three other castles, one after the other, collectively called La Cabaña.[16] I went to see them all and especially the celebrated El Morro, where I counted 120 mounted cannons, with some other batteries still to be completed. I visited the warehouses and all the subterranean rooms; and I was shown the place where Captain Velasco was slain, run through by a sword by an Englishman for refusing to surrender the Spanish flag.[17]

They also build ships in this city because the island has abundant usable timber. I saw one already afloat, called the *San Luis*, with a hundred cannons and nothing but the sails missing. Three others—two seafaring ships and a war frigate—were actually in the process of being built. To avoid being tedious, I will refrain from mentioning many other peculiar features of this island.

On June 18, as the time for departure neared, I carried my effects aboard. On the 19th they fired the departure cannons. On the 20th, which was a Sunday,[18] I boarded at a very early hour, and they were already lifting anchor. We left that port and entered into the very perilous Bahama Channel, where there are many hidden shoals. But with God's assistance and our pilot's experience, we avoided mishap. This channel takes its name from a small island called [Grand] Bahama, not far from the Florida coast. This afore-mentioned island gives its name to many other nearby islands as well, though they are called by other names too, i.e., Lucayas from one of them named Lucayoneca. They are in the Northern Sea [Atlantic Ocean] to the east of the Florida Peninsula. The main ones are Bahama, Lucayoneca, Andros, Cigateo, Abacoa, [New] Provi-dence, Guanahani, Yumeta, Samana, Mayaguana, Yuma [Exuma], Ynagua [Inagua], Caicos, and Triángulo, with a great number of other small ones.[19] All of them belong to the English.

After successfully passing through the aforementioned channel in a few days, we entered the huge gulf, named Mares, which extends to the Bermuda Islands. There are 460 leagues from Havana to the Bermudas. These Bermudas are English, too, and according to Vallemont they are situated between 314 and 316 degrees [64 and 65] of [west] longitude, and between 31 and 33 degrees of northern latitude.[20]

From Havana until we came within sight of these islands there was nothing particularly noteworthy—just some *chubasco*, or tem-pest, which passed quickly. On July 20 the Azores or Terceira Islands were sighted because we had traveled another 480 leagues from the Bermudas. These belong to the Portuguese. They are situated between 347 and 357 [25 and 32] degrees of west longitude and 37 and 42 [40] degrees of northern latitude. That same day we passed within sight of two of these, Corvo and Flores.[21] And here we experienced a powerful tempest, which left me quite apprehen-sive, especially because it occurred at nighttime. My fear intensified because there was a boy in front of me bitterly weeping, begging me to confess him because he kept saying we would perish. When a sailor heard him, he gave him a swift kick that sent him rolling below deck. Yet he aroused so much fear in me that I was trembling from head to foot. While the storm was raging, Father Brà was sleeping soundly even as the entire crew was busy seeking refuge from the storm, which lasted several hours. Eventually, he awoke and, hearing so much commotion on board, asked in Spanish: *Estamus* [sic] *perdidos*? [Are we lost?]—truly the query of a witless person.

Roughly at this latitude, too, we also had a clearing for action. To get a better idea of what this is about, it must be realized that we were traveling in a convoy of three ships: that is, two warships, the seafaring *Castilla* and the frigate *Pallas* (which I had boarded), and another mercantile frigate, the *Rosario*. Because the lead ship was the *Castilla*, which ordinarily preceded the other two, the commander of the *Castilla* had given the two other companion ships copies of instructions on how to steer both day and night in accordance with signals he would send [by day] or from the number of cannon shots he would fire at night.

Suddenly one day there was a novel occurrence. They [the crew] observed that the flagship was flying certain flags. Quickly they took the instructions in hand and saw that this was the signal to prepare for battle with enemy ships. It was almost exactly the noon hour and thus dinner time. Instead of that, everyone went to work preparing for defense. Hurriedly they loaded the cannons and placed numerous rifles and sabers on the quarterdeck. Almost all the large rooms were emptied, so that the boxes and beds of passengers and sailors were tossed from one side to another. Moreover, the stern was disencumbered of the cloths covering the rooms occupied by some ladies along with other women in their service. In very short order everything was in readiness, but we did not see any enemy ship. Indeed, our flagship was eight or ten leagues ahead of us. We stayed there until approximately 21 hours [i.e., 4 P.M.], without eating, and when they saw that the flagship had lifted the signals, everyone burst out laughing.

On July 28 we sighted Cape San Vicente in Europe and on the 30th we passed Cape Santa Maria.[22] On August 2 we were already within sight of Cádiz, where we skirted disaster because we were on a shoal and had only eight fathoms of water beneath us. In spite of the minimal water, our captain wanted to move ahead, but the pilot protested and, in the presence of witnesses, proclaimed that he would relinquish his duty if the captain continued to insist on moving ahead. When the captain saw that everyone disagreed with his opinion, he left the pilot in complete liberty to go wherever he thought fit. For this reason, he turned around and we moved out of sight of Cádiz, but on August 3 we entered the bay without mishap and dropped anchor. On the 5th I went to our monastery, where after a few days I learned that an English frigate named *St. George* was about to set sail for Genoa. With its captain, whose name was Robert Broch [Brock?], we reached an agreement about our transportation to Genoa, paying thirty Spanish pesos for each of us, in turn receiving a cabin in the stern and a place at his table.

On August 29 we set sail, and in twenty-four hours we were in sight of Málaga, where we had a day of calm. On September 6 we came within sight of the island of Ibiza, the lesser island of the Balearics, remaining at that latitude for four days due to lack of wind. Then we entered the Gulf of Lions, below the Balearics facing Africa, where we had a huge storm for two days and two nights during which we had to lay to. The sea was so high and raging, making such a terrible roaring sound, that it caused horrendous fear, and we were already hanging on for dear life. Those two days we ate nothing more than a little bread, which people held with one hand, while with the other they had to stand constantly hanging on firmly to some object so as not to be battered from one side to another by the powerful movement of the ship. We had two other minor storms, and for some days we had to stay in sight of the island of Corsica because of the bad weather.

Finally, on September 13 the coastline of Genoa was sighted, and we arrived there on the 16th, dropping anchor and entering the city that same day. I was very glad to see that I had reached the end of my voyage because I was weary of the many perils we had encountered. Here, after having taken the needed rest, I obtained permission from the most reverend father procurator general to return to my province because I had already advised him of our return to Italy through my letter from Cádiz.

On September 24 I left Genoa on my own and proceeded to Pontedecimo, on the 25th to Voltaggio, the 26th to Novi, the 27th to Tortona, the 28th to Voghera, the 29th to Pavia, the 30th to Binasco, the first of October to Milan, the 3rd to Treviglio, and the 5th to Bergamo, my homeland now dear to me, from which I had been absent seven years and four months. I arrived in Bergamo healthy, but so swarthy and dried-out from the sun and the incommodities and all the travails from long journeys, and especially by sea, that many people did not recognize me because I looked like a coal peddler in a friar's garb; for I had been traveling continuously for seven months, mostly in very hot seasons and climes.[23]

CHRONOLOGY OF
ILARIONE DA BERGAMO'S JOURNEY

1761		Feb 20	sighted Canary Islands
July 8	left Bergamo for Rome	Mar 21	in San Juan, Puerto Rico
Sept 11	arrived in Rome		
Oct	left Rome	Mar 29	left San Juan
Nov 1	at Savona, near Genoa	May 10	anchored at Veracruz
Nov 3	at Genoa	May 17	left Veracruz by land
		May 17	arrived in Antigua
1762		May 19	left Antigua
		May 21	reached Jalapa
Jan 20	left Genoa for Spain	May 28	left Jalapa
Feb 6	anchored at Málaga	May 28	at Perote
Feb 20	left Málaga by land	June 1	arrived in Mexico City
Feb 25	arrived in Cádiz	June–Dec	in Mexico City
July 9	left Cádiz on ship	Dec 20	left Mexico City
July 21	in Gibraltar	Dec 22	arrived in Pachuca
July 22	in Algeciras	ca. Dec 23	Pachuca to Tulancingo
July 26	left Algeciras		
Aug–Jan	in Cádiz		
		1764	
1763			
		ca. Jan 2	returned to Pachuca
Jan 2	left Cádiz for America	ca. Jan 8	to Real del Monte (stayed about four years)
Jan 26	set sail in convoy, 9 ships		

1765		ca. Dec 18	left for Guadalajara
		Dec 24	in Irapuato
Jan–Dec?	in Real del Monte		
		1768	
1766			
		Jan 2	arrived at
Aug 15	in Real del Monte		Guadalajara
ca. Sept	in Mexico City briefly	mid-Feb	left Guadalajara
Oct	in Real del Monte	Feb 22	in Puentezuela
		March	in Mexico City
1767		Apr 18	left Mexico City for
			Italy
June 25	in Mexico City	May 10	left Veracruz
	[expulsion of the	May 29	at Havana, Cuba
	Jesuits]	June 20	left Havana
July	in Mexico City briefly	Aug 3	arrived in Cádiz
ca. Aug	back at Real del	Aug 29	left Cádiz
	Monte	Sept 16	in Genoa
Dec 14	left Real del Monte	Sept 24	left Genoa
Dec 16	in Mexico City briefly	Oct 5	arrived in Bergamo

NOTES

ABBREVIATIONS

BU Michaud, Joseph Fr. *Biographie universelle ancienne et moderne.* Paris: 1843–65. Reprint: 45 vols. Graz, Austria: Akademische Druck- u. Verlagsanstalt, 1966–68.

DM Palomar de Miguel, Juan. *Diccionario de México.* 4 vols. Mexico City: Panorama, 1991.

DP *Diccionario Porrúa de historia, biografía y geografía de México.* 6th ed. 4 vols. Mexico City: Porrúa, 1995.

EC *Enciclopedia cattolica.* 12 vols. Vatican City: Ente per l'Enciclopedia cattolica e per il Libro cattolico, 1949–54.

EM *Enciclopedia de México.* 14 vols. Mexico City: Cía Editora de Enciclopedia de México, 1996.

EU *Enciclopedia universal ilustrada europeo-americana.* 70 vols. Madrid: Espasa-Calpe, 1907–30.

NCE *New Catholic Encyclopedia.* 18 vols. New York: McGraw-Hill, 1967–89.

EDITORS' INTRODUCTION

1. The diaries are Gregorio Martín Guijo, *Diario (1648–1664)*, ed. Manuel Romero de Terreros; Antonio de Robles, *Diario de sucesos notables (1665–1703)*, ed. Antonio Castro Leal; and Francisco de Ajofrín, *Diario de viaje . . . hizo a la América Septentrional en el siglo XVIII.* Antonio de Ciudad

Real, secretary to Alonso Ponce, wrote an extensive narrative about the five-year inspection of Franciscan monasteries in the 1580s, published as *Relación breve y verdadera de algunas cosas . . . que sucedieron al padre fray Alonso Ponce en las provincias de la Nueva España*. Accounts by two Italian travelers are Giovanni Francesco Gemelli-Careri, *Giro del mondo*; and Lorenzo Boturini Benaducci, *Idea de una nueva historia general de la América Septentrional*. In the seventeenth century Antonio Vázquez de Espinosa, a Carmelite missionary, penned a vast *Compendio y descripción de las Indias Occidentales*; English edition: *Compendium and Description of the West Indies*, trans. Charles Upson Clark. Thomas Gage, a English Dominican, wrote *The English American . . . or a New Survey of the West India's*, reprinted as *Travels in the New World*, ed. J. Eric S. Thompson. A royal accountant, José Antonio Villaseñor y Sánchez, described Mexico City in the 1740s in his *Theatro americano, descripción general de los reynos y provincias de la Nueva España, y sus jurisdicciones*. Following his 1803 visit, Alexander von Humboldt wrote a four-volume account, *Voyages aux régions equinoctiales du Nouveau Continent*, translated as *Political Essay on the Kingdom of New Spain*, trans. John Black; abridged version ed. Mary Maples Dunn. Surprisingly, although the central plateau was more heavily populated and also more frequently visited by the few foreign travelers, sources regarding the sparsely populated northern frontier are actually more abundant, due to the presence there of Jesuit missionaries who provided detailed accounts, particularly regarding Indian life. These are too numerous to cite here. See Bernd Hausberger, ed., *Jesuiten aus Mitteleuropa im kolonialen Mexiko: Eine Bio-Biographie*, for an exhaustive listing of published and unpublished material, particularly covering the frontier regions.

2. "Professiones cappuccinorum Brixiae et Bergami (1667–1800)," Biblioteca Civica Angelo Mai, Bergamo.

3. Renato Ravanelli, *Bergamo: History and Art*.

4. William J. Short, *The Franciscans*, 32, 67–70.

5. Padre Silvio da Brescia, *I frati minori cappuccini a Bergamo*, 103ff.

6. *NCE*, s.v. "Franciscans, Capuchin."

7. Ajofrín, *Diario*, 2:318. A summary of Capuchin missions in Tibet and Nepal is in Francisco de Ajofrín, *Carta familiar de un sacerdote en que le da cuenta de la admirable conquista espiritual del vasto imperio del gran Thibet*, 31–40; *EC*, s.v. "Tibet." See also Charles Bell, *The People of Tibet*, 16–17.

8. See Padre Valdemiro da Bergamo, *I conventi ed i cappuccini bergamaschi*, 355.

9. Guido Bustico, "Di un viaggio al Messico nell' anno 1768," *La Geografia: Rivista di Propaganda Geografica* 4, no. 10 (Dec. 1916): 438–39.

10. We are grateful to Dr. Giulio Orazio Bravi, director of the Biblioteca Civica Angelo Mai in Bergamo, the current repository of the manuscript, for bringing this interesting item to our attention.

11. Silvio da Brescia, *I frati minori cappuccini*, 114–17, 139–41.

12. Ilarione da Bergamo, *Viaggio al Messico nell'America settentrionale fatto e descritto da Fra Ilarione da Bergamo, religioso Capuccino con figure, Anno MDCCLXX*, ed. Maria Laura Bruno.

13. México, Dirección General de Estadística, *1er censo de población de la Nueva España, 1790*, 150, table 61; U.S. Bureau of the Census, *A Century of Population Growth . . . 1790–1900*, 11.

14. Ajofrín, *Diario*, 1:67–68; Jonathan Kandell, *La Capital: The Biography of Mexico City*, 236.

15. Ajofrín, *Diario*, 2:319.

16. Magnus Mörner, ed., *The Expulsion of the Jesuits from Latin America*, 19–22.

17. Distressing also are the numerous lines that have been effaced by thorough crossing-out, especially in sections that might excite prurient interest. Whether Ilarione himself expunged this material or whether a later reader chose to play censor is unclear.

CHAPTER 1. BY LAND AND SEA THROUGH ITALY

1. No annotations are provided for the many obscure minor prelates and members of religious orders mentioned by the author who cannot be identified through standard published sources.

2. Ilarione is referring here to the ancient kingdom of the Caucasus, not the American colony of the same name.

3. The sanctuary of Our Lady of Caravaggio, the most important Marian sanctuary in Lombardy, is located two kilometers outside the town. Its origin dates back to the 1432 apparition of the Virgin Mary to a local peasant girl. The sanctuary includes a church begun under the auspices of St. Charles Borromeo in 1575 and completed at the end of the eighteenth century. *EC*, s.v. "Caravaggio, Santuario della Madonna di."

4. Civitavecchia is a port located on the Tyrrhenian Sea about 35 miles (56 kilometers) northwest of Rome.

5. A felucca is a small, light sailing ship with two masts.

6. Ilarione is probably referring to Girolamo Spinola (1713–84; cardinal 1759–84). At one time he was a papal nuncio in Madrid. *EC*, s.v. "Spinola, Girolamo."

7. Albanus and Castel Gandolfo are about twelve miles southeast of Rome.

8. Ripa Grande is a wharf in Rome along the right bank of the Tiber.

9. A pinco is a three-masted merchant ship.

10. The Sanctuary of Our Lady of Mercy of Savona, seven kilometers north of Savona, owes its origin to the apparition of the Virgin Mary to a peasant Antonio Botta in March 1536. *EC*, s.v. "Savona e Noli, Santuari e monumenti più insigne."

11. Scudi were gold and silver coins used in Italy from the fifteenth to the nineteenth centuries.

12. Ragusa is present-day Dubrovnik. In the eighteenth century this, like many other Adriatic cities, was part of the Venetian empire.

CHAPTER 2.
ACROSS THE MEDITERRANEAN TO SPAIN

1. Carmelites are members of the Roman Catholic Order of the Blessed Virgin Mary of Carmel, a mendicant order founded on Mount Carmel in the thirteenth century. *NCE*, s.v. "Carmelites."

2. I.e., the fortified wine known as "sherry," which originated in Jerez and derives its name from that town.

3. The Carthusians are a purely contemplative order founded in France in 1084 by St. Bruno. *NCE*, s.v. "Carthusians."

4. I.e., the duke of Medinaceli. The Medinaceli were a noble Spanish family. In 1762 Luis Antonio, master of the horse for King Ferdinand VI, held the title of duke. *EU*, s.v. "Medinaceli."

5. Gades and Gadir were ancient names for Cádiz, which was founded ca. 1100 B.C. as a Phoenician trading post.

6. Actually 36 degrees, 32 minutes.

7. A Spanish league is equal to 2.6 miles. Giovanni Francesco Gemelli-Careri (1651–1725), a Neapolitan merchant traveler, journeyed around the world between 1693 and 1698. Landing at Acapulco and departing from Veracruz, he visited colonial Mexico during the final stages of his journey. Gemelli published an account of his journey, *Giro del Mondo*, in Naples in 1700; later editions were published in various languages including English. F. A. Nunnari, *Un viaggiatore calabrese della fine secolo XVII*. For the reference to Cádiz, see Giovanni Francesco Gemelli-Careri, *Le Mexique à la fin du XVIIe siècle*, ed. Jean-Pierre Berthe, 261.

8. Cádiz had suffered severe damage from the earthquake of November 1, 1755. The buildings noted by the author may have been under reconstruction. *EU*, s.v. "Cádiz (Historia)."

9. Chiclana is a small village fifteen miles southeast of Cádiz.

10. Santa Catalina castle was constructed in 1598, San Sebastián in 1613. *EU*, s.v. "Cádiz (Militares)."

11. See note 19 below.

12. The first stone of the cathedral of Cádiz was laid in 1721. It was under continuous construction for the remainder of the century. *EU*, s.v. "Cádiz (Edificios)."

13. Retablos, or *reredos*, are ornamental wooden panels behind or at the sides of an altar. Religious paintings are often integrated into the panels.

14. This chapel, located on the Calle de la Amargura, was founded in 1733 by Fray Isidoro de Sevilla. José Rosetty y Pranz, *Guía oficial de Cádiz, su provincia y departamento*, 195.

15. The Capuchin church, Iglesia de Santa Catalina in the Paseo del Sur, was founded in 1614. Ibid., 195.

16. Tomás del Valle (1684–1776), a prelate of piety and austerity, was appointed bishop of Cádiz in 1731. His tenure was marked by considerable charitable activity, creation of hospitals, and expansion of the cathedral. Pablo Antón Solé, *Situación económica y asistencia social de la Diócesis de Cádiz en la segunda mitad del siglo XVIII*, 67–78.

17. Lazaro-Opizio Pallavicini (1719–85) served as papal nuncio in Madrid between 1760 and 1767. He became a cardinal in 1766 and served as secretary of state for Popes Clement XIV (1769–74) and Pius VI (1775–99). *EC*, s.v. "Pallavicini, Lazaro-Opizio."

18. The Casa de Contratación (Board of Colonial Trade) regulated New World commerce and emigration. Besides serving as a passport office, it registered goods shipped between Spain and the Indies, making certain that royal taxes were paid. Robert Ryal Miller, *Mexico: A History*, 125.

19. Between 1756 and 1763, Europe was engaged in the Seven Years' War, which pitted England and Prussia against an alliance of France, Austria, and Russia. (In the American colonies this conflict was known as the "French and Indian War.") The thrones of France and Spain were then occupied by two lines of the Bourbon family. By the agreement known as the *pacte de famille* (family pact) of August 1761, France made a commitment to support Spain, and Spain was obliged to enter the war on France's side if peace were not concluded within eight months. With the accession of Charles III to the Spanish throne later that year, Spain assumed a more

assertive posture toward England, leading to the outbreak of war in January 1762. Walter Dorn, *Competition for Empire 1740–1763*, 373–75.

CHAPTER 3. CAPTURED BY THE ENGLISH

1. A saetía is a small, elongated and swift sailing ship of three masts in use in the Mediterranean from the sixteenth through eighteenth centuries.

2. In 1704, during the War of the Spanish Succession, English forces captured the fortress of Gibraltar from Spain and established a naval base there. Gibraltar is still a British enclave.

3. The Observants, who favored stricter observance of the Franciscan "Rule," developed in the fourteenth century from a reform movement within the Order of Friars Minor (Franciscans); they had their own houses and officers. Short, *The Franciscans*, 53–60; *NCE*, s.v. "Franciscans."

4. Sir George Pocock (1706–92) was commander of the secret expedition to Havana, which set sail in March 1762. The land forces were under the command of George Keppel (1724–86), the third earl of Albemarle. On June 7 British troops landed outside the city; on July 1 the barrage began; on July 30 the fortress was taken; and Havana itself fell on August 13. Juliet Barclay, *Havana: Portrait of a City*, 103–34; *Dictionary of National Biography*, s.v. "Pocock, Sir George"; "Keppel, George, Third Earl of Albemarle."

5. Luis Vicente de Velasco Isla (1711–62), commander of El Morro fortress at the time of the British invasion of Havana, delayed the British capture of it, displaying great bravery. Ilarione's account of his death, however, is wrong. Velasco received serious gunshot wounds just before the fortress fell. When it was taken, the English commanders gallantly permitted him to return to Havana, where he died of infection on July 31. *EU*, s.v. "Velasco Isla, Vicente de"; José Antonio del Río, *Luis Vicente de Velasco e Isla*.

CHAPTER 4. VOYAGE TO THE NEW WORLD

1. By the Peace of Paris (February 10, 1763), ending the Seven Years' War, England restored Havana to Spain, in return for which Spain ceded Florida to England; France ceded to England all claim to Acadia, Canada, and Louisiana east of the Mississippi; and England restored five Caribbean islands to France. Dorn, *Competition for Empire*, 380, 382–83.

2. The Order of Minims was founded in 1435 by the Calabrian St. Francis of Paola (1416–1507). It expanded first in southern Europe and later to the New World and by the end of the eighteenth century included around five hundred monasteries and 14,000 friars. It was a mendicant order, with a strong contemplative element; its monks submitted to a rigorous discipline that included frequent fasting and strict vegetarianism. *EC*, s.v. "Minimi, Ordini regolare mendicante."

3. Translation: "Father San Francisco, either deliver us from this storm or I will deny your miracles; and if I am able to return to my home, I want to take my son from your friars. Nor do I want to give any more charity to them."

4. The existence of the Canaries was known to the ancients, who sometimes identified them with the Elysian Fields, hence the appellation "Blessed Isles." *EU*, s.v. "Canarias (Historia)."

5. The Canaries were rediscovered by the Portuguese in the fourteenth century and awarded to Castile by a papal bull in 1344; Castile took possession of the islands in 1402. *EU*, s.v. "Canarias (Historia)."

6. Teide, a periodically active volcano on Tenerife, has a height of 3,716 meters. *EU*, s.v. "Teide."

7. Madeira is three hundred miles north of the Canaries.

8. Spanish *tiburón* or shark. What the author subsequently describes, however, would appear to be porpoises. This confusion may have resulted from his imperfect command of Spanish.

9. In Spanish America the term *bufeo* is used to designate a dolphin.

10. I.e., *Chrysophrys (Sparus) auratus*.

11. The braccio (pl. braccia) is a unit of measurement equivalent to 0.58 m to 0.68 m, primarily used in measuring cloth; also a unit of measure of water depth equivalent to 1.8 m.

12. Ilarione is probably referring to jellyfish (*Scyphozos discomedusae*).

CHAPTER 5. ISLANDS OF THE CARIBBEAN

1. Saint Martin, one of the Leeward Islands, was first settled by French freebooters in 1638. Ten years later it was divided between France and the Netherlands, and it remains so today.

2. I.e., San Juan.

3. The individuals seen were undoubtedly African blacks rather than American Indians. See note 9 below.

4. Ilarione is referring to the monastery of St. Francis of Assisi. Built during the latter half of the seventeenth century, it was of very simple architecture and without ornamentation. So poor was the institution that King Charles III ordered the royal treasury to provide candles for masses and other ceremonies. Adolfo Hostos, *Historia de San Juan, ciudad murada*, 334–43.

5. Columbus discovered Puerto Rico on November 19, 1493, during his second voyage to America.

6. Specifically, the island of Puerto Rico is approximately 100 miles long and 38 miles wide.

7. The cathedral of San Juan was first constructed of wood in 1521 but rebuilt later in the century. Hostos, *San Juan*, 317ff.

8. The Dominican monastery of St. Thomas Aquinas was first begun during the decade of the 1520s and finished by mid-century. It was badly damaged by hurricanes in 1738 and 1740 and rebuilt during the period of 1761–74. This damage and reconstruction may, in part, account for Ilarione's unfavorable impression. Hostos, *San Juan*, 324–27.

9. The native Indian population, virtually annihilated in the sixteenth century through forced labor and disease, was partially replaced by African slaves. Writers' Program of the Works Progress Administration, *Puerto Rico: A Guide to the Island of Borinquén*, 91.

10. Cassava, also called manioc, is a tropical plant (*Manihot utilissima*) with fleshy root stocks called yuca or yucca, which yield a nutritious starch.

11. Ilarione is referring to the plantain (*Musa paradisisiaca*), the cooked fruit of which is a staple food in the American tropics. It is larger than the ordinary banana (*Musa sapientum*).

12. I.e., they wear very few clothes.

13. In wealthy or middle-class European families, it was then customary to hire wet-nurses to breast-feed children.

14. Guaiacum is a tropical American wood (*Guaiacum sanctum*) resembling lignum vitae.

15. Colonial Spanish pesos were often cut into eighths, each section then equaling one real.

16. Beginning early in the sixteenth century, African chieftains collected black slaves and took them to Portuguese trading posts on the coast for sale. From there, the slaves were transported to the New World in European merchant vessels. By the Treaty of Utrecht in 1713, the contract for supplying the Spanish American colonies with 4,800 African slaves annually, which had previously passed from the Dutch to the

French, was transferred to Great Britain. Basil Davidson, *The African Slave Trade*, 65–66, 81.

17. Here a few words have been rendered illegible by repeated crossing-out.

18. From the earliest days of Spanish colonization in Puerto Rico, it was the custom when slaves first arrived to give them the brand of the government—the so-called *carimba*. This was done to discourage smuggling. Thus slaves found working on plantations without the brand were immediately confiscated by the government. Francisco M. Zeno, *Historia de la capital de Puerto Rico*, 1:157–58.

19. Here three and a half lines, presumably dealing with sex, have been so thoroughly crossed out as to be illegible.

20. I.e., *Sarcopsylla penetrans*, an insect smaller than a flea but with a larger proboscis. The females commonly penetrate below the skin of humans or animals and deposit their eggs, resulting in considerable stinging or more serious consequences for the victim.

21. Since Capuchins go barefoot or wear sandals, Ilarione would have been especially vulnerable.

22. Almost two months before discovering Hispaniola, Columbus and his men had gone ashore on a Caribbean island they called San Salvador; then they sailed through the Bahamas and coasted along the northern shore of Cuba before landing at Hispaniola (La Española) on December 6, 1492. Samuel Eliot Morison, *Admiral of the Ocean Sea: A Life of Christopher Columbus*, 1:300–369.

23. Formerly each nation took its own capital or a principal observatory as the standard meridian from which east and west longitudes were measured; but beginning in the seventeenth century, a majority of geographers used the Greenwich, England, meridian. Based on that standard, Hispaniola is located at approximately 70 degrees of west longitude.

24. Here Ilarione is in error. Jamaica and the other islands are not Windward Islands.

25. Ilarione is incorrect about Newfoundland, which was discovered by John Cabot in 1497 and became a British possession. Though disputed with the French, the island was definitively conceded to Britain by the Treaty of Utrecht in 1713.

26. These islands, never occupied by the Spanish, were colonized beginning in 1734 by British from Jamaica.

27. Girolamo Benzoni (1519–?) from Milan traveled to Spain in 1541 and from there to Puerto Rico, Cuba, Hispaniola, Central America, Ecuador, and

Peru. He returned to Europe in 1556 and later published his *Historia del mondo novo* (1565), English version: *History of the New World*, trans. W. H. Smyth. *Dizionario biografico degli Italiani*, 8:732–33.

28. See chapter 16.

CHAPTER 6. VERACRUZ TO MEXICO CITY

1. Jerónimo de Jerez arrived in New Spain in 1752 and returned to Spain in 1763. Ajofrín, *Diario*, 2:317.

2. The Bethlehemites, who had medieval antecedents, were founded as a charitable order in Guatemala in 1653 and formally established by Pope Innocent XI in 1687. An order of nuns with the same name was established in 1688. Their primary purpose was attending to the sick. According to a German Jesuit contemporary of Ilarione: "They wear practically the same garb as the Capuchins, let their beards grow, wear on their cloaks a copper shield, upon which the birth of Christ in Bethelehem is depicted, and for that reason they are generally known as Bethlehemites." Both orders were abolished by the Spanish Cortes in 1820. *EC*, s.v. "Betlemiti"; *EU*, s.v. "Betlemiti"; W. Junkmann, ed., "Aus dem Tagebuche des mexikanischen Missionarius Bernh. Middendorff aus der Gesellschaft Jesu," *Katholisches Magazin für Wissenschaft und Leben* 2 (1846): 41. See chapter 13, where Ilarione provides a more detailed account of this order, closely paralleling the information provided here.

3. According to a census of 1754, the population of Veracruz was 5,816. Peter Gerhard, *A Guide to the Historical Geography of New Spain*, 361.

4. Ulúa was a variant of Culhua, one of the names the Mexica-Aztecs called themselves. Hugh Thomas, *Conquest: Montezuma, Cortés and the Fall of Old Mexico*, 112.

5. Friar Portogruaro actually died in Veracruz on July 31, 1766, so Iliarione's date is a year off. See Ajofrín, *Diario*, 2:356.

6. For more about Father Paolo Maria da Ferrara, see chapter 15.

7. This small municipality, about fifteen miles northwest of Veracruz, was the original site of the settlement until the end of the sixteenth century. *DM*, s.v. "Antigua."

8. These insects were undoubtedly a variety of the chigoe (*Sarcopsylla penetrans*), also called chigger or jigger, common in tropical America.

9. The Cofre de Perote (13,552 ft), so named because the top resembles a chest, is immediately west of nearby Perote.

10. Jalapa is a herbaceous climbing plant with reddish flowers. Its roots are used in popular medicine as a drastic purgative. *DM*, s.v. "Jalapa."

11. *Forlone* is a variant of *frullone*, a coach with four wheels, two seats, and one or two horses—essentially a calash.

12. Corpus Christi is the Thursday following the first Sunday after Pentecost. In 1763 this was June 2. Frank Parise, ed., *The Book of Calendars*, Calendar 13, 316. For Ilarione's description of the procession, see chapter 16.

13. Manuel Rubio y Salinas (1703–65), after a prominent career in Spain, became archbishop of Mexico in 1748. His tenure was marked by intense missionary activity, the building of parish schools, solicitude for the Indians, and great charity generally. *DP*, s.v. "Rubio y Salinas, Manuel."

14. Joaquín de Montserrat, marqués de Cruillas (1700–1771), served as the 44th viceroy of New Spain (1760–66). His term of office was notable primarily for two severe smallpox epidemics (1761 and 1763) and for continued drainage of the lakes surrounding the capital. *DP*, s.v. "Montserrat, Marqués de Cruillas, Joaquín de."

CHAPTER 7. DESCRIPTION OF THE CAPITAL

1. On Gemelli-Careri, see chapter 2, note 7. Antonio de Solís y Rivadeneyra (1610–86), a Spanish courtier, was the author of *Historia de la conquista de México*, a work highly regarded for both its historical value and style. *DP*, s.v. "Solís y Rivadeneyra, Antonio de." See also the introduction to the Porrúa re-edition of this work.

2. An Aztec legend claimed that their capital was founded in 1325 on an island in Lake Texcoco where they found the symbolic eagle, with a serpent in its beak, perched on a prickly-pear cactus growing out of a rock.

3. Cuauhtémoc, the last Aztec emperor, surrendered to the Spaniards on August 13, 1521. St. Hippolytus of Rome (170–235) was an ecclesiastical writer, antipope, and martyr. His feast is celebrated on August 13. *NCE*, s.v. "Hippolytus, Saint."

4. Mexico City is located at 19.25 north latitude and 99.10 west longitude. Claude Buffier (1664–1737), a French Jesuit, was the author of works on French grammar, philosophy, and religion. The work Ilarione is referring to is probably his *Pratique de la mémoire artificielle, pour apprendre et retenir la chronologie, l'histoire et la géographie*. Jacques Lieutaud (1660–1733) was a French astronomer and mathematician. Philippe de

Lahire (1640–1719) was a celebrated French geometer and author of numerous works on geometry and astronomy. *BU*, 6:116–17; 22: 552–53; 24:514; *Dictionary of Scientific Biography*, s.v. "Lahire, Philippe de."

5. The northern part of New Spain was north of the Tropic of Cancer, thus not in the tropics or torrid zone.

6. The "Lake of Mexico" that surrounded the capital was actually composed of five interconnected lakes named Zumpango, Xaltocán, San Cristóbal, Chalco, and Xochimilco.

7. The royal audiencia in Mexico City served as a supreme court and as a cabinet to the viceroy. The judges, typically numbering six, were called *oidores*. John H. Parry, *The Spanish Seaborne Empire*, 198.

8. Ilarione's population total for Mexico City is too high: his contemporary Francisco de Ajofrín gives a total of 98,000, with 50,000 Spaniards and Europeans; 40,000 mestizos, mulattos, blacks, and mixed castes; and 8,000 Indians. Ajofrín, *Diario*, 1:65. The official census figure for 1790, two decades later, was 104,760. México, *1er censo de población*, 150, table 61.

9. The viceroy's palace was constructed during the sixteenth century on the east side of the main plaza of Mexico City and now serves as the presidential palace. Even today, this is the widest public building in all Mexico. Since an additional story was added to the building in 1927, Ilarione's wonderment at its amplitude is even more understandable. *DM*, s.v. "Palacio nacional."

10. The media anata was the payment by an appointee of half of the first year's salary. Doris M. Ladd, *The Mexican Nobility at Independence, 1780–1826*, 276.

11. Ilarione's manuscript has the term *di concia* (of tanning), the purport of which is unclear; but the court described is clearly the Acordada.

12. The Acordada was a special tribunal established in 1710 to deal with highway robbers. The term also refers to a prison where malefactors were kept. *DM*, s.v. "Acordada." See also Colin M. MacLachlan, *Criminal Justice in Eighteenth Century Mexico: A Study of the Tribunal of the Acordada*.

13. *Gachupín*, a Nahuatl word meaning "wearer of spurs," was a Mexican term for men born in Spain; it often had a derogatory meaning. Francisco Santamaría, *Diccionario de mejicanismos*, s.v. "gachupín." A creole was a person of European ancestry born in the New World. Mulatto women were often used as wet-nurses for the more well-to-do creoles.

14. Spanish colonial laws and customs recognized even more *castas*: *castizos*, offspring of Spanish and mestizo parents; *zambos*, children of Indian and black parents; etc. See Nicolás León, *Las castas del México colonial o Nueva España*, 9.

15. The god's name is usually spelled Huitzilopochtli (Hummingbird-on-the-Left).

16. The great pyramid and temple, currently under excavation, was located just to the northeast of the cathedral.

17. The Spanish claimed that he was struck by a stone thrown by Indians; other versions state that he was killed by an arrow or died from stab wounds inflicted by Spaniards. *DP*, s.v. "Moctezuma II, Muerte de."

18. A number of descendants of Moctezuma were established in Spain, where they held various titles: counts of Moctezuma, dukes of Abrantes, counts of Aguilar de Inestrillos, and counts of Miravalle. *DP*, s.v. "Moctezuma II, Hijos de."

19. Possibly Ilarione is referring to the Aztec pyramid and ceremonial center of Tenayuca, about six miles from the center of Mexico City.

20. Paternoster or Our Father (also known as the Lord's Prayer):

> Our Father who art in heaven,
> hallowed be thy name.
> Thy kingdom come, Thy will be done
> on earth, as it is in Heaven.
> Give us this day our daily bread.
> And forgive us our trespasses
> as we forgive those who trespass against us.
> And lead us not into temptation,
> but deliver us from evil. Amen.

The Ave Maria or Hail Mary (also known as the Angelic Salutation):

> Hail Mary, full of grace:
> The Lord is with thee.
> Blessed art thou amongst women,
> And blessed is the fruit of thy womb, Jesus.
> Holy Mary, Mother of God,
> pray for us sinners
> now and at the hour of our death. Amen.

The Apostles' Creed:

> I believe in God, the Father almighty,
> Creator of Heaven and earth.
> And in Jesus Christ, his only Son, our Lord;
> Who was conceived by the Holy Spirit,
> born of the Virgin Mary,

suffered under Pontius Pilate,
was crucified, died, and was buried.
He descended into hell;
the third day he rose again from the dead;
He ascended into heaven, sits at the right hand of God, the Father
   almighty;
from thence He shall come again to judge the living and the dead.
I believe in the Holy Spirit,
the holy Catholic Church,
the communion of saints,
the forgiveness of sins,
the resurrection of the body,
and life everlasting. Amen.

21. Literary Italian essentially derives from the Tuscan dialect spoken around Florence. In Ilarione's time very different dialects were spoken in the various regions of Italy and were sometimes barely comprehensible to Italians from other regions. Dialect variation is still evident today.

22. The volcano, called Popocatépetl, rises to 17,887 feet.

23. Ilarione has confused Orizaba, between Puebla and Veracruz, with Popocatépetl.

24. See Solís, *Historia de la conquista de México* (1988 ed.), 432, in which he states that it was sulfur, not saltpeter, that the volcano provided.

25. Solís's claim could not be verified. William H. Prescott wrote that Cortés had 905 Spaniards, but he did not give the size of the Aztec army, noting: "I recollect meeting with no estimate of their numbers" (*History of the Conquest of Mexico*, 3:129, n. 27). In his recent history, Hugh Thomas estimated that 100,000 Aztecs and 100 Spaniards were killed in the three-month siege of Mexico-Tenochtitlán. Thomas, *Conquest*, 528–29.

CHAPTER 8. FOODS AND PLANTS OF NEW SPAIN

1. Ilarione has confused the two Mexican terms *tecomate* (a wooden cup or bowl made from a gourd) and *comal* (a flat stone or earthenware slab for cooking maize cakes).

2. Ilarione uses the word *luganeghini*, which refers to a small, thin, nonsegmented sausage eaten in Lombardy and Venice.

3. Pulque, a mildly alcoholic beverage made from the fermented juice of *agave* plants, is described later in this chapter.

4. Between 1614 and 1626 Pietro Della Valle (1586–1652), a Roman nobleman, traveled to Greece, Turkey, Egypt, and Mesopotamia. He spent several years in Persia, where he was favorably received by Shah Abbas. He eventually journeyed as far as India before returning to Europe, where he published an account of his journeys, *Viaggi descritti in 54 lettere familiari*. Wilfrid Blunt, *Pietro's Pilgrimage: A Journey to India and Back*. . . .

5. Atole is a beverage made by mixing corn flour in water or milk and heating it until it reaches a creamy consistency. *DM*, s.v. "atole."

6. In the eighteenth century one common method of time-keeping in Italy was a 24-hour clock with the first hour beginning at 8 P.M. Accordingly, 21 hours would be 4 P.M. This time-keeping is noted by the great German poet Johann Wolfgang von Goethe (1749–1832), who journeyed to Italy in 1786. Goethe, *Tagebuch der italienischen Reise 1786*, 70.

7. I.e., Nahuatl *xocóatl* from *xócoc*, acid, bitter, and *atl*, water. *DM*, s.v. "chocolate."

8. Cacao is a tree (*Theobroma cacao*) cultivated for the seeds, also known as cacao or cocoa beans, which are used to prepared chocolate or cocoa.

9. Tamales are a Mexican dish made with ground maize dough folded around a meat or other filling. They are wrapped in corn husks and steamed.

10. Both the American aloe (genus *Furcraea*) and plants of the genus *Agave* are of the amaryllis family. Ilarione used "aloe" and "agave" interchangeably.

11. Maguey is a species of *Agave*, a fleshy-leaved Mexican cactus.

12. Mescal, from the Nahuatl *mexcalli*, is a distilled alcoholic beverage; mescal resecado is stronger and aged longer. Santamaría, *Diccionario de mejicanismos*, s.v. "mescal."

13. Tepache is a drink made of fermented juices and skin from various fruits, with added sugar. Originally it was made from corn, and it derives its name from Nahuatl *tepiatl*, corn beverage. *DM*, s.v. "tepache."

14. It is said that this image was brought from Spain by a soldier of Cortés and that after the retreat from Tenochtitlán during the Noche Triste it was concealed by him in the place where it was found twenty years later. The Virgin of Los Remedios was considered a patroness of the Spaniards. Fanny Calderón de la Barca, *Life in Mexico*, ed. Howard T. Fisher and Marion H. Fisher, 210–11.

15. Mistela can refer to either a drink made by mixing alcohol and unfermented grape juice or a drink made by mixing brandy, water, sugar, and cinnamon—probably the latter, given the context. María Moliner, *Diccionario de uso del español*, s.v. "mistela."

16. Rosolio is any kind of liquor of low alcoholic content, with a heavy infusion of sugar and made aromatic by addition of essences.

17. Chinguirito is a liquor also prepared from cane. During the colonial period it was strictly prohibited until the edict of December 7, 1796, which subjected it to heavy duties. Jorge Mejía Prieto, *Así habla el mexicano*, 54.

18. Clemole is from the Nahuatl word *tlemolli*, meaning a chile stew or broth. Santamaría, *Diccionario de mejicanismos*, s.v. "clemole."

19. See chapter 6, note 10.

20. These are names for various plants whose roots are used in popular medicine as purgatives. *DM*, s.v. "michoacán."

21. See chapter 14.

22. Ilarione uses the term *braccia*. See chapter 4, note 11.

23. The floating gardens or *chinampas* were begun by the Mexica Aztecs and are still cultivated today, especially in Lake Xochimilco. *DM*, s.v. "chinampa."

24. The insects (*Dactylopius coccus*) are brushed from the cactus, killed by immersion in hot water, dried, and then crushed to make the dyestuff. Santamaría, *Diccionario de mejicanismos*, s.v. "cochinilla"; *DP*, s.v. "Cochinilla (Grana)."

25. Ilarione is referring to the *chicozapote* (*Achras zapote*) tree of thirty meters or more, which produces a spherical fruit five to seven centimeters across; this is the sweetest of the various fruits called *zapote*. The plant, however, is restricted to the southernmost regions, which Ilarione may not have visited. *DM*, s.v. "chicozapote."

26. Peanuts, the fruit or seed of *Arachis hypogaea*, are native to the New World and were still not widely known in Europe in the eighteenth century.

27. There are more than one hundred species of anonaceas, including chirimoya (*Anona cherimolia*), guanabana (*Anona muricata*), and yellow cascara (*Anona glabra*).

28. The *guajave* or *guaje* tree (*Acacia crescencia alata*) produces fruit that is edible in spite of its bad odor.

29. The bracketed material has been introduced by the editors in lieu of deleted illustrations.

30. The camote, derived from Nahuatl *camotli*, refers to the sweet potato (*Ipomoe batatas*). *DM*, s.v. "camote."

31. Chilacayote, from Nahuatl *tzilacayotli* (*tzilac*, smooth; *ayotli*, gourd), is a variety of gourd with a green fruit, spotted white and yellow, with smooth skin. It contains a white fibrous pulp that appears like tangled

hair, from which the sweet *cabellos de ángel* (angel hair) is prepared. *DM*, s.v. "chilacayote."

32. There are two types of pitahaya—the sour (*Lemaireocereus gummosus* [Engelm.] Britt. & Rose, dagger cactus) and the sweet (*Lemaireocereus thurberi* [Engelm.] Britt. & Rose, organ pipe cactus). *DM*, s.v. "pitahaya."

33. Pagua, from the Nahuatl *páhuatl*, is a species of avocado (*Persea schiedeana*) with a sweetish pulp. *DM*, s.v. "pagua."

34. There are many species of chiles (from the Nahuatl *chilli*), including chile ancho (*Capsicum annuum L. gressum* Sendt), chile pasilla (*Capsicum annuum L. longum* Sendt), about two centimeters long, almost black when dry and not very piquant; and chile jalapeño meco (*Capsicum annuum annuum*), spicy and bright red. Ilarione has confused the chile manso, a mild variety, with the chiltepín, which is quite piquant. It is unclear what he was referring to as chilitos redondos. Santamaría, *Diccionario de mejicanismos*, s.v. "chile," "chiltepín"; Janet Long-Solís, *Capsicum y cultura: La historia del chilli*, 72, 145, 149–50.

35. *Hierba de la doncella* is a cultivated succulent herb (*Begonia gracilis*). Maximino Martínez, *Catálogo de nombres vulgares y científicos de plantas mexicanas*, 86, 222.

36. The Perú or *pirul* (*Schinua molle* L.) is a tree, normally four to eight meters in height, of South American origin, which was introduced to Mexico in colonial times. As Ilarione notes, it produces seeds that resemble pepper and are sometimes used as a substitute. It is not, however, quite as useless as he suggests, for its fruits have been used as a popular remedy for bronchitis and other maladies. *DM*, s.v. "pirul."

37. The chayote (*Sectium edule*)—derived from Nahuatl *tzapatli*, spine, and *ayotli*, squash—is a climbing plant with tendrils and produces an oval whitish fruit with spines that is widely used in Mexican cuisine. *DM*, s.v. "chayote."

38. In the time of Jesus, Decapolis (from *deka poleis*, "ten cities" in Greek) was a region south of the Sea of Galilee. See Flavius Josephus, *Jewish War* (Loeb edition), 3:446 and map. The term "Pentapoli" (five cities) refers to unions of nearby cities formed in ancient and medieval times. Ilarione would appear to be confusing the two.

39. *Manzana de la muerte*, or manchineel, is a tropical American tree (*Hippomani mancinella*) with yellowish wood and apple-shaped fruit. Juice for poison arrows was extracted from the fruit. James A. Duke, *Handbook of Medicinal Herbs*, 230.

CHAPTER 9.
MEXICAN OCCUPATIONS AND AMUSEMENTS

1. Ilarione greatly underestimates the number of weavers in colonial Mexico. In 1788 there were 3,167 textile workers; a census five years later counted 9,981 treadle looms. Manuel Miño Grijalva, *Obrajes y tejedores en Nueva España, 1700–1810*, 180, 372–74.

2. Though Ilarione is clearly referring to cigarettes, we have not used this term, which only gained currency in the early nineteenth century.

3. *Fandango* is a general term for a dance as well as for a specific dance of Spanish origin, in which the dancers snap their fingers and stamp their feet.

4. The bamba is an old popular dance, a variation of the huapango, typical of Veracruz. Santamaría, *Diccionario de mejicanismos*, s.v. "bamba." We have been unable to find any reference to the other two dances.

5. In the original manuscript several lines following this sentence have been blotted out.

6. This bracketed section of the text was crossed out, but a later reader supplied these words, which, to judge from still discernible fragments of letters in the crossed-out section, seem to fit.

7. The Alameda Central, the oldest public garden in Mexico City, was created at the end of the sixteenth century. DM, s.v. "Alameda central."

8. Ilarione is referring to Xochimilco, a village and recreation spot south of Mexico City, famous for its flowers and floating gardens (chinampas).

9. Public gardens and a principal promenade in Naples are located at the foot of the hill of Posilipo.

10. *Torquato Tasso's Jerusalem Delivered*, trans. Joseph Tusiani, 334. Torquato Tasso (1544–95) was one of the most renowned poets of the late Italian Renaissance. His *Gerusalemme Liberata* (1575), from which Ilarione quotes (canto 15), is an epic based on the conquest of Jerusalem during the First Crusade. Francesco DeSanctis, *Storia della letteratura italiana*, chapter 11.

11. At various times in the eighteenth century, Spanish monarchs prohibited bullfighting, but the bans did not endure. Timothy Mitchell, *Blood Sport: A Social History of Spanish Bullfighting*, 48, 62.

12. Here Ilarione refers to the practice of some bullfighters of awaiting the bull's onslaught while kneeling on one knee.

13. Ilarione is probably referring to a blade shaped like the Greek capital letter gamma (Γ).

14. Pantalone is a stock figure in Italian comedy of the time: an avaricious and generally lascivious old man who is the butt of jokes.

15. In this variant the roosters are covered so that size, weight, color, etc., cannot be determined until they are released to fight. *DM*, s.v. "tapada."

CHAPTER 10. MEDICINE IN COLONIAL MEXICO

1. The Royal and Pontifical University of Mexico was founded in 1551. Within fifty years there were twenty-four academic chairs, including Latin, rhetoric, philosophy, canon and civil law, scriptures, theology, mathematics, medicine, and the native Mexican languages Nahuatl and Otomí. Schools of mining and fine arts were added in the eighteenth century. *Síntesis histórica de la Universidad de México*.

2. The Colegio de San Ildefonso was founded in 1588 and placed under Jesuit control. New buildings and a chapel were constructed during the eighteenth century. Closed in 1767, following the expulsion of the Jesuits, and reopened and closed again at various times in the nineteenth century, it functions today as the Escuela Nacional Preparatoria. *DP*, s.v. "Escuela Nacional Preparatoria."

3. Jesuits dominated higher education in all but the Royal and Pontifical University. John Tate Lanning, *Academic Culture in the Spanish Colonies*, 32.

4. Ilarione is referring to the Hospital de Jesús, founded by Cortés in 1527. The conqueror's remains rest in an adjacent church (see chapter 13, note 20). *DM*, "Hospital de Jesús"; *DP*, s.v. "Hospital de Jesús."

5. Ilarione uses the world "Gallia" (Gaul), reflecting the tendency of Spaniards and Italians of his day to regard this malady as of French origin. Moliner, *Diccionario de uso del español*, s.v. "gálico."

6. The Hospital de San Hipólito, which accepted patients suffering from dementia, was the first hospital of its kind in the New World. *DM*, s.v. "Hospital de San Hipólito"; *DP*, s.v. "San Hipólito."

7. The Hospital of San Juan de Dios was built and began providing services at the beginning of the eighteenth century. It was run by the order of the Brothers of Saint John of God. *DM*, s.v. "Hospital de San Juan de Dios"; *DP*, s.v. "Hospital de San Juan de Dios."

8. The temazcal is a bath house. Usually built like a low hut, it has a furnace nearby supplying heat and a bed of pine needles on the floor, over which water is sprinkled to produce steam. Frequently the person bathing

uses branches of live oak or bundles of *totomoxltle* (corn husks) to provoke sweating. The session ends with dousing from a bucket of cold water or immersion in a lake. *DM*, s.v "temazcal"; *DP*, s.v. "temazcal."

9. The Otomí and other Otomían-speaking Indians occupied a large territory north and west of Mexico City; many of their descendants still survive. The nomadic Chichimecs lived in northern Mexico and were considered to be less civilized than the Aztecs and other sedentary Indians.

CHAPTER 11. ANIMALS OF NEW SPAIN

1. I.e., *mescalpiques*: fish four to five centimeters in length, which were roasted and then wrapped like tamales. This dish came from the lake regions of the Mexican plateau. *DM*, s.v. "mescalpique."

2. The northwest region of New Spain was called Nueva Galicia; its administrative and religious center was Guadalajara. Ilarione visited this region early in 1768. See chapter 15.

3. The zopilote is not a crow; it is an American vulture (*Coragyps atratus*). L. Irby Davis, *A Field Guide to the Birds of Mexico and Central America*, 17.

4. Ilarione is probably referring to the American raven (*Corvus sinuatus*) or a similar bird (*Corvus corax*). Ibid., 154.

5. Here Ilarione displays the cruelty and callousness that characterized much humor in that age.

6. Ilarione is perhaps referring to the Tamaulipas crow (*Corvus imparatus*), which measures about fourteen inches in length. Ibid., 155.

7. Ilarione is perhaps referring to the chestnut-collared swift (*Cypeloides brunneitorques*) or the Richmond swift (*Chaetura richmondi*), which measure about four to five inches. Ibid., 70.

8. Ilarione is probably referring to the unicolored jay (*Aphelocoma unicolor*). Ibid., 157.

9. Ilarione is probably referring to the military macaw (*Ara militaris*), which measures twenty-seven inches in length. Ibid., 52.

10. There are about fifty species of hummingbirds (Trochilidae) in Mexico. Ibid., 72–87. The term *guachichil* actually applies to a reddish honey bee two to three centimeters in length with a painful sting. *DM*, s.v. "guachichil."

11. The European chamois (*Rupicapra rupicapra*) is not found in the Americas; the reference is probably to the pronghorn antelope (*Antilocapra americana*). Joseph A. Chapman and George A. Feldhamer, eds., *Wild Mammals of North America*, 960.

12. Is this really true or is the author embellishing with stories reminiscent of William Tell?

13. Ilarione uses the term *sancarline*, which can mean chrysanthemums, but does not fit the context here. The word may be regional, but it does not appear in Tiraboschi's definitive dictionary of the Bergamask dialect. Also, the term was unfamiliar to staff we queried at the Biblioteca Angelo Mai in Bergamo. We have, therefore, translated this word as "salamanders," which best seems to fit the context.

14. Ilarione is undoubtedly referring to the iguana.

CHAPTER 12.
MISCELLANEOUS TOPICS AND DISASTERS

1. Tequesquite (composed of sesquicarbonate of sodium and common salt) is a natural salt of ashen color that appears, as Ilarione noted, with the evaporation of salty lake water. It is used as an alkaline in the soap-making process and in cooking and as a medicinal remedy. *DM*, s.v. "tequesquite."

2. The Spanish mark (*marco*) was a unit of weight used for gold and silver; it equaled eight ounces. The peso was a silver coin weighing one ounce and valued at eight reales; thus it was called a "piece of eight." The *patacón* was a silver coin of one ounce. A real was a silver coin valued at one-eighth of a peso. J. Villasana Haggard, *Handbook for Translators of Spanish Historical Documents*, 80, 106–7.

3. See chapter 13.

4. The great flood actually began in 1629, submerging the city for five years. Kandell, *La Capital*, 199–201.

5. Lake Zumpango still exists. However, Lakes Xaltocán and San Cristóbal, located east and southeast respectively of Lake Zumpango, were both drained at the beginning of the twentieth century with the construction of the Canal del Desagüe. Lake Chalco, located south of the capital, was long a main route of commerce and passenger traffic to and from the south and the capital. It dried out after the middle of the nineteenth century. *DP*, s.v. "Xaltocán," "San Cristóbal," "Chalco," and "Desagüe del Valle de México."

6. The extended and expensive attempts to drain the Valley of Mexico lakes are summarized in Jorge Gurría Lacroix, *El desagüe del valle de México durante la época novohispana*.

7. For details about this quake, see María Concepción Amerlinck, *Relación histórica de movimientos sísmicos en la Ciudad de México, 1300–1900*, 26.

8. See the following chapter for Ilarione's account of the expulsion of the Jesuits from Mexico. The Church of La Profesa still stands on the Avenida Isabel la Católica at Avenida Madero. The Philippine fathers were the Oratorians, founded at Rome by Philip Neri in 1575. *NCE*, s.v. "Oratorians."

9. Here Ilarione contradicts his earlier statement about experiencing earthquake tremors only once.

10. On October 15 (the day of Saint Theresa), 1768, Havana was struck by a devastating hurricane—not an earthquake—that tore ships from their anchorage, making them drift out to sea, uprooted fruit trees in orchards, and even lifted buildings from their foundations, moving them elsewhere. Two years earlier, in July and August 1766, there had been severe earthquakes, but in Santiago not Havana. Willis Fletcher Johnson, *The History of Cuba*, 2:116, 117.

CHAPTER 13. RELIGIOUS LIFE IN NEW SPAIN

1. The Metropolitan Cathedral of Mexico City, the largest and most distinguished church edifice in Latin America, was begun during the latter half of the sixteenth century, consecrated in 1687, but only completed in 1813. *DM*, s.v. "catedral de México."

2. The cathedral towers, which have distinctive bell-shaped domes, rise 203 feet above the street level.

3. The Sagrario Metropolitano houses consecrated items from the cathedral, and it is also an independent parochial church. Designed by Lorenzo Rodríguez in the Churrigueresque style, it was constructed between 1749 and 1768. *EM*, s.v. "Zócalo."

4. The multisided Capilla de los Talabarteros (Chapel of the Saddle-Makers), northwest of the cathedral, was demolished in 1823. It was built early but was not the first church; that honor belonged to the Iglesia Mayor, completed in 1525, and later superceded on adjacent land by the Cathedral of Mexico. *EM*, s.v. "Zócalo."

5. The temple of Huitzilopochtli was located northeast of the cathedral, near the intersection of the present streets of Guatemala (Seminario) and República de Argentina. *EM*, s.v. "Zócalo."

6. Between 1530 and 1867 the archbishop's palace was located in the block east of the cathedral and north of the government palace. The building now houses the Meteorological Observatory of the city of Mexico. *DP*, s.v. "Arzobispado, Casa del."

7. The name of the bishopric of Michoacán, with its seat at Valladolid (called Morelia after 1828), was changed to Morelia in 1924; the seat of the Nueva Vizcaya bishopric was at Durango. *EM*, s.v. "Iglesia católica, arquidiócesis de."

8. A racionero, one step below a canon, was a prebendary with the right to receive a share of the income of the cathedral and usually had some choir duties; a medio-racionero was one step lower. *EU*, s.v. "racionero."

9. The Lorenzana chaplains were those supported by Francisco Antonio de Lorenzana y Buitrón, archbishop of Mexico from 1766 to 1772.

10. With a bequest of 100,000 pesos by a wealthy Mexican, plus papal bulls and royal decrees, a collegiate chapter of one abbot and four prebendary canons was established in 1750. Though it is a royal foundation, the abbot was and still is appointed by the papacy. Stafford Poole, *Our Lady of Guadalupe: The Origins and Sources of a Mexican National Symbol*, 178–79.

11. Highway and railway construction destroyed some of the stone monuments; only eight remain today. *EM*, s.v. "Misterios, calzada de los."

12. Ayate is a cloth of maguey or native fibers, used by the Indians of various regions of Mexico as a cloak and to carry fruit and other articles. The Nahuatl word *tilma* is also used for the native cloak. Mejía Prieto, *Así habla el mexicano*, 20; *DM*, s.v. "ayate."

13. According to tradition, the Virgin Mary appeared before Juan Diego, a Christianized Indian, and requested that a church be built there in her honor. She instructed him to gather roses from the rocky ground and take them to the bishop; when he opened his cloak, the image of the Virgin was imprinted on it. In Aztec times this site, the hill of Tepeyac, is said to have been dedicated to Tonantzin, the mother of the gods. *EM*, s.v. "Guadalupe, Virgen de." See below for Ilarione's version of the story of the Virgin of Guadalupe.

14. Ilarione's account of the apparitions is similar to the traditional ones, first published in Spanish and Nahuatl in the 1640s. Poole, *Our Lady of Guadalupe*, 26–28; and William B. Taylor, *Magistrates of the Sacred: Priests and Parishioners in Eighteenth-Century Mexico*, 278, 282–85.

15. The Collegiate Church, completed in 1709, was elevated to a basilica in 1904, and a new structure was dedicated in 1976. The Chapel of the Well (Capilla del Pocito) covered a bubbling spring reputed to have water with miraculous healing powers. (The well is dry today.) The Chapel of the Little Hill (Capilla del Cerrito) was erected in 1660 and rebuilt in the eighteenth century. *DP*, s.v. "Guadalupe, Basílica de"; *EM*, s.v. "Guadalupe, Virgen de."

16. The Virgin of Guadalupe was proclaimed patroness of the city of Mexico on April 27, 1737, and this honor was extended to all of New Spain in 1746. Poole, *Our Lady of Guadalupe*, 176.

17. Ilarione's figures parallel those recorded by his contemporary, the Spanish friar Ajofrín, whose account names the convents and monasteries (*Diario*, 1:67–68).

18. The order of Friars Preachers, commonly known as Dominicans, was founded in the thirteenth century by a Spanish priest, Domingo de Guzmán. Beginning in 1526, members arrived in colonial Mexico, where they established schools and missions, especially in the southern part of the colony. The baroque church of Santo Domingo, all that remains of their great monastery in Mexico City, is located three blocks north of the cathedral. The San Jacinto monastery was located on the street of that name; the Porta Coeli church was founded in 1603 adjacent to the Plaza del Volador. *NCE*, s.v. "Dominicans"; *DP*, s.v. "Porta Coeli."

19. It was called "la Grande" because of its vast size, which extended over two entire city blocks. For more on the Observant Franciscans, see chapter 3, note 3.

20. The bones of Cortés were in the Franciscan church (on the present Avenida Madero) from 1629 to 1794, after which they were moved to the church of Jesús Nazareno (present Avenida República del Salvador). *EM*, s.v. "Cortés, Hernán."

21. Here Ilarione obviously exaggerates the importance of this cleric.

22. The other Observant Franciscan monastery was the Recolección.

23. The order of Hermits of St. Augustine, commonly known as Augustinians, began in the thirteenth century. In 1533 members reached Mexico, where they established monasteries and missions. Their principal church in Mexico City, San Agustín, is extant at the corner of Isabel la Católica and Avenida Uruguay. It now houses a portion of Mexico's National Library. Mercedarians, friars of the order of Our Lady of Mercy, founded in the thirteenth century, arrived in Mexico in the 1520s. *NCE*, s.v. "Augustinians"; "Mercedarians"; "Religious Orders of Men in Latin America."

24. First established in the 1520s as an infirmary for itinerant Indians, the present church of San Cosme is on Avenida Ribera de San Cosme. *NCE*, s.v. "Cosmas and Damian, SS."

25. In Mexico City the principal Franciscan training center for missionaries was San Fernando College, established in the eighteenth century and located three blocks north of the Alameda. Its faculty and graduates were called Fernandinos. *DP*, s.v. "San Fernando [Colegio apostólico]."

26. The order of St. Camillus, Servants of the Sick, was founded in 1582 by Camillus de Lellis. The Discalced (barefoot) Carmelites, a reform order of Carmelites (Our Lady of Mt. Carmel), began in Spain in 1568, and members arrived in Mexico in 1585. The church of San Antonio Abad, south of the main plaza of Mexico City, was erected in 1628 by brothers called Canons of the Order of St. Anthony, the Abbot of Vienna. The monastery and infirmary Ilarione calls "St. Pius of God" was probably the one staffed by brothers of San Juan de Dios. The hospital named for St. Hippolytus of Rome was first built in 1546. The present church, located at the corner of Calle Zarco and Avenida Hidalgo, dates from 1602. *EM*, "Hospitales"; *NCE*, s.v. "Camillians"; "Carmelites, Descalced"; "Antonines (Antonians)"; "Hippolytus of Rome, St."

27. On the Bethlehemites, see chapter 6, note 2. Pedro de San José Betancur, born in the Canary Islands, moved to Guatemala in 1651, when he was twenty-five. He founded a hospital for the poor, a hostel, a school, and an oratory. In 1771 his title of "Venerable" was decreed, but his beatification is still pending. *NCE*, s.v. "Bethlehemites" and "Betancur, Pedro de San José."

28. A Spaniard, Ignatius Loyola (1491–1556), was the principal founder in 1534 of the Society, or Company, of Jesus, popularly known as Jesuits, which for the next two centuries remained the leading arm of the Counter Reformation and an influential order in the Catholic church. Beginning in 1571, members arrived in Mexico, where they established excellent schools and undertook missionary labors on the northern frontier. *NCE*, s.v. "Jesuits."

29. The decree of expulsion was actually dated June 25, 1767.

30. The Jesuits were expelled from Portugal in 1759, France in 1764, and the Spanish empire in 1767. The order was suppressed by the pope in 1773. Among the reasons suggested for the expulsions are Jesuit support of papal authority as opposed to claims of supremacy by heads of state, alleged Jesuit participation in various conspiracies and riots, and envy on the part of other Catholic orders of Jesuit success in the political, economic, and educational spheres. The expulsion is also linked to the Enlightenment—Spain's most enlightened king, Charles III, came to the throne in 1759 with a bevy of advisors imbued with concepts of administrative efficiency and anticlericalism. The Jesuit Order was restored by Pope Pius VII in 1814. Mörner, *Expulsion of the Jesuits*, 19–22, 141–42, 141–45; Richard Herr, *The Eighteenth-Century Revolution in Spain*, 19–24.

31. At the time of their expulsion, the Jesuits had 418 priests and 260 assistants and postulants in New Spain. They maintained more than 100

missions and operated many schools, including 23 *colegios* and 11 seminaries. *DP*, s.v. "Jesuitas."

32. The Baratillo was a market in Mexico City, primarily dealing in used clothing and household items. Originally located in the principal plaza, it was later moved to the Lagunilla and Tepito plazas. *DP*, s.v. "Baratillo, Mercado del." In the colonial era merchants had shops under the *portal* or covered portico, along the south and west sides of *zócalo* or principal plaza of Mexico City. The Montorería was an outdoor market where the stalls were sheltered by canvas awnings. *EM*, s.v. "Parián"; "Zócalo, época colonial."

33. Ilarione accurately notes the popularity the Jesuits enjoyed in much of the country. It is illuminating to compare the account of the German Jesuit Gottfried Bernhard Middendorff, who was deported from Sonora via Guaymas, a sea journey along the Pacific Coast, and eventually overland to Veracruz. As Middendorff shows, the cruelty of the Spanish troops was offset by the love and devotion the Jesuits encountered from all elements of the population throughout the country. Junkmann, "Aus dem Tagebuche des mexikanischen Missionarius Bernh. Middendorff," 21–54.

34. See Octavio Paz, *Sor Juana, or The Traps of Faith*, trans. Margaret Sayers Peden, chapter 9, for a good description of convent life in colonial Mexico, paralleling Ilarione's own account.

35. The Inquisition building, located at the northeast corner of the present República del Brasil and República de Venezuela streets, was erected 1732–36. It later housed the National School of Medicine until that faculty moved to the University City in the 1950s. *EM*, s.v. "Inquisición."

36. I.e., Thomas Salmon, *Lo stato presente di tutti i paesi e popolo del mondo naturale, politico, e morale*.

37. The minor orders of the clergy—such as porter, lector, exorcist, and acolyte—were steps in preparation for the priesthood. They could carry out some ecclesiastical or liturgical functions but not those arising from priesthood, such as celebrating mass, hearing confessions, and administering the sacraments.

38. Inquisition trials were conducted in secret, and punishment of those found guilty varied. Many persons were censored publicly; others were fined, imprisoned, or ordered to do public penance. The death penalty was infrequent—during three colonial centuries in Mexico only forty-three "unrepentant apostates" were turned over to the civil authorities for capital punishment. Additional details, but not the final disposition of the cases mentioned, are in José Toribio Medina, *Historia del tribunal del Santo Oficio de la Inquisición en México*, 295–96.

CHAPTER 14. THE MINES OF REAL DEL MONTE

1. Ilarione's comments about poverty in Mexico City were echoed by contemporary visitors and have been verified by modern scholars, one of whom estimated that 85 percent of the city's population was mired in poverty. Francisco de Ajofrín, who was there in the 1760s, wrote: "For every one hundred people you come across in the streets, you will find scarcely one fully clothed and with shoes." Ajofrín, *Diario*, 1:80. For details about unemployment, famines, and alcoholism, see Kandell, *La Capital*, 254–59.

2. Pachuca is fifty miles north of Mexico City. Real del Monte, now named Mineral del Monte, is six miles east of Pachuca and is still the center of one of Mexico's most important mining regions. It was first settled by the Spaniards in the sixteenth century. *DP*, s.v. "Pachuca."

3. An alcalde mayor is the mayor and chief magistrate of a district.

4. The *quinto real* (royal fifth) was a tax on all silver and gold exploited; at first 20 percent, it was later reduced to 10 percent. David A. Brading, *Miners and Merchants in Bourbon Mexico*, 140, 142.

5. Pedro Romero de Terreros, conde de Regla (1710–81), was born in Spain and emigrated to New Spain in 1732. He began exploiting the mines of Real del Monte first in association with Alejandro Bustamante Bustillo (from 1743 to 1750) and later on his own initiative. He spent much of his vast riches on religious, cultural, and charitable works, making generous contributions to the colleges of Propaganda Fide in Querétaro, Mexico City, Guadalupe, and Pachucha. Romero de Terreros is most famous for having founded the royal Monte de Piedad (pawnshop) in the capital in 1775. Manuel Romero de Terreros, *El conde de Regla, Creso de la Nueva España*, 9, 11, 13–15, 106–15.

6. Giovanni Francesco Gemelli-Careri, *Giro del mondo* (1721 ed.), 6:105–14.

7. Ibid., 6:106.

8. Throughout this section Ilarione uses the Italian word *metale*, whose sole meaning is "metal," though "ore" is clearly the intended meaning. The text has been translated accordingly.

9. In Mexican Spanish, *malacate* can refer to any kind of winch used for lifting weights. *DM*, s.v. "malacate."

10. I.e., *chacuaco* or *chacuaca*, a small furnace for smelting metals. *DM*, s.v. "chacuaco."

11. Temesquitate and tequesquite were local salts used as catalytic agents. Brading, *Miners and Merchants*, 137; Santamaría, *Diccionario de mejicanismos*, s.v. "temesquitate," "temesquite."

12. Cendrada (more commonly *cendra*) is a paste or base of ash used in the oven to refine silver. Moliner, *Diccionario de uso del español*, s.v. "cendrada."

13. This blend is a mixture of sodium and potassium chloride. Ilarione, *Viaggio al Messico*, 107, n. 135.

14. Magistral, used to refine silver ores, is a mixture of ferric oxide and copper sulfate obtained from roasting copper pyrites. Moliner, *Diccionario de uso del español*, s.v. "magistral."

15. A Spanish vara is a unit of measure equivalent to 836 millimeters or about 33 inches. Haggard, *Handbook for Translators*, 84. For braccia, see chapter 4, note 11.

16. Actually the law specified a rectangle staked above the surface, 1,210 yards long and 60 yards wide. Brading, *Miners and Merchants*, 131.

17. During the Middle Ages and early Renaissance, the turbulent Italian city states often invited an outsider to rule and suppress factional discord. This official was known as the podestà and had virtual dictatorial powers.

18. Additional details about the riot can be found in Romero de Terreros, *El conde de Regla*, 93–96; and Doris M. Ladd, *The Making of a Strike: Mexican Silver Workers' Struggles in Real del Monte, 1766–1775*.

19. Gemelli-Careri, *Giro del mondo* (1721 ed.), 6:104–16.

20. The tonnage of precious metals produced in New Spain was 2,812 silver and 24 gold in the sixteenth century; 9,538 silver and 39 gold in the seventeenth century; and 32,488 silver and 91 gold in the eighteenth century. At the time of Ilarione's visit, colonial Mexico supplied half the world's production. *EM*, s.v. "Minería."

CHAPTER 15. EXPULSION FROM MEXICO

1. Archbishop Manuel Rubio y Salinas died July 3, 1765. See chapter 6, note 13.

2. Francisco de Ajofrín (1710–89) was born in the town of Ajofrín in the province of Toledo. Baptized as Bonifacio Castellano y Lara, he adopted his new name when he entered the Capuchin Order in 1740. Sent to New Spain to collect alms for Tibet missions, he arrived at Veracruz on November 30, 1763, and spent the next two and a half years traveling in New Spain from Michoacán to Oaxaca. He later wrote an account of his trip. His companion, Friar Fermín de Olite, remained in

Mexico, where he was ordained as a priest in 1776 and where he died about 1791. Ajofrín, *Diario*, 2:282–85, 317.

3. Francisco Lorenzana y Buitrón (1722–1804) was archbishop of Mexico from 1766 to 1772 during a very distinguished ecclesiastical career notable for charitable works and cultural patronage. Carlos Francisco, marqués de Croix (1699–1786), a Fleming by birth, was the forty-fifth viceroy of Mexico (1766–71). Highlights of his term of office included embellishment of the capital, but also stern measures like the 1767 expulsion of the Jesuits. He also strengthened Mexico's northern frontiers and issued a decree prohibiting the Indians from using their native languages. *DP*, s.v. "Lorenzana y Buitrón, Francisco Antonio de"; "Croix, Marqués de, Carlos Francisco."

4. See chapter 6, note 5.

5. In fact, the archbishop was undoubtedly heeding royal orders to expel foreign clergy. See note 18 below.

6. The distance between the capital and Guadalajara is close to 150 leagues (410 miles).

7. Ilarione confused to the two villages. Tepozotlán, not Cuautitlán, was the site of the Jesuit seminary of San Martín, founded in 1584. The church there is now a museum of colonial religious art.

8. The Church of San Francisco, completed in 1698, was noted for its magnificent art, great tower, and dome covered with glazed tiles. It was adjacent to the Franciscan monastery, which covered four square blocks. *EM*, s.v. "Querétaro, ciudad de."

9. *Mariscal* is marshal in Spanish.

10. The population of Guadalajara was about 21,000 in 1768; it rose from 17,330 in 1742 to 24,249 in 1790. México, *1er censo de población*, 29, table 84.

11. In 1529 Nuño de Guzmán, a merciless president of the audiencia of Mexico, set out from the capital with an army to conquer a vast area to the northwest, later called Nueva Galicia. From Michoacán to Sinaloa, he and his men pillaged the land, burned villages, and enslaved Indians. He eventually founded the towns of Tepic, Culiacán, and Guadalajara. Arrested in 1536 for his misdeeds, he was sent back to Spain and spent many years in prison. Luis Pérez Verdía, *Historia particular del Estado de Jalisco*, 31–149.

12. Guadalajara is actually at 20.30° north and 103.20° west. Ilarione refers to the phenomenon that Guadalajara, although north of Mexico City, has a somewhat warmer climate. The reason is the lower elevation, 5,200 versus 7,415 feet.

13. Ilarione is referring to the San Juan de Dios River.

14. A century before Ilarione's time, Rome, though the spiritual and political capital of Catholicism, was already condemned for moral laxity, even among the clergy; and many observers deplored a religious life based more on observance than on genuine spirituality. Almo Paita, *La vita quotidiana a Roma ai tempi di Gian Lorenzo Bernini*, 117–56.

15. Lake Chapala is actually located southeast of Guadalajara.

16. The bishop of Guadalajara was Diego Rodríguez de Rivas y Velasco. *EM*, s.v. "Guadalajara."

17. The Carnival of merrymaking before Lent ends on Shrove Tuesday, which in 1768 was on February 22. Parise, *Book of Calendars*, Calendar 13, 316.

18. Charles III, who reigned between 1759 and 1788, was dominated by anticlerical ministers, especially the counts of Floridablanca and Aranda, who were influenced by the French *philosophes*. They were also hostile to any person or organization that did not owe primary allegiance to the Spanish crown. The decree Ilarione refers to was dated October 18, 1767, as stated in the letter he received from the archbishop, quoted below. Herr, *Eighteenth-Century Revolution in Spain*, 22, 67, 75, 233.

19. The regular clergy are those who belong to a religious order with its special rule (*regula*), whereas the secular, or "worldly," clergy are primarily curates or parish priests under the control of a bishop.

20. A provisor is an ecclesiastical judge to whom a bishop delegates his authority and jurisdiction for the determination of lawsuits; the title is sometimes used for the vicar general.

21. Juan de Palafox y Mendoza (1600–1659) was bishop of Puebla (1640–55). Following royal orders, he deposed and briefly governed in the place of Viceroy Marqués de Villena, and he served as interim archbishop of Mexico (1642). In Puebla his attempts to force the Jesuits to pay tithes on the income from their properties led to a six-year dispute during which both sides issued excommunications and appealed to the pope and the crown. Finally, an agreement was signed, and in 1655 the bishop was transferred to Osma, Spain. *EM*, s.v. "Palafox y Mendoza, Juan de"; Genaro García, *Don Juan Palafox y Mendoza, obispo de Puebla, Osma, visitador y virrey de Nueva España*, 143–203.

22. Puebla was founded on April 30, 1531. DM, s.v. "Puebla."

23. When the Jesuits plotted to assassinate Bishop Palafox, he fled from Puebla and hid at a mining camp and later at a hacienda from whence he appealed to the king and new viceroy, both of whom supported his position. García, *Palafox*, 170–84.

CHAPTER 16. RETURN VOYAGE TO EUROPE

1. Ilarione is probably referring to the disaster that occurred on July 15, 1733, when a hurricane caused the wreck of twenty-one Spanish ships off the Florida Keys. Salvage crews from Havana refloated several of the ships and recovered all of the royal treasure, but much of the cargo of sugar, indigo, and cochineal was destroyed by saltwater. Robert F. Marx, *Shipwrecks of the Western Hemisphere, 1492–1825*, 209–15.

2. Pierre de Lorrain, known as Abbé Vallemont (1649–1721), was a physician, numismatologist, and "rather mediocre *littérateur*." He was the author of works on coins, gardening, and magnetism and of the *Eléments de l'histoire, ou ce qu'il faut savoir de chronologie, de géographie, de blason, etc. avant que de lire l'histoire particulière* (2 vols., Paris, 1696). Ilarione is probably referring to the latter work. Guillaume Delisle (1675–1726), a key figure in the history of cartography, produced more than ninety highly regarded maps of various parts of the world. His work was epochal in that he broke with the ornamental traditions of the past and instead relied on scientifically accurate data, including precise astronomical observations, as the basis of his craft. *BU*, 42:495–96; *Dictionary of Scientific Biography*, s.v. "Lorrain, Pierre de"; "Delisle, Guillaume."

3. Cuba is in the Greater Antilles, but not in the Windward Islands.

4. Santo Domingo is the early name for Hispaniola.

5. Cuba was discovered by Columbus on October 28, 1492. Morison, *Admiral of the Ocean Sea*, 1:253.

6. In 1511 Admiral Diego Columbus (1480–1526), son of the discoverer and governor of Hispaniola, sent Diego Velázquez (1465–1524?) to Cuba with orders to conquer the island. Joining in this enterprise were many Spaniards, including Pánfilo de Narváez (1470–1528). In 1520 Velázquez, as governor of Cuba, sent Narváez to arrest Cortés in Mexico, but instead he was arrested and returned to Spain. Later Narváez tried to conquer Florida but perished in the Gulf of Mexico. *EU*, s.v. "Colón, Diego"; "Narváez, Pánfilo"; "Velázquez de Cuéllar, Diego."

7. Here several words have been effaced from the manuscript.

8. Other accounts indicate that in the 1760s about one-third of the black and mulatto population of Havana was free. Hugh Thomas, *Cuba: The Pursuit of Freedom*, 13.

9. Ilarione's comment is somewhat obscure. It is likely, however, that he could not disrobe, even in the hot climate of Havana, because of modesty or Capuchin rules.

10. Corpus Domini, usually termed Corpus Christi, is a Christian festival of the Eucharist celebrated on the Thursday after Trinity Sunday, about sixty days after Easter.

11. Actopán is twenty miles northwest of Pachuca.

12. See 2 Samuel 6:12–23.

13. Until about 1790, when the viceroy banned the practice as irreligious, Corpus Christi processions in Mexico City included vulgar images of giants, dragons, the devil, and other grotesque figures. *DP*, s.v. "Corpus, fiesta del."

14. Translation: Whoever kneels before this divine Lord and recites a Creed will gain forty days of indulgences.

15. Robeno is a character, such as a Roman soldier, represented in passion plays in towns during Holy Week. *DM*, s.v. "Robeno."

16. The fort of San Carlos de la Cabaña, named for Charles III of Spain, was built between 1763 and 1774. *Guía de la Habana*, 38.

17. See chapter 3, note 5.

18. June 20, 1768, was a Monday. Parise, *Book of Calendars*, Calendar 13, 316.

19. There are more than twenty islands in the Bahamas, formerly called the Lucayas by the Spanish. Names of individual islands were changed as they passed from one flag to another or as pirates settled on them. All became British after 1783.

20. The Bermuda Islands are a group of about 360 islands, of which only 20 are inhabited. Spanish explorers who visited Bermuda Island in 1515 named it for Juan de Bermúdez. English colonization began in 1612.

21. The Azores are a group of nine islands and several islets, first settled by the Flemish, but assigned to Portugal in 1480 by the Treaty of Algaçovas.

22. Cape San Vicente is at the southwestern tip of Portugal; Cape Santa Maria is on an island off the southwestern coast of Portugal.

23. Ilarione's manuscript actually closes with a paragraph listing the distances between various points on his homeward itinerary. We have omitted this section because, aside from being information of marginal value, it is not a fitting conclusion to the work as a whole.

BIBLIOGRAPHY

UNPUBLISHED SOURCES

Bergamo, Italy. Biblioteca Civica Angelo Mai: Ilarione da Bergamo. *Viaggio al Messico*. MS.
Professiones cappuccinorum Brixiae et Bergami (1667–1800).

PUBLISHED SOURCES

Ajofrín, Francisco de. *Carta familiar de un sacerdote en que le da cuenta de la admirable conquista espiritual del vasto imperio del gran Thibet.* Mexico City: Imprenta de la Biblioteca Mexicana, 1765.
———. *Diario del viaje que por orden de la Sagrada Congregación de Propaganda de Fide hizo a la América Septentrional en el siglo XVIII.* 2 vols. Madrid: Real Academia de la Historia, 1958–59.
Amerlinck, María Concepción. *Relación histórica de movimientos sísmicos en la Ciudad de México, 1300–1900.* Mexico City: Desarrollo Social Sociocultur, 1986.
Antón Solé, Pablo. *Situación económica y asistencia social de la Diócesis de Cádiz en la segunda mitad del siglo XVIII.* Cádiz: Ediciones de la Caja de Ahorros de Cádiz, 1985.
Arzeni, Charles B., and Terri M. Simon. *Plants of Mexico.* Monterrey, Nuevo León: Ron Stearns, 1974.
Barclay, Juliet. *Havana: Portrait of a City.* London: Cassell, 1993.
Bell, Charles. *The People of Tibet.* Delhi: Banarsidass, 1992.

Benzoni, Girolamo. *Historia del mondo novo* (Venice, 1565). Reprinted as *History of the New World*. Translated by W. H. Smyth. London: Hakluyt Society, 1857.

Blunt, Wilfrid. *Pietro's Pilgrimage: A Journey to India and Back.* . . . London: J. Barrie, 1953.

Boturini Benaducci, Lorenzo. *Idea de una nueva historia general de la América Septentrional*. Madrid: Juan de Zuñigá, 1746. Reprint: Mexico City: Editorial Porrúa, 1974.

Brading, David A. *Miners and Merchants in Bourbon Mexico, 1763–1810*. Cambridge: Cambridge University Press, 1971.

Buffier, Claude. *Pratique de la mémoire artificielle, pour apprendre et retenir la cronologie, l'histoire et la géographie*. 4 vols. Paris, 1701–15.

Bustico, Guido. "Di un viaggio al Messico nell' anno 1768." *La Geografia: Rivista di Propaganda Geografica* 4, no. 10 (Dec. 1916): 438–39.

Calderón de la Barca, Fanny. *Life in Mexico*. Edited by Howard T. Fisher and Marion H. Fisher. Garden City, N.Y.: Doubleday, 1966.

Carrión, Arturo Morales, ed. *Puerto Rico: A Political and Cultural History*. New York: W. W. Norton, 1983.

Chapman, Joseph A., and George A. Feldhamer, eds. *Wild Mammals of North America*. Baltimore: Johns Hopkins University Press, 1982.

Ciudad Real, Antonio de. *Relación breve y verdadera de algunas cosas . . . que sucedieron al padre fray Alonso Ponce en las provincias de la Nueva España*. 2 vols. Madrid: Viuda de Calero, 1872–73.

Davidson, Basil. *The African Slave Trade*. Boston: Little, Brown, 1980.

Davies, Keith A. "Tendencias demográficas urbanas durante el siglo XIX en México." *Historia Mexicana* 21 (1972): 481–524.

Davis, L. Irby. *A Field Guide to the Birds of Mexico and Central America*. Austin: University of Texas Press, 1972.

Della Valle, Pietro. *Viaggi de Pietro Della Valle il Pellegrino . . . descritti in 54 lettere familiari*. 3 vols. Rome: Vitale Mascardi, 1650–53.

DeSanctis, Francesco. *Storia della letteratura italiana*. Rome: Newton, 1991.

Diccionario Porrúa de historia, biografía y geografía de México. 6th ed. 4 vols. Mexico City: Editorial Porrúa, 1995.

Dictionary of National Biography. Edited By Leslie Stephen and Sidney Lee. 21 vols. Oxford: Oxford University Press, 1967–68.

Dictionary of Scientific Biography. 18 vols. New York: Scribner, 1970–80.

Dizionario biografico degli Italiani. 41 vols. Rome: Istituto della Enciclopedia, 1960–.

Dorn, Walter. *Competition for Empire, 1740–1763*. New York: Harper & Row, 1940.

Duke, James A. *Handbook of Medicinal Herbs*. Boca Raton, Florida: CRC Press, 1985.

Enciclopedia cattolica. 12 vols. Vatican City: Ente per L'Enciclopedia cattolica e per il Libro cattolico, 1949–54.

Enciclopedia de México. 14 vols. Mexico City: Cía Editora de Enciclopedia de México, 1996.

Enciclopedia universal ilustrada europeo-americana. 70 vols. Madrid: Espasa Calpe, 1907–30.

Gage, Thomas. *The English American . . . or a New Survey of the West India's*. London, 1648. Reprint: *Travels in the New World*. Edited by J. Eric S. Thompson. Norman: University of Oklahoma Press, 1969.

García, Genaro. *Don Juan Palafox y Mendoza, obispo de Puebla, Osma, visitador y virrey de Nueva España*. Mexico City: Librería de Bouret, 1918.

Gemelli-Careri, Giovanni Francesco. *Giro del mondo*. 3rd ed. 9 vols. Naples: F. Mosca, 1721.

———. *Le Mexique à la fin du XVIIe siècle*. Edited by Jean-Pierre Berthe. Paris: Calman Lévy, 1968.

———. *A Voyage round the World*. 2 vols. London, 1704.

Gerhard, Peter. *A Guide to the Historical Geography of New Spain*. Rev. ed. Norman: University of Oklahoma Press, 1993.

Goethe, Johann Wolfgang von. *Tagebuch der italienischen Reise 1786*. Frankfurt: Insel, 1976.

Guía de la Habana. Madrid: Union de ciudades capitales Ibero-americanas, 1990.

Guijo, Gregorio Martín. *Diario (1648–1664)*. Edited by Manuel Romero de Terreros. 2 vols. Mexico City: Porrúa, 1952.

Gurría Lacroix, Jorge. *El desagüe del valle de México durante la época novohispana*. Mexico City: UNAM, 1978.

Haggard, J. Villasana. *Handbook for Translators of Spanish Historical Documents*. Austin: University of Texas Press, 1941.

Hausberger, Bernd, ed. *Jesuiten aus Mitteleuropa im kolonialen Mexiko: Eine Bio-Biographie*. Vienna: Verlage für Geschichte und Politik, 1995.

Herr, Richard. *The Eighteenth-Century Revolution in Spain*. Princeton: Princeton University Press, 1958.

Hostos, Adolfo. *Historia de San Juan, ciudad murada*. San Juan, Puerto Rico: Instituto de Cultura Puertorriqueña, 1966.

Humboldt, Alexander von. *Political Essay on the Kingdom of New Spain*. Translated by John Black. 4 vols. London: Longman, Hurst, Rees, Orme & Brown, 1811–22. Abridged version: Edited by Mary Maples Dunn. New York: Knopf, 1974.

Ilarione da Bergamo. *Viaggio al Messico nell'America settentrionale fatto e descritto da Fra Ilarione da Bergamo, religioso Capuccino con figure, Anno MDCCLXX.* Edited by Maria Laura Bruno. Bergamo: Tipografia Editrice G. Secomandi, 1976.

Johnson, Willis Fletcher. *The History of Cuba.* 4 vols. New York: B. F. Buck, 1920.

Junkmann, W., ed. "Aus dem Tagebuche des mexikanischen Missionarius Bernh. Middendorff aus der Gesellschaft Jesu." *Katholisches Magazin für Wissenschaft und Leben* 1 (1845): 740–98; 2 (1846): 21–54, 179–208.

Kandell, Jonathan. *La Capital: The Biography of Mexico City.* New York: Random House, 1988.

Ladd, Doris M. *The Making of a Strike: Mexican Silver Workers' Struggles in Real del Monte, 1766–1775.* Lincoln: University of Nebraska Press, 1988.

———. *The Mexican Nobility at Independence, 1780–1826.* Austin: University of Texas, Institute of Latin American Studies, 1976.

Lanning, John Tate. *Academic Culture in the Spanish Colonies.* New York: Oxford University Press, 1940.

Lea, Henry C. *The Inquisition in the Spanish Dependencies.* New York: Macmillan, 1922.

León, Nicolás. *Las castas del México colonial o Nueva España.* Mexico City: Museo Nacional de Arqueología, Historia y Etnografía, 1924.

Long-Solís, Janet. *Capsicum y cultura: La historia del chilli.* Mexico City: Fondo de Cultura Económica, 1986.

MacLachlan, Colin M. *Criminal Justice in Eighteenth Century Mexico: A Study of the Tribunal of the Acordada.* Berkeley: University of California Press, 1975.

Martínez, Maximino. *Catálogo de nombres vulgares y científicos de plantas mexicanas.* Mexico City: Ediciones Botas, 1937.

Marx, Robert F. *Shipwrecks of the Western Hemisphere, 1492–1825.* New York: David McKay, 1971.

Medina, José Toribio. *Historia del tribunal del Santo Oficio de la Inquisición en México.* Mexico City: Ediciones Fuentes Cultural, 1952.

Mejía Prieto, Jorge. *Así habla el mexicano: Diccionario básico de mexicanismos.* 4th ed. Mexico City: Panorama Editorial, 1987.

México. Dirección General de Estadística. *1er censo de población de la Nueva España, 1790.* Mexico City: La Dirección, 1977.

Michaud, Joseph Fr. *Biographie universelle ancienne et moderne.* 45 vols. Paris: 1843–65. Reprint: 45 vols. Graz, Austria: Akademische Druck- u. Verlagsanstalt, 1966–68.

Miller, Robert Ryal. *Mexico: A History*. Norman: University of Oklahoma Press, 1985.

Miño Grijalva, Manuel. *Obrajes y tejedores en Nueva España, 1700–1810*. Madrid: Instituto de Cooperación Iberoamericana, 1990.

Mitchell, Timothy. *Blood Sport: A Social History of Spanish Bullfighting*. Philadelphia: University of Pennsylvania Press, 1991.

Moliner, María. *Diccionario de uso del español*. 2 vols. Madrid: Editorial Gredos, 1989.

Morison, Samuel Eliot. *Admiral of the Ocean Sea: A Life of Christopher Columbus*. 2 vols. Boston: Little, Brown, 1942.

Mörner, Magnus, ed. *The Expulsion of the Jesuits from Latin America*. New York: Alfred A. Knopf, 1965.

New Catholic Encyclopedia. 18 vols. New York: McGraw-Hill, 1967–89.

Nunnari, F[ilippo] A. *Un viaggiatore calabrese della fine secolo XVII*. Messina: Tipografia Mazzini, 1901.

Paita, Almo. *La vita quotidiana a Roma ai tempi di Gian Lorenzo Bernini*. Milan: Rizzoli, 1998.

Palomar de Miguel, Juan. *Diccionario de México*. 4 vols. Mexico City: Panorama, 1991.

Parise, Frank, ed. *The Book of Calendars*. New York: Facts on File, 1982.

Parry, John H. *The Spanish Seaborne Empire*. London: Hutchinson, 1967.

Paz, Octavio. *Sor Juana, or The Traps of Faith*. Translated by Margaret Sayers Peden. Cambridge: Harvard University Press, 1988.

Pérez Verdía, Luis. *Historia particular del Estado de Jalisco*. Guadalajara: Universidad de Guadalajara, 1988.

Poole, Stafford. *Our Lady of Guadalupe: The Origins and Sources of a Mexican National Symbol*. Tucson: University of Arizona Press, 1995.

Prescott, William Hickling. *History of the Conquest of Mexico; with a Preliminary View of the Ancient Mexican Civilization; and the Life of the Conqueror, Hernando Cortés*. 3 vols. New York: Harper & Bros., 1843.

Ravanelli, Renato. *Bergamo: History and Art*. Bergamo: Grafica & Arte, 1997.

Río, José Antonio del. *Luis Vicente de Velasco e Isla*. Santander: Diputación Provincial, Institución Cultural de Cantabria, Instituto de Estudios Marítimos y Pesqueros "Juan de la Cosa," 1976.

Robles, Antonio de. *Diario de sucesos notables (1665–1703)*. Edited by Antonio Castro Leal. 3 vols. Mexico City: Editorial Porrúa, 1946.

Romero de Terreros, Manuel. *El conde de Regla, Creso de la Nueva España*. Mexico City: Ediciones Xochitl, 1943.

Rosetty y Pranz, José. *Guía oficial de Cádiz, su provincia y departamento*. Cádiz: D. F. Joly, 1878.

Salmon, Thomas. *Lo stato presente di tutti i paesi e popolo del mondo naturale, politico, e morale.* 32 vols. Venice: Giambatista Albrizzi, 1742–65.

Santamaría, Francisco. *Diccionario de mejicanismos.* Mexico City: Editorial Porrúa, 1959.

Short, William J. *The Franciscans.* Wilmington, Del.: Michael Glazier, 1989.

Silvio da Brescia, Padre. *I frati minori cappuccini a Bergamo.* Bergamo: Industrie grafiche Cattaneo, 1958.

Síntesis histórica de la Universidad de México. 2nd ed. Mexico City: UNAM, 1978.

Solís, Antonio de. *Historia de la conquista de México: Población y progresos de la América Septentrional, conocida por el nombre de Nueva España.* Madrid, 1684. Reprint: Mexico City: M. A. Porrúa, 1988.

Tasso, Torquato. *Torquato Tasso's Jerusalem Delivered.* Translated by Joseph Tusiani. Rutherford, N.J.: Fairleigh Dickinson University Press, 1970.

Taylor, William B. *Magistrates of the Sacred: Priests and Parishioners in Eighteenth-Century Mexico.* Stanford: Stanford University Press, 1996.

Thomas, Hugh. *Conquest: Montezuma, Cortés and the Fall of Old Mexico.* New York: Simon & Schuster, 1994.

————. *Cuba: The Pursuit of Freedom.* New York: Harper & Row, 1971.

Tiraboschi, Antonio. *Vocabulario dei dialetti bergamaschi antichi e moderni.* 2 vols. Bologna: Forni, 1873.

United States. Bureau of the Census. *A Century of Population Growth, from the First Census of the United States to the Twelfth, 1790–1900.* Washington, D.C.: GPO, 1909.

Valdemiro da Bergamo, Padre. *I conventi ed i cappuccini bergamaschi.* Milan: Lodovico Felice Cogliati, 1883.

————. *I conventi ed i cappuccini bresciani.* Milan: Cesare Crespi, 1891.

Vásquez de Espinosa, Antonio. *Compendium and Description of the West Indies.* Translated by Charles Upson Clark. Washington, D.C.: Smithsonian Institution, 1942.

Villaseñor y Sánchez, José Antonio. *Theatro americano, descripción general de los reynos y provincias de la Nueva-España, y sus jurisdicciones.* 2 vols. Mexico City, 1746–48. Reprint: 2 vols. Mexico City: Editorial Nacional, 1952.

Webster's Geographical Dictionary. Springfield, Mass.: G. & C. Merriam Co., 1960.

Writers' Program of the Works Progress Administration. *Puerto Rico: A Guide to the Island of Borinquén.* New York: University Society, 1940.

Zeno, Francisco M. *Historia de la capital de Puerto Rico.* 2 vols. San Juan: Gobierno de la Capital, 1959.

INDEX